NEW WAYS THROUGH THE GLENS

Telford's Bridge at Dunkeld

NEW WAYS
THROUGH THE GLENS

Highland Road, Bridge and Canal Makers of the
Early Nineteenth Century

A. R. B. HALDANE
D.Litt.

DAVID & CHARLES : Newton Abbot

ISBN O 7153 6080 9

Printed in Great Britain
by The Pitman Press Bath
for David & Charles (Holdings) Limited
South Devon House Newton Abbot Devon

THIS BOOK IS DEDICATED
TO THE MEMORY
OF
THREE GOOD FRIENDS
OF THE
SCOTTISH HIGHLANDS

THOMAS TELFORD
Civil Engineer

JOHN RICKMAN
Clerk Assistant to the House of Commons

and

JAMES HOPE
Writer to the Signet

PREFACE

THE history of the roads of the Highlands has always been closely associated with the name of General Wade and it is probably not unfair to say that for very many people Highland roads of any antiquity pass under the generic name of Wade Roads. The road system to which this name is popularly applied embraces many roads which were made by the military roadmakers long after Wade's death in 1748, but some of these were planned by him, and, though he did not live to see them made, it is neither un-natural nor unfitting that the name of the pioneer should in this way be perpetuated. While the work of Wade and the other military roadmakers of the eighteenth century is thus generally recognised and to some extent familiar, much less is known about the period of road-making which immediately followed, or of the great transition by which, within the space of a few years, the military roads of the Highlands came to be replaced by a system of roads for civilian use from which the road system of today has been directly evolved.

By the end of the third quarter of the eighteenth century the constructional work of the military roadmakers who followed Wade had virtually ceased, and in the last quarter of the century road work in the Highlands was largely confined to maintenance of the hundreds of miles of roads of varying quality which the work of the Army had brought into being. This maintenance work was carried out with waning enthusiasm and decreasing efficiency, and when the eighteenth century closed communications in the Highlands consisted of about 800 miles of roads, many of them ill-constructed, most of them in poor repair, some no longer usable and few if any suited to the needs of a poor but peaceful people. It was to bring the communications of the Highlands into line with contemporary needs, to check the flow of emigrants and to bring work and livelihood to a people impoverished, bewildered and embittered by social and economic changes beyond their ken or their control, that in the first years of last century the Government turned its attention to road and canal construction. During the first quarter of the nineteenth century more than £1,500,000 was spent under the direction of two Commissions appointed by

PREFACE

Parliament in 1803, with Thomas Telford as their Engineer, on the making of new roads and bridges in the Highlands and on the construction of the Caledonian Canal.

Of the work of Wade and the military roadmakers who followed him few traces now remain, save the Tay Bridge at Aberfeldy, the ruins of the High Bridge over the Spean, the winding track over the Corrieyairack Pass and here and there stretches of grass-grown road and small stone bridges interesting to the historian, the antiquary or the pedestrian rather than to the serious traveller; but much of Telford's work remains. Not a few of the bridges in use today are his work, and very many of our modern Highland roads follow closely the lines of the roads he made. It is fair to say that the work done between 1803 and 1823 was the real foundation and origin of modern communications in the Highlands.

The work which was carried out in these first twenty years of last century was without precedent in character and in magnitude. The pages which follow are an attempt to tell the story of the making of what came to be known as the Parliamentary Roads, of the men whose work it was and of the difficulties which they met and surmounted, with some account of the work on the Caledonian Canal. Of the life and work of Thomas Telford much has already been written, but the variety and extent of the interests and activities of that great Engineer were remarkable, and those who have written of him have necessarily dealt with much besides his work in Scotland. These pages are devoted solely to his work in the Highlands.

It would seem more natural that the story of the building of roads, bridges and Canal should be written by an engineer rather than by a lawyer. This book lays no claim to be in any sense a technical treatise, and those who wish to study the purely technical aspects of the Commissioners' work will find in it but little interest. My aim has been rather to attempt to reconstruct from contemporary sources and on broad lines the story of how, mainly by the thought, labour and imagination of a great engineer, a devoted public servant and a prominent Edinburgh lawyer, there was accomplished during the first quarter of last century a work for the Highlands of Scotland which in scope, originality and lasting benefit has yet to be equalled.

The main source for the study of the work of the Commissions is contained in the Reports dealing with Roads, Bridges and Canal which were presented to and published by Parliament from 1803 onwards. These Reports contain much detail—technical, financial and statistical. Yet, dry and factual as they are, the Reports do not entirely obscure the human drama nor the difficulties, perplexities and final achievements of the men whose work they record. No one studying them could fail to realise that many records in the form of Minutes, correspondence and other documents must have been left, which, if they could be found, would tell a far fuller and more interesting story, and my first task was to trace these fuller records.

It was known that while the Commissions were centred in London much of the detailed work was done in Edinburgh, and exhaustive search was made in both cities. Little success was at first achieved, and it began to appear that the record of the Commissioners' work must rest solely on the printed Reports. Then, when hope was waning, I learned that among the vast body of Parliamentary and other papers in the Record Office of the House of Lords there had quite recently been found a large accumulation of documents which appeared to relate to the building of roads in the Highlands. Cheered by this knowledge and armed with the requisite authority I visited the House of Lords at the first opportunity. The material there consists of many hundreds of original and copy manuscript letters—including some original letters of Thomas Telford—reports, memoranda, contracts and other documents relating chiefly to the making of Highland Roads and Bridges after 1803 and to the construction of the Caledonian Canal. The greater and by far the most interesting part of the material relates to the years from 1803 to 1823, a period which covered the main constructional work. The material, which is contained in eight large boxes, is extremely miscellaneous in character and, while some of the documents have at some stage been arranged in date, a large proportion were found in the now dusty bundles in which no doubt they had been originally tied. When and in what circumstances such an incomplete and miscellaneous body of documents came to be assembled in the House of Lords is something of a mystery. It seems possible that they were hurriedly gathered together from papers saved at the time of the fire which destroyed the House of Commons in 1834, and that they were thereafter housed in the

Victoria Tower, where they now live in the company of the master copies of Acts of Parliament and very many other precious and irreplaceable documents.

To the examination of this accumulation in 1953, 1954 and 1955 I devoted what hours could be spared from professional work during periodical visits to London. Every facility was afforded to me in my work and I wish to thank most warmly Mr M. F. Bond, Clerk of the Records in the House of Lords, and his staff for the unfailing help and kindness I received from them.

Among the documents included in the House of Lords collection were found a very large number of letters from James Hope, W. S., the Commissioners' Agent in Edinburgh. The existence and substance of these letters still further strengthened my conviction that in Edinburgh must surely still exist much material of importance; but here the results of search and inquiry were no less discouraging than they had initially been in London—and even more baffling, for the area of search was so much more limited, and it was hard to think that a large body of documents could have entirely disappeared. Yet so it began to seem, and I had almost reconciled myself to doing without what I could not have, when among the House of Lords documents was found a letter from James Hope to John Rickman written in 1824 in which Hope reported his removal from his office in Queen Street to a new office at the north-west corner of what is now Moray Place, and the storage of papers connected with his work for the Commissioners. Hope's letter supplied the key to the problem. In the basement of what are now the offices of The Hope Trust in 31 Moray Place were found at last the letter books of James Hope, and my thanks are due to the Hope Trustees and to Mr Hope Campbell for allowing me access to these letter books and permission to make extensive use of them. Without this, the story of the work of the Commissioners would have been quite incomplete, and this book would have been deprived of a considerable part of such interest as it may possess.

While the material in the House of Lords Record Office consists largely of original documents, that in Moray Place consists only of copies of letters written by James Hope in his capacity of Agent to the Commissioners and no original documents were there found. Not all the letter books have survived, and many of the letters in the volumes discovered are copies of letters to John

Rickman, the originals of which had already been found in the House of Lords. But among the many hundreds of pages in these fourteen volumes of Hope's letter books are a very large number of letters of great interest—to Thomas Telford, to John and Joseph Mitchell the Road Inspectors and to countless other correspondents throughout Scotland. Incomplete though it be, the material which thus came to light in London and Edinburgh went far to supplement the printed Reports, and to enable the story to be told of the great work for the Highlands which was done in the first quarter of last century.

While the documents in the House of Lords collection and the letter books of James Hope constitute the most important part of the manuscript sources available, two other sources bearing mainly on the construction of the Caledonian Canal call for mention. When the construction of the Canal was commenced in the autumn of 1803, work was started simultaneously at the Eastern and Western ends, and for four years the supervision of the work at the Western end was entrusted to an Engineer called John Telford, who may or may not have been a relation of his more eminent namesake Thomas. During these four years John kept a letter book. Many of the copy letters contained in it are of purely technical interest, but not a few are of a more personal nature and throw light on the hardships and human problems of the men who worked in the Great Glen in these early days. The book is in the possession of Mr Frank Whyte, who was until 1960 Engineer and Manager of the Caledonian Canal and through his kindness this too has been made available.

The other manuscript source of some importance consists of a collection of letters passing between Thomas Telford and John Rickman, the Secretary of the Commission, relating to Canal matters. This collection is now in the possession of the Ministry of Transport, by whose permission I have been enabled to make use of the letters.

Of the printed sources, the official Reports of the Commissioners have been extensively used, while Robert Southey's *Journal of a Journey in Scotland in 1819* and numerous other records of contemporary Highland travel contain much of interest. One other printed source, however, deserves special mention. In 1824 Joseph Mitchell succeeded his father as Chief Inspector of Highland Roads, a post which he held until the end of the Commissioners' work in 1863. After his retiral, Joseph occupied his later years by writing his Reminiscences, and the two volumes which were published in 1883 contain much of interest bearing on Mitchell's work as an engineer and on conditions in the Highlands in the first half of last century.

In addition to those mentioned I have received help and kindness from many whom I would wish to thank. As on previous occasions the great resources of the Signet Library, Edinburgh, have been at my disposal, and to the late Dr C. A. Malcolm and the staff of that Library I am deeply grateful. In addition to the help which I received from him in my search for sources, Dr Malcolm took a large share of the laborious task of checking the references and supplied me with valuable material about contemporary Edinburgh. The acknowledgment here made can be but an inadequate tribute to the memory of that fine scholar and kindly man.

The resources of Edinburgh Public Libraries have also been available to me and valuable help has been received from Mr Minto and his staff. The Bank of Scotland have made available certain of the Bank's early letter books while the late Mr James Little of Craig, Langholm, kindly allowed me to quote from letters passing between Thomas Telford and Andrew Little which were in his possession. I have received much help and kindness from the Institution of Civil Engineers. The executors of the late Sir Alexander Gibb have allowed me to quote from letters passing between John Rickman and Robert Southey, copies of which are in their possession. Use has also been made of the resources of the Institute of Historical Research in London and of the Scottish Central Library. Miss Jean Dunlop (now Mrs Munro) has allowed use to be made of her valuable and unpublished thesis on the British Fisheries Society, while Dr C. T. McInnes, late Curator of Historical Records, H.M. Register House, Edinburgh, has kindly read my manuscript. My thanks are also due to the Editor of *The Scotsman* for permission to use material contained in an article contributed by me to that paper in 1948.

The help of my Wife has throughout been constant and invaluable.

Edinburgh, 1961   A.R.B.H.

CONTENTS

LIST OF PLATES

NOTE ON THE ILLUSTRATIONS

The Frontispiece and Plates 5, 9, 10 and 13 are reproductions of pictures executed by T. Allom and W. Purser for inclusion in *Scotland* (two volumes) by William Beattie M.D. (1838). Plate 1 is reproduced by courtesy of the National Portrait Gallery, Edinburgh. Plate 2 is reproduced from an engraving by Cousen of 'Lochaber no more' by J. Watson Nicol, by permission of Radio Times Hulton Picture Library. Plate 3 is a reproduction of a portrait by Samuel Lane, 1822. The original of this portrait is in the possession of the Institution of Civil Engineers by whose courtesy the reproduction is here included. Plate 4 is from an engraving in the House of Commons by Samuel Bellin after a portrait by Samuel Lane and is reproduced by courtesy of the Lord Great Chamberlain and the Speaker of the House of Commons. Plate 6 is a reproduction of a picture by Kay executed about 1814. The reproduction of the original letter of Thomas Telford (Plate 7) is by courtesy of the House of Lords Record Office. Plate 8 is from an engraving in *Speyside* by John Longmuir (1860). Plate 11, a portrait of Glengarry by Raeburn, is reproduced by courtesy of the National Gallery of Scotland. Plate 12 is a reproduction of an early print in the author's possession. Plate 14 is reproduced from a drawing executed by Thomas H. Shepherd included in the volume *Modern Athens or Edinburgh in the 19th Century* (1831). Plate 15 is from a portrait by Sir George Reid, P.R.S.A., in the possession of Inverness Town Council, by whose courtesy it is reproduced.

Despite an extensive search it has proved impossible to trace any picture of James Hope.

Thanks are also due, in the case of this new impression, for the provision of new prints or permissions: Plate 1, Society of Antiquaries; Plate 3, Brian Bracegirdle; Plate 4, Crown copyright—reproduced with the permission of Her Majesty's Stationery Office; Plates 6 and 8, Edinburgh Public Libraries.

ABBREVIATIONS USED IN REFERENCES

H.R. & B.	Reports of Commissioners for Highland Roads and Bridges
C.C.	Reports of Commissioners for the Caledonian Canal
H. of L.	Papers in Record Office, House of Lords
Hope	James Hope's Letter-Books
J.T.	John Telford's Letter-Book
Mitchell	Joseph Mitchell's *Reminiscences of my Life in the Highlands*
Telford	Letters of Thomas Telford to John Rickman
Southey	Southey's *Journal of a Journey in Scotland in 1819*

THE ROADS OF THE HIGHLANDS BEFORE 1800

THE magnitude and speed of the changes in human life seem destined to increase as the years go by, and there is little sign that slackening in the pace of these changes, or limitation of their scope, is to be looked for. On the contrary; all the indications are that both will increase, bringing with them the growing problem of how successfully man can adapt his institutions, his body and above all his spirit and culture to the changes going on around him, and of which far from being the master he may well become the slave. Looking back on the last two centuries in the United Kingdom, it is very evident that this acceleration of the changes in human life began to make itself apparent about the beginning of that period. England was then on the threshold of the Industrial Revolution which, with the stimulus of new discoveries and inventions and extending markets at home and abroad, was to bring vast changes in the lives of millions. Growing knowledge and increasing capital resources were soon to transform agricultural methods, and with them the face of the rural districts. In Scotland the changes came somewhat more slowly, but the time-lag was not a great one, and long before the end of the 18th century sweeping changes were in progress not only in the industrial belt of Central Scotland, but in the rural districts as well.

In the Highlands, the latter years of the century witnessed a remarkable transformation. The process which was then under way was far from complete when the 18th century ended, but already the social and economic life of the people was changing fundamentally, and long before the middle of last century conditions in the Highlands had altered beyond all recognition. The changes which had then taken place in the life of the people of the Highlands had been accompanied by great developments in the communications of the area. Some will see in these developments the cause of the vast improvement which was taking place, particularly in the agricultural districts. Others may prefer to look on them as the outcome of such changes. Cause and effect are closely interwoven and not to be easily unravelled, but the fact remains that the first quarter of the 19th century saw, in a few short years, a forward surge in the opening up of the country which far exceeded what had been achieved during all the centuries which had gone before.

It has been said that the history of Highland road construction starts with the work of General Wade. So far as concerns the mountainous area, enclosed by a line running from Dumbarton by Crieff and Perth to Aberdeen and Inverness and so down the Great Glen to Fort William, this is true. In this great expanse, Wade in his road work could fairly claim to be, in every sense of the word, breaking new ground. In the Lowlands and on the fringes of the Highland area, particularly along the east coast, the position appears to have been somewhat, though not greatly, different. Here a start had been made in the construction and maintenance of some form of primitive roads, but even here road construction was mainly confined to the immediate neighbour-hood of the towns, and little provision had as yet been either required or made for traffic between them.

Among the responsibilities placed on the Justices of the Peace in the early years of the 17th century, was the duty of supervising and repairing roads leading to market towns and churches, but the powers then vested in them seem to have been little more than pious expressions of hope, and not for another fifty years were the Justices armed with any practical means of enforcing these powers. Then in 1669 the system of Statute Labour was introduced. By an Act of that year tenants and cottars were ordered to give six days' labour with a horse and cart in each of the succeeding three years, and four days' labour thereafter.[1] Those tenants who failed to provide the required labour, were liable to have their goods confiscated to the value of 30s Scots for a man and horse, and an early form of local assessment was im-posed on owners of land, who were made liable for an annual payment of 10s for each £100 Scots of the value of their land.

During the next half century the amount of Statute Labour due by the occupiers of land was varied by successive Acts of Parliament. In some districts the local schoolmaster was charged with the task of compiling the lists of those liable for this service; but it was a service grudgingly given, and it is not difficult to

[1] *Acts of the Parliament of Scotland* (Rec. ed.), vol. 7, p. 574

picture how thankless was the schoolmaster's task, and how meagre or how imaginative must have been the reports which the Justices of the Peace made each year to the Privy Council of the state of the roads under their care.

Passive resistance and active opposition to these statutory duties of road-making led in the early years of the 18th century to a growing practice of commuting them for a money payment. While this did something to lighten the load for tenants already burdened with payments in kind and in 'services' for the land they occupied, it can have done little to solve the problem of road-making. The value of a day's work was assessed at only 3d, and, though later the sum was raised in some districts to 6d, the total sum collected can have been little more than a token payment, wholly inadequate even in days when labour was cheap. It was an age when the construction and maintenance of roads depended, like much else, on the degree of energy and public spirit of the landowners and principal tenants, with wide variations from utter neglect to earnest endeavour.

Contemporary records show how unsatisfactory and inadequate were the existing arrangements. In Aberdeenshire about 1720, a meeting of proprietors held after Proclamation in the Parish Churches unanimously agreed 'that the whole highways and bridges within the said County should be repaired, amended and built with all convenient diligence'.[1] Their aims were high but their task was great. On the estate of Grant of Monymusk it was said that there was 'not one wheel carriage on the esteat nor indeed any one road that would allow it',[2] and Grant had reported that he could not get his wife from Aberdeen to Monymusk by coach. Twenty years later it was reported that there was no road in the County of Aberdeen on which wheels of any kind could be dragged,[3] a state of affairs which is less surprising when it is recalled that not until the middle of the century did a stage coach start running—or should one say moving?—twice a week between Edinburgh and Glasgow.

If these were the conditions prevailing on the fringe of the Highlands and in the relatively prosperous farming lands of Donside, what must the conditions have been in the Highlands themselves? Here, in the more populated glens and in the flatter land

[1] Alexander W., *Notes and Sketches illustrative of Northern Rural Life in the Eighteenth Century*, p. 85   [2] ibid.   [3] ibid.

by the sea, rough roads, tracks, or cobbled ways over bogs, had no doubt been made for foot traffic and for horses loaded with panniers or dragging sledges. For the rest, communications through nearly the whole vast area were little better than they had been for many centuries, moor, glen and mountainside traversed only here and there by the paths of men and the tracks of beasts.

George Wade, the real pioneer of Highland road-building, came to Scotland in the summer of 1724. Conditions in the Highlands at that time called for a soldier with strength and experience. The Union of the Parliaments was looked on by Scotland as a matter of unpleasant necessity whereby she had surrendered much and received little in return. The situation was tense and unquiet. Measures for the pacification and disarmament of the country after the Rising of 1715 had met with little success. Jacobite sympathies were strong among the clans, and the short Rising of 1719 had shown the danger from abroad. In 1724 Lord Lovat had presented to George I a Memorial on the conditions of the Highlands, with suggestions for dealing with the situation. 'The use of arms in the Highlands', he had written, 'will hardly ever be laid aside until by degrees they [the Highlanders] begin to find they have nothing to do with them.'[1] Wade was sent to Scotland to report, and in 1724 received the King's Commission as Commander-in-Chief in Scotland which he was to hold for fifteen years.

Wade's preliminary report in the summer of that year had made small reference to roads, though his instructions authorised him to repair and improve the roads linking the garrisons at Fort William, Fort Augustus and Inverness. Some doubt has been suggested as to the exact year when Wade started his road work, but he himself has left on record that he started work between Fort Augustus and Fort William in 1725. The main work of road-building was carried out during the next nine years, but some work was continued till 1736 when the High Bridge over the Spean was completed, and an entry in the House of Commons Journal shows a final payment of £1,000 'to Lieutenant General George Wade upon account for building a stone bridge over the River Spayen, near Fort William' in March 1737.[2]

[1] Burt's *Letters . . . from the North of Scotland*, II, p. 258
[2] House of Commons Journal, 1738

During these twelve years the roads actually constructed were: (1) from Inverness to Fort William following the south side of Loch Ness; (2) from Inverness to Dunkeld by Drumochter Pass; (3) from Fort Augustus by the Pass of Corrieyairack to Dalwhinnie; and (4) from Dalnacardoch by Tummel Bridge to Crieff. The total mileage by modern reckoning is slightly less than the 250 miles mentioned in the inscription on Wade's bridge over the Tay at Aberfeldy. The difference appears to be accounted for largely by a cross road, the exact route of which is not certain, from the barracks at Ruthven near Kingussie to join the road from Fort Augustus at Dalwhinnie. It may be, too, that Wade was responsible for the road by Glen Roy to join the Corrieyairack road, but this is still unproved. Whatever the exact figure, the field of controversy is narrow, and Wade's claim that he made 250 miles of road in the Highlands must be very near the truth.

Our knowledge of the details of Wade's work on the Highland roads comes partly from his own reports, but largely from an account of the work written by Edward Burt who in 1725 had been appointed 'Receiver and Collector of the unsold Forfeited Estates in Scotland'. Work on the roads was carried out entirely by military labour, and three to five hundred men were employed. In addition to their army pay they received extra pay ranging from 2s 6d a day for subalterns to 6d a day for private soldiers. Financing of the work was arranged through the newly established Royal Bank of Scotland, money being taken on horseback from Edinburgh to Fort William for payment to the garrison and for the men employed on the roads. No work was done in winter and spring. The road-making season was from May to October, and Wade himself appears to have gone south in the autumn of each year, returning to Scotland the following summer.

With unskilled labour and primitive tools no high standard of construction was possible. Burt, it is true, reported the new roads as being 'now as smooth as Constitution Hill', but it is difficult to avoid the conclusion that this was either a gross overstatement or a sad commentary on the state of the streets of contemporary London.[1] Wade himself speaks of travelling on the Inverness road in his coach 'with great ease and pleasure' through Drumochter Pass to the end of Loch Garry in Perthshire.[2] The standard

[1] *Letters . . . from the North of Scotland*, II, p. 193   [2] ibid., II, p. 213

width of the roads was sixteen feet, but this varied considerably. Where soft ground had to be crossed, the foundations were made with successive layers of stone of diminishing size, the top layer and the surface being gravel. For the most part the roads followed straight lines, but where steep gradients were met with, as in the crossing of the Corrieyairack Pass, traverses were made. Gunpowder was used on rocky ground. Describing the road from Inverness to Fort William on the south side of Loch Ness, Burt tells how 'the miners hung by ropes from the precipice over the water to bore the stone in order to blow away a necessary part from the face of it'.[1] At first rivers and streams were crossed by fords. Later it was found that these were so liable to be obstructed or obliterated by floods that many bridges became necessary. A total of forty stone bridges constructed by Wade included bridges over the Garry, the Tummel, the Spean and the Tay.

Only in places have the routes used by Wade been used for the roads of today. From Dalnacardoch to Aberfeldy the modern road follows Wade's line pretty closely, while the road from Fort Augustus by Corrieyairack remains largely as he made it. This route, long since abandoned for general use, continued to be used by sheep and cattle drovers until the end of last century.

The outcome of Wade's work in Scotland was a singular blend of failure and success. He had gone north charged with the task of disarming the rebellious clans and subduing the Highlands. Yet five years after he left, these clans were again bearing, in support of the Stuarts, the still serviceable arms which he had failed to take from them, while Prince Charles Edward was using Wade's road system in the preliminary manoeuvres of a campaign in which Wade's own part was far from distinguished. Were the

---

[1] Nearly a century later Joseph Mitchell, then Chief Inspector of Roads in the Highlands, writing of Highland Road development since Wade's time, made this comment on Wade's work: 'The usual practice in the roads constructed by General Wade was to excavate all the earth and turf until the gravel appeared when the Road surface was then dressed and formed on it; and the excavation and rubbish being thrown on either side, the Road (generally not more than 12 feet wide) was left in the form of a ditch. No great inconvenience was occasioned by this mode of construction in Summer; but in Winter it evidently formed a complete receptacle for snow.

'There existed another defect of no less consequence in the formation of these Roads. They were generally conducted in a series of direct lines over the irregular surface of the country, crossing and passing over the numerous hillocks without any regard whatever to easiness of acclivity. Consequently the wreaths of snow were formed and retained by these irregularities of the Road.' Report by Joseph Mitchell to Lord Colchester, 26 January 1828. Printed with 14th Report of Commissioners for Repair of Highland Roads and Bridges Appendix D.

outcome of Wade's mission between 1725 and 1740 to be judged on this alone, it must then be judged something of a failure, and it is on his work as a road-builder that his claim to fame must rest. What was the range of his vision as he planned his roads? Did he look on them purely as part of a military plan or did he see beyond? These must remain matters for speculation, but reading his periodical reports, the clear impression is of growing emphasis on road- and bridge-building as his true purpose. The soldier in him seems to give way progressively before the engineer and the administrator, the success of each year's work estimated in the miles of road constructed and the number of bridges built. 'I have had so much plague, vexation and disappointments', he writes to his friend Duncan Forbes of Culloden, Lord Advocate, about the construction of the Tay Bridge at Aberfeldy, 'that staggers my philosophy.'[1] Neither his projects nor his energy were curbed from London. Year after year the sums needed were voted by Parliament with a regularity which suggests that here, too, the angle of vision on the Highland problem was changing.

In the Highlands themselves criticism of Wade's work went far to justify it. The roads, it was said, opened the country to strangers and weakened the attachment of the clansmen to the chieftains, while remote districts were laid open to invasion; but the feeling was not entirely one of opposition. 'The Highlanders', Wade wrote as early as September 1726, 'from the ease and conveniency of transporting their merchandise begin to approve and applaud what they had first repined at and submitted to with reluctancy.'[2]

The credit for the major part of Highland road-making belongs to those who came after him, but to Wade belongs the distinction of being the first to recognise in practical fashion that the problem of the Scottish Highlands was then, as it remains today, largely one of communications. His achievement, limited as it was in scope, marks the start of a great work by which in the years to come Highland Glens and Passes, trodden successively by raiding clans and cattle thieves, by drovers and by the pack-horse of the travelling merchant, were brought at last to serve more adequately the needs of changing times.

[1] Salmond, J. B., *Wade in Scotland*, revised ed., p. 18
[2] *Inverness Scientific Society and Field Club Transactions*, vol. V, p. 156

Wade was succeeded in 1740 as Commander-in-Chief in Scotland by General Clayton, and for the next fifty years the extension of the military roads in the Highlands was carried on more or less continuously under a succession of military commanders. The actual construction work was still done by military labour, for many years under the direct supervision of Edward Caulfield who became Inspector of Roads with headquarters at Inverness. It is probable that some at least of this later road construction had been planned by Wade, though he himself had no direct part in any work after 1737. Under Clayton in 1741 and 1742 a military road from Stirling to Crieff was constructed,[1] and when Sir John Cope succeeded Clayton in 1743, the road from Dumbarton to Inveraray was put in hand at an estimated cost of £4,258. This was considered by the Lords of the Treasury to be excessive compared with the £3,270 which was the cost of making the whole stretch of the road from Crieff to Inverness in 1730; but even then costs were tending to increase.

The Rising of 1745 called a halt to road work, but it was soon resumed with renewed vigour and purpose, and between 1746 and 1748 was concentrated on the road from Dumbarton to Inveraray. Two years later, in 1750, when expenditure on the Inveraray road had almost ceased, work was started on the road between Stirling and Fort William by Lochearnhead and Tyndrum which remained the chief objective for the next two years. It was about this date, too, that the military road was built from Blairgowrie, by Braemar and the Upper Don, to the newly constructed military base at Fort George on the Moray Firth, some ten miles from Inverness, and reference to the building of bridges on this road and the erection of milestones in 1757 appears to show that by that date the Fort George road was nearly complete.

The records of the next few years contain references to new roads, through Strathbran from 'Conton in Ross-shire to Pollew', and from Fochabers to Strathbogie, but in August 1767 Caulfield, who as Inspector had for the past thirty-five years exercised a close control under successive commanders in Scotland, was succeeded by Colonel Skene, and the Treasury took advantage of the change to try to check the growth of what was proving a heavy and grievous charge on public funds. The concern felt by

[1] H. of C. Journals, vol. 24, pp. 127, 411

the Treasury was not unreasonable, for shortly after Colonel Skene succeeded Caulfield, he estimated that no less than 858 miles of military road had been completed, almost all in the Highlands, while 139 miles were under construction. These roads had been made largely by unskilled labour, many of the earlier ones at high speed, and in the circumstances it was inevitable that the cost of their repair and upkeep was rapidly increasing. It is probable, too, that as time passed, the sense of urgency, purpose and direction progressively waned. Hitherto the cost of repairing the military roads had been met each year out of Army Funds made good by a vote of Parliament in the following year, but from 1770 onwards, while a fixed annual sum of £500 was allowed for maintaining the original roads made by Wade, the estimated cost of maintaining the roads made since his time had to be laid before Parliament each year for approval. Despite this change, however, the cost of repair did not diminish nor did the efficiency of the work increase, and when in 1784 and 1785 General Mackay, then commanding the Forces in Scotland, reported to the Treasury on the state of the 682 miles of military roads then under his care, his report brought to light a state of affairs reflecting little credit on his immediate predecessors. 'No regular system', he writes, 'seems to have been laid down in carrying on this business. . . . These roads have in many places been very ill-conducted and, excepting a few stages, are at present in very bad repair. . . . The number of bridges upon these roads amount to 938. Many of them are insufficient, some ruinous, and others of those that were first built, injudiciously constructed and ill-executed.' 'Until the complete survey of these roads was made by Major Fraser,' he wrote in a covering letter of remarkable candour, 'the truth is we were all groping in the dark and for my own part I had no idea of the very bad order in which he reports them.'[1]

The reports which General Mackay made to the Treasury were detailed and comprehensive, and many of his recommendations for improving the system of road maintenance and controlling the cost were adopted. The employment of military labour on the roads ceased after 1790, and from that date onwards the work was carried out by civilian labourers working for a daily wage. Mackay had recommended that contractors should

[1] *Inverness Scientific Society and Field Club Transactions*, vol. V, pp. 378-9

be employed, and had his advice been followed some of the problems of the later years might well have been avoided.

The extent of the military roads in the Highlands had passed its peak, and from now onwards a policy of gradual reduction was adopted. The total of 682 miles of road reported by Major Fraser as being in some sort of repair in 1783, had been reduced by 1799 to just under 600, the annual sum spent on them falling from £7,000 in the period 1770 to 1783 to rather under £5,000 between 1783 and the end of the century. Three main lines of road were then in being: From Callander a road led by Loch-earnhead to Tyndrum, where it joined another which came up Loch Lomond and so by Arrochar and Inveraray to Dalmally. From the junction at Tyndrum the road led on over the Black Mount to Fort William, Inverness and Fort George. From Inverness a second road went by Aviemore, Dalwhinnie and Blair Atholl to Dunkeld and so up Strath Bran to Amulree and Crieff. The third main road ran from Fort George by Grantown and the Upper Don to Braemar, and south by Glenshee and Blairgowrie to Perth.

Besides these main military roads, a number of subsidiary roads which had been made since Wade's time were still in existence, but of these only two were north of the Great Glen. A road from Contin to Poolewe first appears in the records about the year 1760. It seems to have been kept in some sort of repair during the next twenty years, but after that there is no reference to work on it, and in a paper which Sir Kenneth MacKenzie read to the Inverness Scientific Society in 1899, he records that in the last year of the 18th century Lady Seaforth on her way to Lewis could only get as far as Loch Achanalt, fifteen miles from Contin, where her coach became a complete wreck.[1]

The only other military road to the north of the Great Glen ran from Fort Augustus to the barracks at Bernera at the foot of Glenelg, which had been built about 1722 to guard the narrow Kylerhea crossing to Skye. It is not certain at what date work was started on this road, but provision for it was made in the estimates laid before Parliament each year from 1770 to 1784. The first estimate included a sum for building an inn at Aonach in Glenmoriston, where three years later James Boswell and Samuel Johnson spent a night on their way to Skye and talked

[1] *Inverness Scientific Society Transns.*, vol. 5, p. 382

with the soldiers at work on the road.[1] The standard of work on the Bernera road must have been even lower than that attained on the other military roads, for when in 1803 Telford reported on the roads of the Highlands then in existence, he noted that 'from Fort Augustus there are just the vestiges remaining of what was once a military road to Bernera opposite the back of the Isle of Skye'.[2]

The total sum of public money spent on the military roads between the start of Wade's work and the end of the 18th century was probably well in excess of £300,000, and reading the somewhat confused records of the times it is impossible to avoid the conclusion that much of this was ultimately wasted. Central control was lacking and local supervision appears to have been slack. The military roads were initially intended for a purpose which, as time passed, came to be increasingly out of touch with the needs of the times. The problem of maintenance, too, had never been fully appreciated, and few had given thought to the effect of the Highland climate on long stretches of little-used roads passing through areas whose resources in men and money would have been in any event inadequate for the task of upkeep.

The second half of the 18th century saw a steady increase in the number of hardy travellers who ventured on journeys through the Highlands, and their records and comments serve to construct some picture of contemporary Highland travel, whether by the military roads or by such subsidiary roads as local efforts had made. The Judges of the Court of Session rode on circuit until far beyond the middle of the century.[3] Lord Lovat in 1740 had taken eleven days to go by coach from Inverness to Edinburgh, breaking his axle three times on the way, while thirty years later Boswell and Johnson found no roads fit for wheels north of Inverness. John Knox,[4] travelling in the Highlands in 1786 on behalf of the British Fisheries Society, noted the remarkably small extent of military roads in use considering the sums which had been spent. Bishop Forbes visiting the Northern Highlands in 1762 had found the road through Ross-shire to the north 'remarkably

[1] Boswell's *Journal of a Tour to the Hebrides*, edn. 1775, p. 149
[2] Survey and Report, 1803
[3] In March 1799 Colonel Anstruther, then Superintendent of the Military Roads in the Highlands, reported, 'To such a degree did the want of safe and easy intercourse between the Northern Counties affect even the ordinary administration of Justice, that until of late years the Counties of Sutherland and Caithness were not required to return jurors to the Northern Circuits at Inverness.'
[4] A Scottish bookseller and philanthropist living in London

good', but Knox found no roads in Sutherland, Caithness or Ross-shire, failing apparently to notice or to record the short-lived road from Contin to Poolewe which was to wreck Lady Seaforth's coach a few years later. 'Two Highways,' he reported, 'traverse the Highlands but the communications between them are miserable', and from him we first hear the complaint, so often to be echoed by succeeding generations, that only a path leads eastward across the Moor of Rannoch from Kingshouse. 'Through a considerable part of the year', he wrote, 'the inhabitants of each respective glen or valley may be considered as prisoners strongly guarded by impassable mountains on one side, by swamps and furious torrents on the other. They disappear from the public eye and are only seen by their neighbours in the low countries when the calls of their families lay them under the unavoidable necessity of venturing upon the arduous enterprise of a winter's journey.' Of the quality of such roads as existed Knox was very outspoken. 'It is hardly agreed upon by travellers', he writes, 'which is the line of road, everyone making one for himself. Even sheep follow better routes, understanding levels better and selecting better gradients.' The common rate of travel he reckoned as being only one mile an hour.[1] Knox must have been a far-sighted man, for already he was advocating the construction of new roads for civilian use and calling attention to the magnitude of the task, not only of making but of maintaining them. 'For this', he wrote, 'able engineers are needed with at least three to five hundred soldiers and as many Highlanders to help.' Organised and paid labour, he foresaw, must replace the hopelessly inadequate efforts of men giving unwilling Statute Labour such as he saw in Skye. Here, the inhabitants were working on different parts of the island 'under the inspection of the gentlemen and tacksmen and accompanied each party by a bag-piper. Some were eight miles from home with no lodging.'[2]

The journey which Knox undertook and the criticisms which he made on the lack of roads were not without result, for a few years later the British Fisheries Society decided, with Parliament's support, to undertake the construction of a road from Contin near Dingwall to the newly-established fishing village at Ullapool. The road was surveyed by George Brown of Elgin about 1790,

[1] Knox, J., *Tour through the Highlands of Scotland*, p. CXLIV
[2] op. cit., p. 136

and the estimate of cost was little short of £8,000 which the Government considered excessive. Kenneth Mackenzie of Torridon, however, offered to undertake the work, influenced as he later wrote by 'the avidity for labour and the necessities of the poor', and in the spring of 1792 a contract was entered into with him for the making of forty miles of road, at fourpence to eightpence a yard according to the nature of the ground, and a large number of bridges. This road was completed in 1797 at a total cost of £4,582, the Fisheries Society acting as agents between the Treasury and the contractor. Mackenzie's road fell quickly into disrepair, and when only twelve years later Telford and his colleagues were faced with a demand for its renewal, the inadequacy of Mackenzie's price and the poor quality of the work became all too clear. Telford's adverse comments were no doubt justified, but the work Mackenzie did provided employment at a time when this was much needed, and the efforts then made by the Fisheries Society may well have helped to show the way for the great project of Highland road-making soon to be undertaken.

As the century drew to a close other travellers were on the move through the Highlands with varied fortune. Mrs Grant of Laggan in her *Letters from the Mountains* wrote of her journey from Inveraray to Oban. 'The endless Moor,' which she describes, 'without any road except a small footpath through which our guide conducted the horses with difficulty', was probably the high ground lying between Loch Fyne and Loch Awe, through which the drovers of the time brought the Island cattle on their way to the Lowland trysts. The best accommodation on Loch Fyne was, she tells us, a thatched inn with clay floor where beside a peat fire the travellers ate trout, eggs, kippered salmon, new-made butter and barley cakes.[1] Dorothy Wordsworth about the same time, going from Dumbarton to Ballachulish and on over the Black Mount, found that the inns varied from wonderfully good to wretchedly bad, but she records that an excellent road led from Ballachulish to Glencoe and from Dalmally towards the Pass of Brander, where twelve years earlier Thomas Newte had described the road as being 1,000 feet up on the side of Ben Cruachan, without a parapet.[2]

[1] Mrs Anne Grant of Laggan, *Letters from the Mountains*, I, p. 12
[2] Thomas Newte, *Prospects and Observations on a Tour in England and Scotland, 1791*, p. 39

If the records left by travellers through the Highlands in this second part of the 18th century are too slender, too scattered and indeed too contradictory to afford material for any comprehensive view of the state of contemporary Highland Roads, the broad outlines of the picture which emerges are reasonably clear. Despite the great mileage of roads made by General Wade and his successors communications remained, with few exceptions, primitive and inadequate. Wheeled transport was still a rarity. Travel must be on foot or at best on horseback, while through many a Highland glen and over many a Highland moor the way which the traveller followed was marked only by the feet of the men and the hooves of the beasts of bygone centuries. The military roads, themselves ill-made, uncared for and now little used, were fast falling to ruin, and soon only a small remnant was to be left to the future care of the men whose great work for Scotland this book records.

2

OLD PROBLEMS AND NEW PLANS

As the old Military Roads of the Highlands moved from neglect to decay, large sections of the population of the country through which they passed were faring little better. The sweeping changes which the fifty years since Culloden had brought to the people of the Highlands had been matched by few constructive efforts to enable them to adapt their way of life to new conditions, and now as the 18th century drew to a close the lives and fortunes of thousands in the glens had sunk to a low ebb.

The end of the political revolution which was attempted in 1745 marked the start of a great social revolution, and as night fell on Culloden Moor the current of life in the Highlands imperceptibly but irrevocably set into a new course. For centuries past the social organisation of the Highlands had been feudal in character. At the apex of the social structure was the Chieftain, to whom all within the area of the clan owed an allegiance resembling more closely the relationship of parent and child than that of master and servant. Immediately below the Chieftain came the tacksmen holding for and from him on long leases areas of land of varying, but often considerable, extent. Below the tacksmen, and holding directly from them, came tenants and sub-tenants, working small parcels of land for which they paid rents, mainly in kind or in labour on the tacksmen's land, with some small rights in the grazing of the common hill. It was a system with little to commend it to the eye of the agriculturalist or the social reformer, but one which for long had been not unsuited to the needs of the times. For the Chieftain it gave the prestige and security of a large following against the frequent times of war or clan quarrels. For the tacksmen it offered a position of some social importance, a rent roll from the smaller tenants much in excess of that paid to the Chieftain, and cheap labour available almost at call. For the small tenants and sub-tenants the advantages were less obvious. For them, tenancies secured by more than custom and tradition were virtually unknown. With none but primitive implements, little learning

15

and no capital, they lacked the means, the knowledge or indeed the urge to improve the small scraps of land impoverished by constant cropping from which they won their meagre crops. Seed-time and harvest brought peremptory if untimely calls to work the ground or reap the crops of the tacksmen. So situated, they won a bare livelihood; seldom far from the verge of actual want; their status and indeed their very existence dependent on an ancient way of life; vulnerable and defenceless in the face of changes; marked out by Fate as the first to suffer when new times came.

Yet with so much to endure and so little, it seemed, to enjoy, it is doubtful how heavily the primitive and precarious nature of their existence weighed on the minds and spirits of these humble clansmen. If their resources were slender their needs were simple. If lack of learning put beyond their reach the improvement of their lot, so did it bring, if not contentment with, at least acquiescence in a condition than which they knew no better. Their duties and obligations were limited. In return for their services to the tacksmen and their ultimate allegiance to the Chieftain, they enjoyed the status of family membership and that measure of security which came from being one of a clan in days when security meant much.[1]

In the social structures which had thus grown up in the glens, while the final authority remained with the Chieftain the practical working of the system rested with the tacksman. To him had in effect been delegated all but the ultimate headship, and on him largely depended the welfare and happiness of the vast majority of the Highland people. In a widespread area like the Highlands, it was inevitable that great variations of character, intelligence and ability should be found among a class of men on whom depended so many and so much. Some paid little heed to the welfare of those who were dependent on them, supplementing their other sources of income with the rents and services exacted from their tenants, and caring for little else. Some were active and knowledgeable farmers, working the land in their own occupation

[1] Many years later when the condition of the small tenants of the Highlands at this period was under review, their status was thus described; 'They were entitled to security of tenure, subject to rent and services as the descendants or successors of those subordinate members or dependants of the family who in former ages won the land for the clan and maintained the fortunes of the Chief by their swords. This claim to security of tenure is held to have been in some sort transmitted to existing occupiers.' (Crofters Commission Report 1884, p.5)

Plate 1   General Wade

Plate 2   The Emigrants

with the help of their tenants. Some were careless, some benevolent and some intelligent; but some were exacting taskmasters,
severe and unscrupulous.[1] In the many reassessments of the social
and economic life of the Highlands in the 18th century which
have been attempted, the position, functions, merits and demerits
of the tacksmen have taken a prominent place. The judgments
passed by contemporary writers and those of more recent times
have varied no less than the character and qualities of those men
of whom they wrote, but critics and adherents alike find common
ground in their recognition of the tacksman as the lynch-pin of
the social structure, the removal of which would bring quick and
fundamental changes to the whole edifice.

Within two years of the failure of the Rising of 1745, there
took place in Scotland an event which at once foreshadowed
changes to come and made these changes inevitable. For centuries past, many of the great landlords and even some of the
smaller landed proprietors in both Highlands and Lowlands had
exercised wide powers of jurisdiction over the people living within
their lands. In many instances the powers so exercised enjoyed
no official recognition, but in not a few cases powers of jurisdiction
had, through ancient custom or by express grant, come to be
recognised by King and Government as hereditary rights per-
taining to the lands held. These rights were commonly known as
Heritable Jurisdictions. Wide and recognised powers of this
nature had long been exercised by certain of the great Highland
landowners, while over a large part of the Highland area the
jurisdiction of the chieftains, though not enjoying official recognition, had been tacitly accepted. In days when the King's Writ
ran little further than his arm could stretch, the exercise of jurisdiction by chieftains and landowners in remote areas was a
necessity. King and Parliament acquiesced in what they could
not prevent or themselves replace. Over a wide area some form
of justice was thus available to people to whom otherwise it would
have been denied, and it is probable that in the great majority of
cases chieftains, responsible for and dependent on the loyalty and
well-being of their clansmen, applied with reasonable if rough
equity the rules of right and wrong.

With the failure of the Rising of 1745 and the forfeiture of
many Highland estates which followed, the rights of jurisdiction

[1] Crofters Commission Report, pp. 5-6

which pertained to these forfeited estates became merged in the Crown, but throughout Scotland, in Highlands and Lowlands alike, many rights of Heritable Jurisdiction remained—some recognised and still more unrecognised—and the Government lost little time in bringing to an end a system which constituted a challenge and a danger to the central authority and which, in the Highlands at least, had largely contributed to the existence and growth of a divided loyalty. Those claiming rights of Heritable Jurisdiction were called on to submit claims for compensation on the extinction of rights, which not only carried with them prestige and status, but were in many cases of considerable monetary value.[1] The amounts claimed have been variously reported, but the total appears to have been not far short of £600,000, and following a searching examination by the Court of Session payments totalling over £150,000 were made. Many of the claims and awards were in respect of Jurisdictions in the Lowlands and the south of Scotland, but the existence and importance of these rights in the Highland area can be judged by the fact that the Duke of Argyll received no less than £21,000, the Duke of Gordon £5,282, the Earl of Moray £4,200, the Duke of Atholl £4,023 and the Earl of Breadalbane £1,000, while numerous smaller payments were made.[2] By an Act of 1746/7 Heritable Jurisdictions were abolished, and a damaging blow had fallen on the position and prestige of the Highland Chieftain and thus on the social structure which for centuries had sheltered the dwellers in the glens.[3]

While the sudden abolition of the rights of absolute authority which the chieftains of the Highlands had for so long exercised was an outward and visible sign of the changing times, it was in fact only one symptom of sweeping changes which were already taking place. The severe methods of repression which were adopted towards the Highlands by a Government shaken by two serious Risings in the space of thirty years, the military occupation of the Highlands and the work on the military roads all had their effect, and despite fierce resentment and bitter feelings in the

[1] Certain of these hereditary rights included the valuable rights of holding Fairs and Markets and of collecting the market dues, while in one case compensation was claimed for the loss of the office of 'Hereditary Keeper' of the Water of Tay and of the Rivers, Waters and Burns running into the same' with the power to hold Courts 'against takers of smouts [sic] kipper and fishes in forbidden times'.

[2] Acts of Sederunt 1532-1790, p. 419

[3] 20 George II, ch. 43

Highlands there were few who in their hearts did not feel that the old times had irrevocably passed away. With the changing times, too, had come almost inevitably a change of outlook. So long as the presence of large numbers of people in the glens was a real or at least a potential advantage to the chieftains, the old system of tacksmen and their tenants had served; but now all was changing. Many estates were in the hands of the Commissioners on the Forfeited Estates; from others the chieftains had been forced to fly after Culloden, while even in those cases where they remained, the numbers of their clansmen had ceased to be a matter of pride.

With the changing times came a new view of the use and functions of the tacksman. His peculiar position, which had hitherto been justified and indeed required in the old structure, was now seen to constitute only a superfluous and useless cog in the social machine which the new times were bringing into being. As the need for large followings passed, Highland lairds and chieftains came to view less kindly the existence of a favoured class standing between them and their tenants. The difference between the low rents paid by the tacksmen and those which they received seemed a high price to pay to middlemen for services which were now of little value. As the status of chieftainship diminished, so did its material advantages grow in importance. Profits from land ownership must now compensate for loss of prestige and power.

If the redundancy of the tacksmen was becoming yearly more obvious, their elimination from the social structure was not so easy. Many of them had long leases of their lands, and while some did little to justify their existence others were good managers of land, honestly serving the best interest of tenants whose welfare and livelihood depended entirely on them. But with the changing times the trend towards a new order was inevitable. As time passed the rents of many of the tacksmen were progressively raised. Some adapted themselves to the changed conditions by means of better farming methods; others emigrated, in many cases taking with them tenants bound to them by ties of long association or financial dependence. Others abandoned their farms, leaving their tenants to face the new conditions, deprived of the leadership and protection which for so long had sustained them— bewildered participants in a game where all the rules were changed.

While the growing unpopularity of the tacksmen and the pressure to oust them from the social system were bringing disruption and distress to the Highland glens, other factors were at work. The rapid settlement of the Highlands which followed the final defeat of the Stuart cause and the opening up of the country by means of the new military roads were bringing north in growing numbers economists, writers and social reformers, but with them others whose interest was less altruistic. With the coming of the second half of the 18th century a great revival had started in Scottish agriculture. New and better implements and growing knowledge of what could be achieved by land drainage, liming and better stock-breeding had put into train a process of improvement which over a long period to come was to bring a transformation in farming methods. Much land in the Lowlands and the south of Scotland which had hitherto afforded only poor grazing came under the plough, and stock-breeders in those districts, in search of new grazings, turned their eyes to the north. Improved farming methods, lower wage bills and rising prices enabled the men from the Lowlands to offer tempting rents, and Highland agriculture was entering on an era in which the low rented tacksman and the small tenant would have no place. Some tacksmen, faced with demands for higher rents from their lairds or chieftains, themselves raised their tenants' rents, or, if they farmed themselves, adopted farming methods which called for less labour. Others left the glens, leaving the field open for farmers from the south who were able to offer rents far beyond the means of the smaller tenants who stayed behind. Simultaneously with the rise in rents had come a rise in prices, caused partly by increasing demands from the growing industry of the Midlands and the north of England and partly by the American War, producing together conditions in which only those with capital, knowledge and enterprise could prosper. Gone were the days when small patches of arable land, dug, sown and reaped with prodigious labour could support large numbers of people paying small rents largely in kind or in services. The new farming was to a great extent stock farming calling for larger farming units, with more enclosing of land and growing encroachment on the common land and the hill ground. With the disappearance of the tacksmen, too, and the growth of absentee landlordism, money rents were coming more and more to be demanded in place of the produce and the field labour which had formerly been gladly accepted.

The redundancy and gradual elimination of the tacksmen and the growing competition from Lowland farmers would in themselves have proved fatal to the fortunes and livelihood of many of the small tenants; but Fate now dealt them a further blow. For centuries past the main livestock in the Highlands had been cattle. These cattle, owned in large numbers by the tacksmen and larger tenants, and in much smaller numbers by the sub-tenants, grazed in summer on the common hill-ground of the clan, being brought down in the autumn to pass the winter months on the stubbles and lower lands of the glens. As conditions in the Highlands became more settled, drovers from the south started to come north in the autumn to buy beasts for the Lowland markets, and during the 18th and much of the first half of the 19th centuries a busy if speculative droving trade existed. The existence and management of this cattle stock for a time interfered little with the arable farming of the glens, and until well into the second half of the 18th century sheep played a very small part; but soon after 1760 large-scale sheep-farming started to spread rapidly from the south of Scotland, and soon the growing competition for farms in the Highlands was further stimulated by the demands of the sheep-farmers. The new farming proved an added blow to small tenants already threatened with dispossession and extinction, for large-scale sheep-farms demanded wide areas of that hill ground in which common grazing rights had been enjoyed, while only a fraction of the population could now find employment in the new and unfamiliar trade of shepherding.[1]

To suggest that all these changes came about suddenly would be to ignore the facts, and would do less than justice to many of the landowners in the Highlands. If some landlords and some tacksmen were apathetic and unthinking, there were many who were not so. With not a few the old feelings of responsibility for the poorer tenants still remained strong, and there were not lacking instances where low rents continued to be accepted from old tenants in the face of higher offers. Tacksmen with long

---

[1] 'This [sheep-farming] not only requires much fewer people to manage the same track of country, but in general an entirely new people who have been accustomed to this mode of life are brought from the Southern parts of Scotland.' (Telford's *Survey and Report*, 1802)

leases clung to their lands, fortified in many cases by the possession of much of the stock and implements on the estate, and resisting for themselves and their tenants the inroads of the new flow of the tide. The spread of sheep-farming, rapid in some areas, was more gradual in others. In Glengarry the change to sheep was delayed until the end of the 18th century, while in other parts of west Inverness-shire, the Islands and the north-west its progress was slow.[1] But such areas of resistance were the exception rather than the rule. 'The Lairds', wrote Telford in 1802 in his Second Survey and Report, 'have transferred their affections from the people to flocks of sheep and the people have lost their old veneration for the Lairds.' The pressure of economic change was steadily mounting, and as the 18th century neared its end the last strongholds of the old order were yielding one by one.

The first serious signs of emigration from the Highlands followed closely on the beginning of the movement to dispossess the tacksmen. The emigration was partly from Inverness-shire but mainly from the Hebrides, and while the total numbers involved can only be conjectured, the numbers who left in the ten years from 1763 to 1773 have been reliably estimated as being in the region of 10,000.[2] Many of these were tacksmen or large tenants with capital, education and initiative, but with them went very many of the smaller tenants, linking their fortunes in North America with those of the men to whom for so long they had looked for livelihood and leadership. Close on the heels of these first emigrants went a second wave in the last years of the 18th and early years of the 19th centuries. While it seems reasonably certain that the first emigration must be closely associated with the eviction of the tacksmen, the responsibility for the later movement lies partly with over-population and rise in rents and partly with the spread of sheep-farming.[3]

The fluctuations of fortune which the past two centuries have brought to the Scottish Highlands have throughout presented to those responsible for their solution problems of peculiar complexity. If the answer to the Highland problems of today seems

[1] Haldane, *The Drove Roads of Scotland*, ch. 11
[2] Adam, 'The Highland Emigration of 1770' *Scottish Historical Review*, XVI, pp. 281-2
[3] Adam, 'The Causes of the Highland Emigration of 1783-1803', *Scottish Historical Review*, XVII, p. 73. 'In some few cases a greater population than the land can support in any shape has been the cause of emigrations; such was the Island of Tiree.' (Telford's Survey and Report, 1802)

yet uncertain it can be small wonder that the economists and politicians of the late 18th century found their task difficult. With the opening up of the country in the second half of the century, Highland problems had come to have a new-found prominence and urgency. Signs of distress and disruption among the Highland people were all too evident, but as to the causes and the cures there was, among contemporaries, little unanimity. Some saw in the consolidation of small farms and the enclosure of large areas of grazing for large-scale stock-farming a cruel and unjustifiable hardship on the small occupiers dispossessed, while others, admitting the hardship, regarded it as an inevitable consequence of the change to that type of farming to which the Highlands were best suited. To one school of thought the chief wealth of the Highlands lay in its large population, and to its adherents emigration seemed an unmitigated evil to be discouraged at all costs.[1] Others, conscious of the growing over-population, looked on emigration as an inevitable consequence and a reasonable solution.

The views of the opponents of emigration were soon to gain support and cogency from a new factor. After the Rising of 1715 six companies of men locally recruited had been raised and successfully used to check plunder and preserve the peace. Though these companies were later disbanded they formed the nucleus of the 42nd Highlanders, The Black Watch, and were the predecessors of the famous Highland regiments to come. With the progressive recession of memories of 1745 came the idea of enlisting for the public service the military qualities of those men who had come so near to restoring the Stuarts. Stimulated by the success which had already attended the raising of the earlier companies, William Pitt, the elder, embarked on the raising of Highland regiments on a more extended scale. 'I sought for merit wherever it was to be found', he declared in his speech in Parliament at the beginning of the American War in 1766. 'It is my boast, that I was the first minister who looked for it and I found it in the mountains of the North. I called it forth, and drew it into your service, a hardy and intrepid race of men. Men who, when left by your jealousy became a prey to the

---

[1] 'The late and present emigrations from the Highlands which some view with pleasure and too many with indifference ought to be considered as a great national calamity.' George Dempster, *A Discourse containing a Summary of Proceedings of the Directors of the British Fisheries Society since 25th March 1788*

artifices of your enemies and had gone nigh to have overturned the State in the war before the last. These men, in the last war, were brought to combat on your side, they served with fidelity, as they fought with valour, and conquered for you in every part of the world.'[1]

By the end of the century the exploits of the Highland regiments in Europe, Canada and America had enormously enhanced their reputation both in the army and in the eyes of the public, and the growing flow of emigrants from the Highlands was looked on as a grave threat to the future recruitment of an outstanding part of the Armed Forces of the Crown. Contemporary views as to the probable effect of emigration on recruiting for the army were by no means unanimous. The Earl of Selkirk, one of the advocates of emigration, writing just after the turn of the century, considered that those who were leaving Scotland were not of the class likely to be recruits, and that in any event the general rise in rents and growing independence of those tenants who remained in the Glens would soon bring an end to extensive recruiting from the Highlands.[2] Doctor John Macculloch supported the view that the occupation of even a small area of land made tenants averse to leaving it for the army, and regarded the so-called threat to the forces as arithmetically absurd, based on gross exaggeration of the number of Highland recruits.[3] More than half a century later, in the course of their review of the conditions prevailing in the Highlands between the break-up of the clan system and the early years of the 19th century, the Crofters Commission reported, 'It may be doubted whether enlistment in the regular army was for any length of time generally popular or entirely spontaneous. The evidence on this subject is conflicting. Martial traditions and hereditary attachments on the part of the tenantry, transmitted authority and personal popularity on the part of the Chief had no doubt a preponderant influence in eliciting those contributions to the national defence before the American War which we now regard with admiration and wonder. Promises of favour on one side and dread of dis-

---

[1] Rev. F. Thackeray. *History of Earl of Chatham*, vol. II, p. 62. Joseph Mitchell refers to the raising of 1,100 men in nine days by the Earl of Sutherland at Pitt's request in 1759, of 800 in Lord Reay's Country in 1792 and of 1,000 on the Sutherland Estates in 1800. (*Reminiscences*, vol. 2, p. 89.)

[2] Selkirk, *Observations on the Present State of the Highlands etc.*, 1805

[3] Macculloch, *The Highlands and Western Isles of Scotland*, IV, p. 143

pleasure on the other in connection with the land were, towards the end of the last and the beginning of the present century, when many Highlanders enlisted, perhaps more operative causes.'[1] In this, as in so much else affecting the Highlands, contemporary opinion was divided and confused, but there is little doubt that, whether well or ill founded, fears of a serious threat to Britain's military resources came to constitute a potent force.

So long as the clan organisation and the tacksman's position remained firmly established, the population of the Highlands was scattered far up the glens, but as the break-up of the clan and growing enclosure steadily reduced the area of land available for the small tenants there started a gradual move to the coast and a concentration, as if for mutual support, of those made homeless. It may be that for some the move was not unconnected with an instinctive feeling that their days in Scotland were running out, and that the only future lay overseas, but to others the sea offered, not only a means of escape but a new chance of livelihood. For nearly two centuries fishing round the coast of Scotland had been vigorously and successfully exploited by the Dutch, and not a few efforts had been made to stimulate the industry in Scotland. Men like James Anderson and David Loch had championed the cause of the fisheries. A Committee of the House of Commons had reported favourably on their future possibilities and in 1786 John Knox made a long journey through the Highlands which culminated in the establishment of the British Fisheries Society. The aims of the Society and of its promoters were ambitious. In an extensive tour of the west coast and the Islands a Committee of Inquiry visited possible sites for fishing stations in Skye, Harris, Mull, Canna and Lewis, while on the mainland Ullapool, Lochinver, Assynt, Gruinard, Torridon and Lochewe were among the many sites considered on the whole line of the coast from Arran to Dornoch.[2]

The constant and unpredictable movement of the herring shoals had always been a difficult problem. 'The herring be indeed a whimsical as well as migrating animal', wrote one of the advocates of the fisheries in 1791,[3] while some doubted whether the Highlander would ever come to look on fishing as more than a

[1] *Crofters Commission Report*, 1884, p. 6
[2] Knox, *A Tour through the Highlands* . . ., 1786, p. 275. Dunlop, 'The British Fisheries Society 1786-1893' (unpublished thesis, 1952)
[3] Newte, *Prospects and Observations on a Tour in England and Scotland*, 1791, p. 85

part-time occupation. Each of these criticisms was to prove well founded, but the new plans went forward. With the aid of public subscriptions large areas of land were bought at Ullapool, at Tobermory and at Stein in the north-west of Skye. The public imagination had been touched. Generous contributions came from Scots abroad. Clan Ranald offered a free gift of sites on Canna and South Uist, while Captain Huddard of the Royal Navy, who had already done work on surveys of the coasts of these islands, offered to make, free, a survey of the west coast of Scotland.[1]

The Ullapool plans in particular were comprehensive and ambitious. Fifteen hundred acres of land had been acquired and soon contracts had been placed for the building of a workshop, a school and an inn besides curing and barrelling houses, a salt store and workers' houses, while a Customs House for clearing vessels inward and outward bound had been established on Isle Martin in the mouth of Loch Broom. Thomas Telford acted as general surveyor and engineer, his services being at first paid and later given free. The Society for the Propagation of Christian Knowledge had co-operated in payment of a schoolmaster, and plans were afoot for importing flax for the inhabitants to spin as a subsidiary industry.[2]

In the early years of the British Fisheries Society attention was thus concentrated on the west coast. The sea lochs and the coastal waters, sheltered by the islands of the Hebrides, afforded many tempting sites for fishing stations. At that time the herring shoals were appearing in western waters with a regularity sufficient at least to appeal to the sanguine temperament of the fisherman. Arnisdale on Loch Hourn was already a fishing village of some importance, and despite the objections of the Revenue and the opposition of the saltmakers in the south there were hopes that ways could be found of overcoming the difficulties which the complex Salt Laws presented. The primitive but intensive corn cultivation hitherto practised in the glens could, it was claimed, be with advantage replaced along the coast by potatoes and flax. 'The leaking showers which fall out in the Highlands during the months of May, June and July', wrote

---

[1] By 1788 £33,000 of the total of £150,000 aimed at had already been raised by public subscription, including £5,000 from Scots in Bengal. (George Dempster, *Discourse . . . British Fisheries Society*, 1789)
[2] Dempster, ibid.

George Dempster, one of the chief supporters of the Society, 'render that Country remarkably fit for flax husbandry.'[1] The prospect of thriving fishing villages on the western seaboard, inhabited by men and women drawing an ample livelihood alike from sea and land, seemed no mere dream, and to many it must have appeared that the solution of Highland problems was almost in sight. In an honest belief that here lay the solution lies the justification of those who encouraged the drift to the coast, but it does little to lighten the burden of blame on some who forced this movement ruthlessly and with small regard to those displaced.[2]

The high hopes of the Society for the West Coast Fisheries were to be disappointed. The whimsies of the herring resulting in a movement of the shoals from west to east, were to divert attention from Ullapool, Mull and Skye to Wick and the north-east coast. The harvests from the coastal waters of the west proved too meagre and too intermittent to support the dwindling hopes of men and women already dispirited by change of conditions. Hardship and apathy continued, and with them emigration. The Skye station of the Society was abandoned in 1837, that in Mull two years later, while in 1847 the Ullapool station, of which so much had been hoped, was sold to Mr Mathieson of Lewis.[3]

The dispossession and distress which followed the break-up of the clan system and the elimination of the tacksmen coincided closely with the emergence in the Highland economy of a factor which must at first sight have appeared to many as almost a divine intervention. For many years past the alkali used in the manufacture of soap and glass and in bleaching had been obtained from a substance known as barilla, largely imported from Spain. The import of barilla had for long been subject to duty, but about 1781 the rate of duty was progressively and steeply raised, and during the French War the trade was virtually at a standstill. It was known that the alkali could be obtained by a more expensive and cumbrous process by burning the seaweed known as kelp, and as the supply of barilla dwindled so did the demand for the kelp product increase. Kelp occurred in very large quantities all along the many thousands of miles of Scotland's western coast-

[1] Dempster, ibid., p. 7

[2] Southey, p. 136. It would seem, too, that undue reliance on the possibilities of coastal fishing led to the size of these early crofts being fixed too low, a defect which is apparent in very many of the crofts and small holdings of today.

[3] Dunlop, op. cit., ch. XI

line, the weed for burning being obtained by cutting every third
year or by collecting the more valuable drift weed brought in by
the sea. Shortly after the end of the Napoleonic War the duty on
barilla was again reduced, so lowering the price of alkali produced
from kelp to an uneconomic figure, but it has been estimated that
during the years when the demand was at its peak the annual
value of the output from western Scotland may have reached
£400,000 with forty to fifty thousand people dependent on it.[1]
If the great bulk of this harvest went to the owners of the large
coastal or island estates, the collection of the weed provided much
welcome employment, but contemporary writers are almost unanimous in their view that the benefits of this sudden and short-
lived windfall were in most cases wastefully dissipated and in not
a few totally misapplied. For the workers, the wages earned in the
collection and burning of the weed did little more than supplement their income at a time when the fishing on the west coast was
deteriorating. To them the transitory and fortuitous nature of the
kelp revenue was not apparent. The more reliable and more permanent resources of their crofts were thus neglected, and the
collapse of the kelp industry shortly after 1820 hit them hard.[2]
For the big landowners in the west and in the Islands the large
sums received during the heyday of the industry offered a golden
opportunity of carrying out improvements on roads, cottages and
farm buildings which would have gone far to reduce the distress in
the hard days to come. Instead, the rise in revenue was, it seems,
in most cases used as a means of borrowing on the security of their
estates large sums for unproductive expenditure, much of it outside the Highlands.[3]

So, as the century drew to a close the problems of Highland
Scotland mounted.[4] Destitution, apathy and emigration were the
visible symptoms of a disease, the ravages of which all could

[1] Mitchell, I, Ch. xxv. 'I think I was present, in 1826,' wrote Mitchell, 'at the
burning of the last heap at Dunvegan, which they said would fetch £8 to £10 per ton.'
[2] There was at this time no organised Poor Relief in Scotland. Destitution in
each parish was met solely by voluntary collections at the church doors.
[3] Mitchell sums up the position in these words: 'Kelp, therefore, when it was
substituted for barilla ... brought nothing but one series of unmitigated misfortunes
both to the proprietors and people.' (Mitchell, I, 207)
[4] 'The history of the economical transformation which a great portion of the
Highlands and Islands has during the past century undergone,' wrote the Crofters
Commission in 1884, 'does not repose on the loose and legendary tales that pass from
mouth to mouth; it rests on the solid basis of contemporary records and if these were
wanting it is written in indelible characters on the surface of the soil.' (*Crofters
Commission Report*, p. 2)

recognise, the true nature of which few could define and the cure for which none could find. The diagnoses pronounced were as numerous and as varied as the cures suggested. Over-population, rack-renting, insecurity of tenure and sheep-farming, each in turn were blamed. Controlled emigration, fishing, abolition of services, leases and new methods of farming each were in turn prescribed. While the doctors disagreed the patient suffered. Yet, even in their disagreement one common ground was slowly becoming apparent, in their prescriptions one ingredient common to nearly all.

For over half a century expenditure on the construction and upkeep of the military roads in the Highlands had been a recurring item in Government budgeting. Yet, for all the labour and all the money which had gone in this work communications in the Highlands remained sadly deficient, a deficiency which, as the century neared its end, was fast becoming increasingly apparent. 'The Highlands were at peace; the Government had no longer reason to apprehend rebellions and civil wars; the feuds of rival clans had been fought out and the turbulance of the people had been subdued; but in civilisation and industry these remote mountain districts were at least 50 years behind the Lowlands of Scotland and all parts of England. The value of military roads had been proved by the tranquillity of the Country, and it was now evident that more extended communications were neccessary for the development of its natural resources.'[1]

To the advocates of the fishing industry, the importance of improved communications was all too clear. Without good roads, especially between west and east, the herring fishers would be hampered in disposing of their catch, in getting supplies for boats and crews, or in receiving early news of the erratic movement of the shoals. It was at the instigation of the fishing interests that the new road from Dingwall to the west coast was put in hand, and it was the construction of this road which decided the Society to choose Loch Broom rather than Loch Ewe or Gairloch for the site of a fishing station.[2] For the farming community the new Highland Society urged the need of new and better roads, while in the Statistical Account and the new Agricultural Surveys which were fast appearing, one writer after another wrote of the same weakness and the same need.

[1] H.R. & B. Final Report, March 1863   [2] Dunlop, op. cit., ch. III

The thoughts which were thus slowly shaping themselves in men's minds were not confined to roads alone. For more than a quarter of a century economists and engineers had toyed with the idea of a great waterway from east to west to bring into fruitful union the wealth and industry of the east coast and the rich coastal waters of the west and to remove, for naval and civilian shipping alike, the hazards of the exposed and dangerous passage by Cape Wrath and the Pentland Firth. For the important cattle-droving industry a canal through the Great Glen would afford favourable sites for trysts, where breeders and dealers from the north could sell their beasts without incurring the costs and delays of the long journeys to Crieff and Falkirk. A canal, too, it was claimed would result in the cultivation of thousands of acres of waste land along its banks and the opening of limestone and slate quarries, while facilitating the marketing of the oak, fir and birch woods in Glengarry, and the pine forests in Glen Moriston and on the shores of Loch Arkaig.

If the ultimate aims and purposes of the planners remained divergent and debatable, the means to those ends were thus approaching some measure of unison. Whether for agriculture, fishing, social welfare or central authority, new ways through the glens were now seen to be long overdue. If they achieved nothing more they would give work, hope and livelihood to thousands, and would surely check the insidious flow of emigrant ships. So, by different paths and with hesitant steps the planners had come at last to stand on common ground. The stage was set, the audience impatient, the actors ready and waiting to take their call, chief among them the great engineer, who in the years to come was to play so large a part.

3

THE LAUNCHING OF TWO GREAT PROJECTS

On 27 July 1801 Nicholas Vansittart, Joint Secretary to the Treasury, sent to Thomas Telford, Civil Engineer, the preliminary instructions which were to mark the beginning of a great work for the Highlands. Telford was already familiar with the Highlands and their problems, for during the last ten years he had acted as surveyor to the British Fisheries Society. His instructions from the Treasury now were to select the most suitable fishing stations on the west coast, to plan safe and convenient communications between the mainland and the islands and to consider the possibility of inland navigation from the east coast to the west.

To this formidable task Telford set himself with a speed and energy which during the next thirty years were to mark all he did. His first journey in the late summer and early autumn of 1801 took him through Lochaber to Fort William and up the Great Glen to Inverness. From there he went by Dingwall up the northeast coast to Wick, returning to Inverness and so along the south shore of the Moray Firth to Peterhead. Fear of bad weather and enthusiasm for his task hurried his steps. 'The apprehension of the weather changing for the worse', he wrote to his friend Doctor Currie at Liverpool, 'has prompted me to incessant hard labour so that I am now almost lame and blind.'[1] Telford's distrust of the weather proved, for once, unfounded. 'Never was there a season more favourable for making Surveys', he wrote subsequently to his friend Andrew Little at Langholm. 'I passed along the Western and Central Highlands, from thence to the extremity of the Island and returned along the Eastern Coast to Edinburgh, and scarcely saw a cloud upon the Mountains' top. It would require a Volume to specify anything like the particulars of this journey. I shall therefore only say that every part of my Survey exceeded my expectations and I did not leave anything unaccomplished which came within the compass of my Mission, and I am now possessed of Data which will enable me to make out Plans

[1] Letter to Dr James Currie, October 1801

and Reports which I trust will be satisfactory.'[1] Little missed
Telford's observation during that first journey, and by 17 October
he was able to write to Vansittart that the result of his survey
showed 'that the whole of the objects which their Lordships have
in view are not only practicable but are capable of being formed
into one intimately connected system which would very evidently
have a striking effect upon the welfare and prosperity of the
British Empire'. Of the proposed canal through the Great Glen
he wrote that he was convinced that it could be formed, that he
had observed no serious obstacles on any part of its line and that
by means of it 'the fisheries would not fail to be improved and
much extended.[2]

Telford's imagination and enthusiasm had been deeply
stirred by all he had seen and heard in the Highlands, and during
the next few months he waited, with impatience but growing
hope, for further instructions. 'Never when awake—and perhaps
not always when asleep,' he wrote to Andrew Little in April 1802,
'have my Scottish Surveys been absent. . . . If they [the Govern-
ment] will only grant me £1,000,000 to improve Scotland, or
rather promote the general prosperity and welfare of the Empire,
all will be quite well and I will condescend to approve of their
measures.' Telford had not long to wait. Impressed by the
encouraging nature of his first Report, the Lords of the Treasury instructed him to continue his surveys during the summer of 1802. His first instructions had limited his terms of
reference, but in making his second survey he was directed to
inquire into the wider question of the causes of emigration. By the
early spring of 1803 his second Report was complete. 'I have
endeavoured', he wrote to Little on his return, 'to make the
Northern proprietors sensible of their own interests and to convince the Government and the public that the Nation at large is
deeply interested in the proposed improvements.'[3] Much of the
second Report was devoted to plans for the construction of
new roads both north and south of what was already referred
to as the 'Caledonian Canal', and of bridges over the larger
rivers. Of the country north and west of the Great Glen he
wrote, 'It is incalculable the loss which the public has sustained

[1] Letter to Andrew Little, 30 November 1801
[2] Letter to Vansittart, 7 October 1801
[3] Letter to Andrew Little, 18 February 1803

Plate 3   Thomas Telford

Plate 4   John Rickman

and are about to suffer from want of roads in this country.'[1]

As to emigration, Telford saw in the introduction of sheep and the consequent change in the economy of Highland estates the main cause. 'From the best information I have been able to procure,' he reported, 'about three thousand persons went away in the course of the last year, and if I am rightly informed three times that number are preparing to leave the country in the present year'; but he was careful not to pass judgment on those who had preferred the new ways to the old. Some, he pointed out, considered that economic changes should be allowed to take their course; others saw great hardship and injustice in people being driven from their native country to make room for sheep-farming. 'In whatever light', he concluded, 'the foregoing statements may be viewed, there is another on which there can I think be no difference of opinion. This is that if there are any public works to be executed, which when completed will prove generally beneficial to the country, it is advisable these works should be undertaken at the present time: the Caledonian Canal and the roads and bridges before mentioned are of the description here alluded to; they will not only furnish present employment but promise to accomplish all the leading objects which can reasonably be looked forward to for the improvement in the future welfare of the country whether we regard its agriculture, fisheries or manufactures.'[2]

The speed with which the Government took action on Telford's second Report was a measure of their alarm at the distress in the Highlands and the growing emigration with its threat to recruitment for the Services. A Select Committee of the House of Commons was appointed to go into all the matters arising from Telford's Surveys, and three months later their work was complete. 'The improvement of internal communications by means of Roads and Bridges, essential in itself, and for the introduction of all subsequent improvements could not but occupy the early attention of the Committee. They were naturally led to this subject indeed by the existence of the Military Roads, which although made for a particular purpose, and with little or no regard for such ascents and descents as do not impede the passage of an Army had become so useful in a Country destitute of better Roads, as to demonstrate the greater benefit which could not but result from

---

[1] Telford's *Survey and Report*, 1803   [2] ibid.

a judicious extension of what had been done, and the Report which was under the consideration of the Committee developed a consistent plan of internal communication.'[1] As to the roads and bridges, the Select Committee advised that Telford's recommendations should be accepted, but that as the cost of their construction was more than could be met locally, one half should be provided from public funds, the remaining half to be contributed by those local proprietors deriving benefit from them.[2]

On the question of the canal there seems to have been rather more doubt. One of the arguments for its construction was that it would avoid the dangers both from foreign attack on shipping in the English Channel bound for the east coast ports and from bad weather on the long passage round the north of Scotland. No evidence appears to have been available as to losses from the first cause, but the Committee had before them a Report prepared in the early months of 1803, on losses to shipping from weather during the previous three years. The Report, which was largely the work of Captain Gwyn, the commander of the latest of the series of Government galleys which had been stationed on Loch Ness since Wade's time, showed that in these three years fifty-three ships varying from fifty to one thousand tons had been totally lost on the northern passage, and twenty-nine driven ashore or damaged, with losses of merchandise ranging from wheat flax, hemp and hides, to iron, lime, timber and tar. Losses were reported from the Outer Isles, from Orkney and Shetland, from Cape Wrath and the Pentland Firth, and on the assumption that many more were unreported owing to the remoteness of the area and the lack of communications, it was estimated that they represented a total loss in money of well over three hundred thousand pounds.[3] The Select Committee appear to have taken the not unreasonable view that this was largely guesswork, but their conclusion was that whatever the actual figure, the present route for shipping was highly dangerous. Loch Ness, they observed, never froze; winds were only dangerous from November to February, while good anchorages in Loch Ness and Loch Lochy, and many other natural features, favoured the making of a canal through the Great Glen. The work, they considered,

[1] H.R. & B. 9th Report, 1821
[2] H.R. & B. Report of Parliamentary Committee, June 1803
[3] 3rd Report of Committee on Caledonian Canal, 2nd Appendix

would give much-needed employment and might check emi-gration, and their final conclusion was in favour of 'a measure highly conducive to the prosperity and happiness of that part of Scotland in which it is situated and of great importance to the general interest of the whole United Kingdom'. As the sum in-volved was far beyond local resources, they recommended that the work be done solely out of public funds,[1] accepting Telford's rejection of a proposal that a branch of the canal should link the Great Glen with Loch Duich.[2] Of the whole project for roads and canal, the Committee reported to Parliament that 'they have not recommended that the smallest additional burden be thrown on the public unless to prevent that emigration which will de-prive the country of its hardiest and bravest protectors who have distinguished themselves most conspicuously by sea and land, and with a view to improve that commerce which must amply repay the pecuniary assistance your Committee have thought it their duty to advise'.

On 15 June 1803 Mr I. Hawkins Brown rose in the House of Commons to move the House to grant a sum up to £20,000 for the making of roads and bridges in the Highlands,[3] and before the end of the following month the Royal Assent had been given to the Acts of Parliament setting up the two parallel Commissions charged with the construction of roads and bridges in the High-lands of Scotland and the making of the Caledonian Canal.[4]

The constitution of the two Commissions which now took up their heavy tasks showed the importance which the Government attached to the projects and the careful thought which had been given to their execution. The Chairman of each was Charles Abbot (later Lord Colchester), the Speaker of the House of Commons, who for more than twenty-five years was to take a leading part in the work, acting as Chairman from 1803 to 1817. The Treasury ensured close control by the presence on each Commission of Nicholas Vansittart, who had issued the first instructions to Telford and who had since become Chancellor of the Exchequer. The British Fisheries Society, which had been closely connected with the plans from the start, was strongly represented by the presence on each Commission of a number of

---

[1] Report of Parliamentary Committee, June 1803
[2] Telford had also advised against a suggestion that Loch Eil should be connected by canal with Loch Shiel. Telford, *Survey and Report*, 1803
[3] *New Annual Register*, 1803, p. 200   [4] 43 George III, chs. 80 and 102

its directors, including Vansittart, Charles Grant the Member of Parliament for Inverness-shire, and Sir William Pulteney, whose work was later commemorated in Pulteneytown, the original name given to the fishing port of Wick. At a time when human life was shorter than it is today, it was fortunate indeed for Scotland that not a few of these men, together with their three great servants, lived to see the completion of the work entrusted to them.

If the importance of the work now to be put in hand was evident to all, it is doubtful if any realised the full magnitude or complexity of the tasks to which the Commissions were committed. The last quarter of the century had seen a great increase in the number of travellers to the north, but none the less the Highlands of Scotland remained a little-known area. Maps were few and poor, and the most reliable survey which had yet been made had long lain and still lay forgotten and undisturbed on the shelves of the King's Library. Despite the many years and the large sums which had been spent on the military roads, the few that remained in use were rapidly falling into disrepair. Even the journey from Perth to Inverness was a long hazardous adventure, while off the beaten track, and in all but a few of the Highland Glens, travel must be on foot or at best by pony. Even between London and Edinburgh a letter took four days, and few would have cared to estimate with any exactness the time of its delivery in Inverness by way of Aberdeen.

Money was scarce, tools were primitive, and there were few with the resources or the experience to undertake with much hope of success any but the smallest and simplest jobs. If in these conditions large-scale road-making seemed a formidable task, how must the project in the Great Glen have seemed to the ordinary man or woman? To construct across Scotland a waterway over sixty miles in length and of a minimum depth of twenty feet; a waterway rising to an elevation of one hundred feet and draining an area of twelve hundred square miles of the most mountainous part of the Highlands; here was a pioneer work without parallel or precedent which surely must have staggered the imagination of all but a few.

When Thomas Telford received in the summer of 1803 the final orders which launched him on his work in the Highlands, he had already, at the age of forty-six, attained a position of great eminence in his profession. His father, a shepherd in the valley of the Dumfriesshire Esk, had died while Thomas was still very young, and his boyhood had been a hard one. After serving an apprenticeship as a mason in Dumfriesshire, he came to Edinburgh about 1780 where there was ample scope for masons in the building of the New Town; but after two years he went to England. Here, first in London and then at Portsmouth, he quickly set himself to gaining experience and amassing knowledge and information far beyond the ordinary scope of a stonemason. 'Knowledge', he wrote about this period, 'is my most ardent pursuit; a thousand things occur which would pass unnoticed by good easy people who are contented with trudging on in the beaten path; but I am not contented unless I can reason in every particular.'[1] In 1787 Sir William Pulteney, who was later to be closely associated with Telford's work in Scotland, took him to Shropshire where he was soon appointed Surveyor of Public Works. In Shropshire he was concerned in works of great variety, while continuing studies on an immense range of subjects bearing directly or even remotely on his professional work; but already there were signs of the direction in which his genius and his later work were to develop. This was the age when men's minds were full of the great possibilities of canal construction, and in this development Telford took a full share. In 1793 he was appointed engineer and architect of the Ellesmere Canal to connect the Severn with the Mersey, and in the next year he became engineer to the Shrewsbury Canal. Telford seems to have had a genius for storing in his mind for later use not only a stupendous volume of miscellaneous knowledge, but with it a recollection of the men whose merits and experience could be used in other spheres of work, and many of those who were associated with him in his work at this time were later to share in his Scottish work. 'Telford's is a happy life', wrote his friend Southey at a later date, 'everywhere making roads, building bridges, forming canals and erecting harbours—works of sure, solid, permanent utility; everywhere employing a great number of persons, selecting the most meritorious and putting them forward in the world in his own way.'[2]

It was about this time that Telford first became connected with work in Scotland, advising the British Fisheries Society in connection with plans for the building of a harbour at Wick, and

---

[1] Letter to Andrew Little, 1 February 1796   [2] Southey, p. 54

by 1796 he was already acting as official engineer to the Society. The new plans for the Highlands were, in their early stages, centred mainly on the development of the fishing industry off the Scottish coasts. When, therefore, an engineer of eminence and wide experience was called for to carry out the survey of the Highlands in 1801, Telford's selection, first as reporter and surveyor and soon as permanent consulting engineer to the Commissions, was as natural as it was fortunate.

The Commissions which were appointed by the Acts of 1803 were Parliamentary Commissions, responsible to Parliament to whom annual Reports of their work were to be submitted. The members of the Commissions were Members of either the House of Commons or the House of Lords, and their Chairman was the Speaker of the House of Commons. It was thus clear that, though all the constructional and much of the administrative work would be done in Scotland, an official Secretary would be needed to deal with the committee work in London. To this problem Charles Abbot, Chairman of the Commissions, was able to supply the answer. For some years past the idea of collecting reliable information about the numbers and occupations of the inhabitants of these islands had been gaining ground. Abbot was much interested in the project, and a paper recently written on the subject by a young man called John Rickman had been brought to his notice. In the closing weeks of 1800 Abbot introduced in the House of Commons the Bill which resulted in the first census based on returns made by the local clergy, and to Rickman was given the difficult task of collecting and analysing the mass of information of varied quality and accuracy which resulted from the inquiry. Rickman's industry and accuracy impressed Abbot, and on the appointment of the latter in 1801 as Keeper of the Privy Seal in Ireland, he took Rickman to Dublin as his private secretary, a position which Rickman retained on Abbot's return to London in the following year as Speaker of the House of Commons.[1]

Rickman's interests, like Telford's, were wide and varied, and with Telford he shared a boundless energy and a passion for knowledge and accuracy. His chief interest lay in economics, and just as Telford set himself to the study and mastery of any subject which bore however indirectly on the problems of a civil engineer,

[1] Williams, *Life and Letters of John Rickman*, pp. 46, 51

so Rickman's range of interests embraced subjects so varied as vital statistics, local laws, tides and clocks, weights and measures and currency. His first objective was to avoid being deceived or deceiving others; his sole aim and ambition to serve his fellow men. Qualities and characteristics of such a severely practical nature seemed perhaps hardly calculated to endear him to his fellow men, more especially as he expected of others the high standards which he applied to himself. A man who could write of his own recent marriage, 'I lately imported a wife from the country by way of experiment; I think it will answer; we shall see', would seem, if his comments were to be taken seriously, to be deficient in certain human qualities, while the terms of a letter written years later, taking to task his idle and wayward daughter Ann, aged sixteen, would seem to strengthen the impression that the man was a dry and humourless prig.[1]

Yet with it all he was not in fact the friendless pedant which his interests and certain of his letters would suggest. Apparently lacking in literary taste and with little facility for composition, he yet numbered among his closest friends Charles Lamb and Robert Southey. 'This Rickman', wrote Lamb in 1800, 'lives in our Buildings, immediately opposite our house; the finest fellow to drop in a-nights, about 9 or 10 o'clock—cold bread and cheese time—just in the wishing time of the night when you wish for somebody to come in. . . . He is a most pleasant hand; a fine rattling fellow; has gone through life laughing at solemn apes . . . oppressively full of information . . . a great farmer . . . thoroughly penetrates into the ridiculous wherever found . . . understands the first time (a great desideratum in common minds) . . . you need never twice speak to him . . . does not want explanations . . . up to anything, down to anything whatever . . . a perfect man', and in another passage, 'I never saw a man that could be at all a second or substitute to him in any sort.'[2]

Such, then, was the man who returned from Ireland in 1801, to act for twelve years as Secretary to the Speaker, for over twenty-six years as Clerk at the Table of the House of Commons, and for twenty-five years as Secretary to the Commissions for Highland Roads and Bridges and the Caledonian Canal. The coming years were to show that those very peculiarities of tem-

---

[1] Williams, ibid., p. 116
[2] *The Letters of Charles and Mary Lamb.* Ed. E. V. Lucas, pp. 220-1.

perament and taste which made him appear at times lacking in humanity fitted him in an unusual degree for the career to which he was called. For almost a quarter of a century his Road and Canal Reports were to prove masterpieces of accurate summary and condensation, his letters models of clear thinking and logic. Seldom indeed has Fortune matched more closely work and worker.

The posts of secretary and consulting engineer to the Commissions having been satisfactorily and, as it was to prove, most adequately filled, there remained the question of providing for the dispatch of business in Scotland, including such legal and financial problems as might arise. It was clear that, without this, the delays in communication between London and Scotland would be an almost insuperable obstacle, and that it was essential for the Commissioners to have an agent in Scotland. Whoever was appointed to fill the post must have much legal and some financial knowledge, while initiative and a high sense of responsibility would be called for.

James Hope, the man on whom the choice fell, belonged to a branch of the Scottish legal profession, the history and functions of which were, and perhaps to many still are, something of a mystery. The wide powers of local jurisdiction in Scotland, which came to an end with the passing of the Act of 1748, had in most cases been exercised with moderation and reasonable justice by those landowners who possessed them; but moderation and justice had not always been in evidence, and those who considered themselves the victims of injustice had long enjoyed, both in theory and in practice, the inalienable right of appealing to the King. As the King could not personally deal with all these appeals, they came to be heard for him by his Council, and in such cases the King's intervention was signified by the use of a Royal Signet which was attached to such documents as came before, or were issued by, the Council. As time passed and the system of appeals became established and organised, the custody and use of the King's Signet for this purpose came to be entrusted to an official of the Court who, about the middle of the 15th century, became a Minister of State in his capacity of Royal Secretary This Secretary had a staff, the members of which came to act both as servants of the Crown and to some extent as legal advisers to those who brought their problems and their grievances before the Council.

In course of time the volume of business before the Council increased, and it became necessary to have more than one Signet for use on official documents, and at this stage the King's Secretary entrusted the use of one Signet in ordinary cases to a member of his staff who acted as its Keeper, retaining the other for use in cases where the King himself was closely and personally concerned. In this way what we now call the Signet Office came into permanent existence, with clerks attached to it for the transaction of day to day business, and when James V formed into a single unit the whole machinery for the administration of justice in Scotland, the Signet Office and its clerks, or 'Wryttaris to the Singnet' as they came to be called, were recognised as part of the new College of Justice. By the end of the 16th century, besides the Keeper of the Signet the writers engaged in the regular work of the office had increased to eighteen. Many of these now had places of business of their own from which they conducted not only business directly connected with cases coming before the King's Council, but private legal practice, and together they had come to form a corporate body with power to make rules for their own government and to regulate by examination admission to their ranks. From now on the numbers admitted to this branch of the profession increased steadily, and by the beginning of the 19th century had grown to over six hundred.[1] The close connection, first with the King's Court and later with the College of Justice, made it necessary that most of those practising as Writers to the Signet, as they were now called, should practise in Edinburgh, which thus became, as it has remained to this day, the natural home and centre of this branch of the legal profession.[2]

So, as the years passed, Edinburgh was growing to be the centre of the legal as well as of the cultural life of the country. At the end of the 18th century and for very many years to come, nearly all the landed proprietors in Scotland had their legal advisers in Edinburgh, Writers to the Signet for the most part, who made their wills and their complex family trusts, arranged the heritable bonds which were then almost the sole means of investment or of estate financing, and guided through the Courts

[1] The origin and history of the Writers to the Signet were reflected in the fact that until quite recent times only members of that profession had the right of presenting at the Signet Office documents requiring the imprint of the Royal Signet.

[2] *History of the Society of Writers to the Signet*, 1890

the lengthy and involved lawsuits, without which, it almost seemed, no gentleman's estate would be complete. To the Roll of this ancient Society of Writers to the Signet was added on 1 March 1799 the name of James Hope. Hope had started practising as a lawyer in 1784 when he acquired the business of James Walker of Dalry, another Writer to the Signet whose daughter he later married. James Walker was subsequently to marry Hope's sister—Hope thus finding himself in the unusual, and maybe embarrassing, possession of a father-in-law who was at the same time his brother-in-law. As a boy James Hope had attended the High School with Sir Walter Scott, who later mentioned him as one of his class-mates who had become well known and distinguished in the Law.

Through his own family and his close connection with the Walkers of Dalry, Hope was the fortunate possessor of that wide circle of friends and relatives round which many a successful legal business has been built, and soon he was in busy practice, numbering among his clients some of the leading landowners in the country. An ardent Tory, at a time when political feelings ran high, he was for many years agent for that party in the Lothians, and it is on record that at one stage he felt himself compelled, on political grounds, to decline to act for one of the largest Whig proprietors in Scotland. How James Hope came to be chosen to act as agent in Scotland for the newly formed Commissions is not known. At the time of his appointment, the wide scope and infinite complexity of the work ahead can hardly have been foreseen, and it is probable that all that was then in contemplation was the need for a lawyer possessed of sound knowledge and absolute integrity to advise the Commissioners on the intricate legal problems which beset the early stages of their work. However that may be, the years to come were to leave no room for doubt that, as with Telford and Rickman, the choice of James Hope to act for the Commissioners in Scotland in that summer of 1803 was indeed a happy one for the Scottish Highlands.

Reading today the printed Reports of the two Commissions, with the faded letters and such other contemporary papers as the passage of a hundred and fifty years has spared, it is easy to trace the distinctive roles played by these three men in the great undertaking to which they gave so much. Telford, on Highland moors and in the Great Glen, faced and solved engineering problems of a nature and on a scale far beyond previous knowledge or experience. Hope in Edinburgh wrestled with difficulties calling for skill in law and finance and no less for wide understanding of human nature, while in London Rickman held in his hands the threads of the whole complex undertaking, keeping them from enravelment and confusion, and labouring into the small hours to preserve the records of the work. As the years passed, each in his sphere gave his contribution, essential and complementary to the work of his colleagues, making together a whole so complete and satisfying in its entirety that the work of each came at last to appear logical, natural and almost simple. But the reality was very different. The clear division of functions, the dovetailing of one with another and the smoothness and efficiency with which the whole complex machinery moved, was achieved only as the laborious outcome of work, thought and imagination. Great as the problems must have appeared to the men who faced them in the autumn of 1803, the experience of the years to come was to show that they were in fact immensely greater and more complex than any could then foretell. That they were successfully overcome was largely due to these three great public servants, whose work in the course of the next thirty years was to attain to heights of quality never perhaps surpassed in the history of the professions to which each belonged.

4

PROBLEMS OF THE EARLY YEARS

DURING the closing years of the 18th century the Highland Society of Scotland, which had been founded in 1784, had played a leading part in urging the need for new and better communications in the Highlands. So, when Telford was commissioned to report on the project in 1801, he sought their advice. His questions to the Society were directed to getting their views as to the best lines of road, the probable effect of these and of the proposed canal on the fisheries and agriculture of the Highlands, and as to the extent to which local interests should be asked to contribute.[1] That Telford himself considered that local interests should share in the cost is evident from what would today be considered the somewhat leading nature of the questions he addressed to the Society.

The Highland Society appointed a Committee to deal with the whole matter, and in December 1802 they made their Report. They appear to have had no doubt that the cost of the new roads should be shared in some degree by the local proprietors, but as to the canal they showed a wise discretion, observing that they had no means of forming an opinion as to the extent to which commercial interests would be ready to contribute, 'other than by reference to that general spirit of liberal enterprise which distinguishes the commercial body'.[2] The Parliamentary Committee which virtually decided the matter, recommended that while the canal should be made at public expense, the cost of the roads should be shared equally between the Government and local interests. 'A general systematic scheme of roadmaking was not to be expected from the united efforts of local proprietors', wrote the Commissioners at a later date. 'They were as yet unaccustomed to association for public objects; their moor and waste lands yielded a scanty income; and many were jealous of the invasion of their fortresses by the outer world. Had they been left without encouragement and direction the Highlands would probably have remained a wilderness for more than half a cen-

[1] C.C. vol. 1, Appendix, p. 21   [2] ibid.

44

tury.'[1] 'The system', wrote Sir John Sinclair, 'was wisely contrived. Private enterprise being thus embarked in the same bottom with the public fund, less of idle enterprise and design and less of waste and want of economy in expenditure was to be expected than what generally is found to take place in the management of public money'.[2] It was easy to decide that the expense of the roads should be shared, but a system which is familiar enough today was then quite untried, and when in the autumn of 1803 the Commissioners took up their task, the 'common bottom' of which Sir John Sinclair wrote, was launched on uncharted seas.

The Act of 1803 which brought into being the Commission 'for making Roads and building Bridges in the Highlands of Scotland', had made provision for the grant of a sum of twenty thousand pounds as the first instalment of the sum which would eventually be required to meet the Government's half of the cost. The money was to be invested in the purchase of Exchequer Bills or India Stock, or lodged in the Bank of England.[3] Exchequer Bills were in fact purchased through Messrs Hoares' Bank, and these Bills were subsequently sold from time to time to meet the cost as the work in Scotland proceeded. From the start the Bank of Scotland in Edinburgh was closely connected with the project for the new roads, and here a deposit account bearing interest at four per cent was opened in the names of John Rickman and James Hope for the Commissioners, fed as occasion arose through the Bank's agents in London, Messrs Coutts. In those days funds in London were considered as being of more value than funds in Edinburgh, and consequently when money was transferred from London to Edinburgh, the Bank of Scotland credited to the Commissioners' account with them a sum representing a gain on the exchange amounting to four per cent on the sum involved, for twenty to twenty-five days. Conversely, on the rarer occasions when money was sent from Edinburgh to London, a loss on the exchange was suffered, unless a period of forty days was allowed to elapse before the money was needed in London.

During the two weeks following their appointment the Commissioners met repeatedly to consider the many problems which

[1] H.R. & B. Final Report, 1863
[2] Sinclair, *General Report of the Agricultural State of Scotland*, II, xvi, Appendix I, p. 228
[3] 43 Geo. III, ch. 80

faced them. Their first task was to make known in the Highlands the Government's offer of help in road- and bridge-building, and for this purpose they wrote to the Conveners of the counties in the northern Highlands, besides putting notices in two Edinburgh newspapers, *The Edinburgh Courant* and *The Caledonian Mercury*, and two Glasgow papers, *The Courier* and *The Herald*. The Treasury had made available a number of earlier surveys of proposed new roads, with estimates of the cost of the work. These surveys and estimates were out of date, and Telford, who was now officially appointed engineer to the Commissioners, was instructed to re-survey certain of the routes. Tools for road-making were known to be very scarce in Scotland, and one of Telford's first tasks was to build up a store collected from all parts of the country. These were to be kept at Fort Augustus to be available at cost to the chosen contractors, the Government galley on Loch Ness being pressed into service for transport.[1]

The object of the Government and their offer of financial help having been made known in the Highlands, the Commissioners set themselves to devising plans for dealing with such applications as might be received. It was decided that when a new road was asked for, Telford should be directed to make a preliminary survey and prepare an estimate of the total cost, one half of which estimate would in the normal case be the measure of the Government's contribution. If Telford's Report were favourable, the local proprietors who had put forward the application would be required to deposit in the Bank of Scotland one half of the estimated cost, and then and not till then Telford would lay out the route in detail and prepare specifications on the basis of which tenders would be invited by advertisement.[2]

In the first few months of the work it was not known to what extent the early enthusiasm for the Government's plan would be reflected in applications from the Highlands together with definite promises from local proprietors to put up their share of the cost, but it soon became apparent that there would be no lack of applications. Highland proprietors were quick to see the great advantage of having their estates opened up by roads made partly at the expense of the Government, while many saw their way to doing their share at small expense. The steep rise in agricultural rents which had taken place within recent years had

[1] H.R. & B. 1st Report, 1804   [2] ibid.

borne hardly on such of the old tenants as had retained their holdings in the face of rising competition, and by the early years of the 19th century many rents were in arrear. In such cases the proprietor had the opportunity of getting his tenants to undertake road work, which not only helped to clear off the arrears of rent, but enabled the proprietor thus to provide his fifty per cent contribution to the road at small cash outlay.

It was clearly impossible even for a man with the energy and physical strength of Telford to undertake preparation of all the surveys and estimates, and from an early stage he was forced to rely partly on surveyors working under him. Few at that time had the professional experience needed and, as soon became apparent, still fewer were competent, to prepare a reliable estimate of cost. This part of the work was made doubly difficult by the fact that the early years of the 19th century were years of rising costs, a rise in which the work on the new roads and the canal were themselves to play no small part.

While Telford wrestled with the technical problems Rickman and Hope had their hands equally full. Much thought had been given to the question of how those proprietors who were unable to offer contributions in labour were to provide their shares of the cost. There appeared to be two alternatives. The half share due from local contributors must either be paid into the Bank of Scotland or satisfactory security must be found for its ultimate payment. Despite the rise in the rental of many Highland estates which had followed the development of sheep-farming, the increase in stock prices and the rise in the price of kelp, ready money in any considerable quantities was not easily available, and it was soon apparent that few were able and none were prepared to make immediate payment to the Bank of Scotland.

The other alternative was not attractive. Today a bond over land, or a mortgage as it would be called in England, is not one of the simplest of legal documents. In the early 19th century it was truly formidable in length and complexity. To make matters worse, a bond over land grants security for the payment of money already advanced, whereas the problem before the Commissioners was to secure a future payment by a proprietor or, worse still, by a group of proprietors. There was a further difficulty. The estimate of cost made by Telford and his surveyors formed the basis for calculating the shares due from the Government and from the local contributors respectively, but it was foreseen that in many cases the ultimate cost might prove to be greater; and for such excess the contributors would be solely responsible.[1] Under Scots law a bond over land cannot be granted for an unspecified sum. This meant that the liability of the local proprietors for any excess over the estimated cost could not be secured by bond, but must rest solely on their personal obligation.

But the legal problems did not end even here. In the early years of the 19th century, and indeed for very many years to come, a large number of the estates in the Highlands were entailed, the complicated laws which regulated entailed estates narrowly restricting the rights and powers of the person for the time being in occupation of such an estate. The Montgomery Act of 1770 had extended these powers to allow the owner for the time being, who was called 'the heir of entail in possession', to grant the long leases which were urgently needed to permit improvements in the methods of agriculture. Now the Highland Roads and Bridges Act of 1803 allowed the heir to borrow on the security of his estate or even to sell part of it to enable him to contribute his share to the cost of road-making, the capital value of his estate being preserved and restored by means of a sinking fund to be set up for the purpose. The provision removed what would otherwise have proved an almost insurmountable obstacle in the path of the Commissioners, but it still further complicated the problems of James Hope and the many and novel legal documents which he had to devise and draw.

Thus difficulties beset the Commissioners on every side, and in the first few weeks it must have seemed to them and their advisers that in these strange seas their frail barque was to suffer early shipwreck. It is not known who solved the main problem of finance, but it seems probable that the credit should go to James Hope who was closely in touch with the business men of Edinburgh. For more than a century past, much of the commerce of Scotland had been financed by means of bills or promissory notes. Currency in the shape of gold, silver or even copper had long been scarce. At the time of the Union of the Parliaments the total value of the currency in circulation was estimated to be not more than £150,000, and by the middle of the 18th century the total had still further dwindled through the

[1] H.R. & B. 1st Report, 1804, Appendix B

excess of imports to Scotland over exports from the country. Before the establishment of the Bank of Scotland in 1695, the largest holders of currency in the country were merchants and shopkeepers in Edinburgh, many of whom had started the practice of making loans against the promissory notes of their customers. The issue of notes by the Bank of Scotland and later by the Royal Bank eased the situation, but currency remained in very short supply, and certain of the mercantile firms continued the practice of discounting their customers' bills, a form of business which many found more profitable than the ordinary business of a merchant.

About 1728 the new Royal Bank and the old Bank of Scotland started the system of cash credits, by which credit up to agreed limits was given against promissory notes signed by reputable applicants supported by two guarantors, without security other than the personal obligation of the borrower and his backers, and twenty years later the British Linen Company did much to develop the system through agencies in many of the Scottish towns. It was a system well suited to the needs of the public and of the growing banks. For the public, it provided means of financing business at a time when new activity was beginning to stir in the commercial life of the country, while it helped the growth of the banks by getting into circulation their notes and enormously extending their business. The banks, too, through their directors and officials, were in most cases well placed to assess the reliability and standing of those who approached them.

Meantime the trade in droving cattle from the Highlands and Islands was rapidly expanding. The new system of cash credits was a boon to the drovers—many of them men of little substance— who were thus able to obtain from the banks in the Lowlands sufficient cash to enable them to offer to the farmers and breeders in the north the strong temptation of a small cash payment for their cattle, the balance being met by means of bills payable after the sale of the beasts at Crieff. These bills passed from hand to hand, often for long periods, many of them finding their way ultimately into the hands of the merchant bankers or banking firms who, if all went well, would get them cashed at Crieff or Falkirk where many of the bills had been made payable.[1] So it came about that by the end of the century the drawing and dis-

[1] Haldane, *The Drove Roads of Scotland*, p. 48

counting of bills were operations with which the public, the prosperous mercantile houses and the banks had long been familiar.

In the last weeks of 1803 Hope wrote to James Fraser, the cashier of the Bank of Scotland, inquiring whether the Bank would advance to local landowners the amount of their contributions against promissory notes or bills granted by these owners. Hope did not conceal the difficulty in which the Commissioners were placed, but pointed out that the Bank was in a good position to satisfy itself as to the security offered.[1] Since the ultimate repayment of these bills at the end of one or at most two years would include interest on the money advanced, the transaction was good banking business; but the part played by the Bank of Scotland in the years to come suggests that a genuine desire to help in this work for the welfare of the Highlands influenced powerfully the decision of the Directors, and, little over a week after his first approach to the Cashier of the Bank, Hope was able to report that the Bank had consented to the plan.[2] To no-one was the new plan more welcome than to John Rickman, to whom the intricacies of Scots conveyancing were something of a mystery. 'Now that I have before my eyes', he wrote to Hope in November 1809, 'the formidable appearance of an Heritable Bond, I feel more sensibly the convenience of the other mode of contribution by means of the Bank of Scotland'.[3] The first advance agreed to under the new plan was for the erection of bridges in Easter Ross, but from now on advances against bills were regularly made by the Bank and, though the more complex method of bonds over land had in some cases to be resorted to, a formidable obstacle in the path of the Commissioners had been largely surmounted.[4] As payment by the contributors of any excess over Telford's estimate which might arise in the course of the work could not be secured either by bonds or by bills, this remained in every case dependent solely on the personal obligation of the contributors.[5]

[1] Hope, 8 December 1803   [2] H.R. & B. 1st Report, 1804
[3] H. of L., Rickman to Hope, 1 November 1809
[4] Despite their complexity, bonds over land had been described by Hope in an early letter to Sir George Mackenzie of Coul as being 'the only security in consequence of which they [the Commissioners] can make sure of their money without risk of cavil or importunity.' (Hope, 21 November 1803)
[5] In those cases where the method of a heritable bond was used to secure the half share payable by the local proprietors it became the practice for the Commissioners to advance the whole of the cost of the road. In this way the legal obstacle that a heritable bond must be for money already advanced was overcome.

The earliest applications for Government help in road and bridge construction came from large individual landowners or groups of landowners in the Highlands. The Government's object from the start was to achieve the construction of roads which would be of value to the community rather than to the individual, and at an early stage it became apparent that some method must be devised of dividing equitably the financial burden of work which would benefit many. General agreement on this point was not easily reached, but after long discussion Inverness-shire decided to levy for the purpose a uniform assessment on all landowners in the county. At first the assessment was not to exceed one shilling sterling on one pound Scots of valued rent, and since at that time this represented only £3,600 sterling per annum for the whole county, the prospects of speedy progress in road-building seemed remote[1]; but at least it was a step in the right direction, and soon Ross-shire, Sutherland and Caithness followed the example of Inverness-shire. Rickman described Ross-shire's effort as 'pitiful', but none the less, the action of these three northern counties 'laid open before [the Commissioners] an uninterrupted scope of improvement over a space not over-estimated at One hundred and thirty miles in length, averaging at fifty miles in breadth'.[2] Public-spirited proprietors continued to get from the Bank of Scotland advances against bills signed by themselves and their friends, but now they and the Bank knew that, at least in the case of roads approved by the county, the assessments, small as they were, would eventually be available to repay their initial outlay, while it was open to these individuals to withhold payment of their own assessment to reduce their liability to the Bank. Hope's correspondence at this time shows that many forms of security were offered to the Bank of Scotland by would-be borrowers. Some asked for advances secured only on the county assessments, but the Bank strictly and prudently adhered to the rule that advances could only be made against the full and unqualified obligation of the borrowers, the bills signed by them to be payable at latest in two years' time, interest to be charged at five per cent and each bill to bear the name of at least two reputable persons.

[1] '. . . the proposed rate has been accommodated to the general ability of the heritors, many of whom possess property inferior to their public spirit . . .' (H.R. & B. 1st Report, 1804)
[2] H.R. & B. 9th Report

If some of the initial problems were being brought to solution Rickman, Telford and Hope had still much to worry them. Rickman's task as secretary was no sinecure, but as problems of policy and procedure gave way to those of actual road planning and construction, the focus of the picture shifted increasingly from London to Edinburgh and the Highlands. The early months of the Commission's work saw a steady flow of memorials and petitions directed to the Commissioners, a flow probably far in excess of what had been foreseen. Most, if not all, of these meant surveys, estimates and specifications. Telford's enthusiasm and energy were unlimited, but his time had to be divided between his many responsibilities in Scotland and elsewhere, and as time went on an increasing burden fell on James Hope. Hope had originally been appointed to advise the Road and Bridge Commissioners on the sufficiency of the security offered by Highland proprietors for payment of their contribution, but soon he was acting as their recognised agent in Scotland, the extent and variety of his responsibilities steadily increasing as the months passed. The arrangement with the Bank of Scotland for discounting bills had gone far to ease the financial difficulties, but a host of others had arisen in their place, and soon in his office in Princes Street Hope was beset with problems legal, financial and before long technical as well.

Telford was responsible for appointing the surveyors to report on those routes where new roads were asked for; but good surveyors were scarce. Many of those sent to the Highlands had much to learn, and no doubt their task was made less easy by the conflicting views of those they sought to please. 'Is it that the surveyors will not listen to the desires of the inhabitants', wrote Rickman in exasperation to Telford, 'or that the inhabitants do not know what they want?'[1] Some, like Langlands the surveyor for Islay, Jura and part of Argyllshire were superficial in their work. 'I am not ever convinced of the accuracy of Langlands' surveys', wrote Hope to Rickman in the summer of 1805.[2] Some were stupid, others merely slack, while one, Wilson, sent to Caithness in the late autumn of 1808 virtually disappeared from human ken, only to emerge in the following spring. Hope seems to have had his own idea as to the cause. 'Your hospitable Country ruins him', he wrote to James Trail of Hobbister in January, and a few

[1] H. of L. Rickman to Telford, 6 March 1806   [2] Hope, 12 August 1805

weeks later, reporting to Telford the arrival of the spring thaw, 'I wish it may also recall poor Wilson to life and activity'; but an agency more powerful than the spring was needed, and in April Hope wrote to Telford that the errant surveyor's daughter 'had passed thro' Foss on her way North in the intention of conducting him home again'.[1]

With all their shortcomings—and in the early years they were many—the surveys had to serve for the specifications of the work which Telford drew. One copy of these was kept in Hope's office while another was deposited locally, often with the parish minister or a local estate factor, for the inspection of intending offerers who were to be shown the line of the proposed roads by local guides paid by the Commissioners. Hope then advertised the work for tender in the local newspapers and waited developments with what, in the early years, must have been some interest and no little anxiety, while far to the north the local guides were being walked off their feet by a large and varied clientèle.

Hope had not long to wait in doubt, and soon offers and inquiries began to reach him. Some came from local landowners, a few from genuine contractors with at least some knowledge of road work, but many came from men without knowledge, experience or resources. Architects and masons, gardeners and nurserymen, vintners, farmers and ordinary labourers were among the offerers, while many described themselves as 'undertakers', a designation which seems in those days to have been applied to what would now be called 'general contractors'. The variation in the offers when they came was as perplexing as the variety of the offerers. Some were far above Telford's estimate of cost, others much below, while in the case of one road on Loch Fyne the amount of the highest offer was five times that of the lowest.[2] The closing date for receiving offers had been fixed by Rickman and Hope. It often happened that bad weather held up would-be offerers on their way to the Highlands or delayed their inspection of the route, and in such cases an extension of time was allowed; but often late offerers had no such excuse. To Hope fell the difficult task of deciding whether the excuse was good or bad, holding the balance as fairly as he could between the punctual and the laggards, and resisting the persuasions of those who sought for hints as to the amount of the Commissioners' estimate or the tenders of their competitors.

When the closing date arrived, the whole of the offers, with Telford's comments and such information as Hope could get about the offerers, were sent to Rickman for the final decision of the Commissioners. Their task was no easy one. Many offers received were far in excess of the estimate and these could be discarded at once. Others might be close to the estimate, but not infrequently some were appreciably below it. These low offers were in the early years a source of much discussion and no little embarrassment. Telford's official estimate had determined the limit beyond which the Commissioners would not go in their offer of half the cost. If tenders above the estimate were accepted the contributors must thus bear the whole of the excess. There was therefore a natural temptation for local contributors to prefer low offers to higher ones, regardless of the experience, resources or integrity of the offerers. Some of these, honest but ignorant, had based their offers on guesswork and optimism; others in straitened circumstances had been tempted by the Commissioners' offer of an advance payment for tools and supplies, while not a few had omitted from their calculations any allowance for storms, led into fatal error by inspection in dry weather of routes many of which passed through the wettest areas in the whole of Scotland.

As time passed the sheep became distinguishable from the goats, the knowledgeable from the ignorant, the solvent from the bankrupt, but the experience was bought at high cost, and meantime not a few contracts fell to well-meaning incompetents or light-hearted adventurers, to the grief and loss of all concerned. Offers came from all quarters; from Edinburgh and Glasgow; from Fife and Perthshire; from Berwickshire and Ayrshire. Hope did his best in the interests of all concerned to dissuade from long and fruitless journeys those who were palpably unsuitable or ignorant; but many paid no heed, wasting their own time and that of the Commissioners and their servants in preparing and submitting offers which stood no chance of acceptance. In an attempt to mitigate the loss to so many who could ill afford it, the Commissioners had decided to make compensation payments to unsuccessful tenderers—three guineas to those north of the Grampians and five guineas to those further south. Their Second Report showed payments of £148 to unsuccessful offerers for roads through Glengarry and between Fort William and Arisaig, and in the following year the total had risen to £242. It was soon apparent that the system of payments was leading to abuse and waste of time, and payments for such 'near misses' were first restricted to the three offerers nearest the successful tender and finally discontinued.

Telford's standards were high. His specifications had been carefully prepared, and he had no intention of allowing deviation from them or of accepting poor work. 'Good contractors are a scarce commodity,' wrote Hope to Sir George Mackenzie of Coul in 1807, 'and it is our business to remove, not to find, difficulties for them'[1]; but the relatively few good contractors were not always the lowest tenderers. An apparent saving in the contract price was dearly won if it led to poor workmanship or the bankruptcy of the offerer, and as time passed the Commissioners found 'increasing reasons for dealing as little as possible with the adventurers who are attracted by such [road contract] advertisements'.[2] If this was plain to Telford, Rickman and Hope, it was less so to the contributors in the northern counties, who expected the lowest tender to be accepted. In the early years of their work the Commissioners shared this latter view, and not a few low tenders were accepted in the knowledge that the contractor would be the loser. 'I am afraid', wrote Rickman to Hope, 'that Scott will be ruined if he undertakes the Dunbeath road on the terms of his own offer, and yet I do not see how you can warn him of his danger without displeasing the heritors of Caithness.'[3] Wiser counsels came with time and dearly-bought experience, but hard words and hard thoughts had come and gone before Rickman could write to Hope, 'That affair [the building of the road from Corran Ferry to Kinlochmoidart] I think has proved sufficiently that the personal character of our contractors is of much more importance than the small differences upon which the contributors expect preference to be given.'[4]

If contractors with knowledge and experience were scarce, those with adequate resources were fewer still. Very many of the contracts for road-building into which the Commissioners were now entering involved sums of three, four or five thousand pounds.

[1] Hope, 26 January 1807
[2] H. of L. Rickman to Hope, 27 July 1809
[3] H. of L. Rickman to Hope, 2 September 1809
[4] H. of L. Rickman to Hope. 23 September 1809

Some were even larger, and to make such contracts without reasonable security for their execution would have been gross folly, involving serious risk of loss both to the public and to the local contributors. To guard against this the Commissioners laid down from the start a strict and salutary rule that before a contract was accepted the contractor must find security—or 'caution' as it is called in Scotland—that the work would be completed; and to Hope fell the delicate and difficult task of assessing the value of the security offered. If the contractor seemed competent and his offer reasonable for the work involved, the Commissioners were satisfied with security up to about one third of the contract price; but where the offer was a low one or the offerer lacked experience the security must be greater. Hope did his best to discourage the inexpert. 'You must excuse my being plain with you', he wrote to Henry Elder, a Glasgow mason who had offered to build the Glendaruel road. 'The offer you make is much lower than according to my ideas the work can be executed at and I am naturally led to be diffident of your experience.'[1]

Offers of security showed a bewildering variety. Some came from local landowners, and most though not all of these could be accepted without hesitation. Some came from small farmers, local merchants or personal friends of the contractor. All these called for careful inquiry both as to the character of the 'cautioners' —as the offerers of security were called—and as to the security offered, which was often found to be worthless or already pledged for other obligations. The contractor offering for a difficult stretch of road in central Ross-shire in the autumn of 1812 put forward as his guarantors a group of five or six small local farmers; but Hope's growing experience stood him in good stead, and Rickman was warned not to accept the offer, as the situation of the guarantors 'does not admit of their making up even a small loss without impossible hardship, and a considerable default would ruin the whole of them'.[2] Guarantors who lived outside the jurisdiction of the Scots Courts were as a general rule not regarded as satisfactory by the careful Scots lawyer, 'but', as he wrote to Telford, 'we must not be *chusers* when contractors with guarantors are so rare'. Soon Hope was corresponding with private friends, local clergymen, landowners and sheriffs, collecting and assessing such facts as he could obtain at the cost of much

[1] Hope, 21 March 1807   [2] Hope, 17 September 1812

hard work and some hard words. The motives, too, of the cautioners varied widely. Some were influenced by a genuine desire to help in road-making for the good of the community. Some acted in sincere, but often misplaced, friendship for the contractor. Some hoped for a share in the profits on the contract or on the supply of meal and provisions to the labourers, while not a few hoped that payments during the course of the work would enable the contractor to meet debts already owing by him to themselves.

Hope was a careful lawyer, and as a careful lawyer should he aimed at clarity and certainty in all he did, having each step firm before proceeding to the next. Never in his previous legal practice had clear thinking and firm bargaining been more needed. Never had it been so hard to achieve. Like Telford, he was launched on work without precedent in scope or in character, and like a mariner off an uncharted coast he must rely largely on his own initiative, his own reckoning and his own judgment. His colleagues could help him little, and he would look in vain among his text-books for guidance on many of the problems which now beset him, or for styles and precedents to follow in the documents he drew. Overestimate of his own abilities was certainly not among his faults. The drafting of the first contract for road construction—on the Arisaig Road—had caused him much anxious thought. Few lawyers welcome extensive revision of their work, but Hope had no false pride in matters touching the interests of the Commissioners, and the covering letter which went with the draft to Telford asked that it be amended 'with the least delicacy'.[1] Years later, with twenty years' experience of work for the Commissioners behind him, Hope could still write to Rickman of some minor imperfection in the work of his own staff, 'Often, often do I go wrong daily; but never do I entrust to others my own duty without repenting of it . . . some day or other I shall hope to learn some approximation to wisdom.'[2] Even when others erred, Hope would preface his correction with an acknowledgment of his own shortcomings, and to the last he remained in his own estimation the pupil rather than the master.

In Rickman, Hope had a good friend and a firm ally, for if one characteristic more than another marked the secretary of the

[1] Hope, 3 July 1804
[2] H. of L. Hope to Rickman, 30 May and 9 June 1823

57

Commission, it was his passion for accuracy and hatred of error. For the rest, Hope's work in these early years was frustrated, complicated and generally bedevilled by loose thinking, ignorance or plain illiteracy in those with whom he dealt. Even the Commissioners, with Rickman at their elbow, were not beyond reproach, and one of the earliest documents sent by Hope for their signature came back imperfectly executed. Hope had but recently been appointed law agent to the Commission, and in the circumstances it needed a fearless servant to return the document to London for the word 'witness' to be added to the signature of the witnesses; but returned it was, and the Commissioners may well have reflected that if their agent in Edinburgh was scrupulous in small things he would be no less careful in great.[1]

If the Commissioners could on occasion be careless by Hope's high standards, his correspondents in Scotland erred repeatedly. Local proprietors, once the construction of a road had been agreed in principle, were only too apt to regard the matter as virtually complete, ignoring the many complex requirements of the Commissioners and the Act of Parliament under which they worked, and causing untold labour and needless correspondence for Hope. Among the contractors the level of general education was not high. Some wrote with difficulty and none wrote at all when it could be avoided, while with some, simple arithmetic was a little-known art. During the winter of 1806 John Faichney, an Oban mason, had tendered for making a road between Broadford and Portree, and his offer had been accepted. It later transpired that a mistake had been made in Faichney's calculations and that his offer was £1,000 less than he had meant; and in despair he wrote to Hope. 'His agitation and misery, poor creature, excite my compassion', wrote Hope to Telford.[2] The mistake involved tedious correspondence with Faichney's cautioner and the local contributors, all of whom would be affected by any alteration in the price; but all ended happily and the Commissioners allowed the harassed contractor to amend his offer.

It can hardly be doubted that much of the enthusiasm in the Highlands which greeted the Government's offer of help in road construction came from genuine concern for the welfare of the country, but behind this lurked here and there traces of self-interest. The applications for assistance which reached the Com-

[1] Hope, 25 April 1804   [2] Hope, 23 January 1807

missioners came mainly in the form of memorials prepared by the legal advisers of the applicants, high-sounding, plausible and persuasive. In framing them their authors had perhaps at times allowed themselves to be carried away by their own eloquence or on occasions by the wishes and interests of their clients; but very many were wise and practical estimates of local needs. To Telford and his surveyors fell the task of discriminating the good plans from the bad, while Rickman and Hope must soothe feelings ruffled by unwelcome decisions. Questions of priority, too, threatened to be difficult and delicate. 'From what I see of the individuals interested in that country [Inverness-shire]', wrote Hope to Rickman early in 1805, 'I am satisfied that there will soon be a keen struggle whose road should be first proceeded with.'[1] In Ross-shire, too, troubles were seldom far to seek. 'I am afraid', wrote Rickman to Telford, 'the affairs of Ross-shire will perplex you not a little, but if difficult to manage on the spot they become quite unmanageable at this distance and I am afraid must remain so while the caprices of individuals are suffered to have so great a sway'[2]; and only two days later, 'Their county squabbles may be sport to them but they are murder to our time and the Commissioners.'[3]

In the autumn of 1803 when the Commission started its work, Sir George Mackenzie of Coul was Convener of the County of Ross. Rickman described him as 'a man of some genius but not of that kind which facilitates business',[4] and indeed Sir George's part in the subsequent negotiations over roads and bridges in Ross-shire suggests that the qualification in Rickman's appreciation of the Convener was something of an understatement. Rickman, Telford and Hope all at one time or another crossed swords with the Ross-shire Convener. 'A rash individual,' wrote Hope of him, 'who has no control over his mind, or pen or memory and whom, from his incessant relapses, there is no possibility of keeping him right.'[5] 'No doubt', wrote Rickman to Telford in the summer of 1806, 'you have received an angry letter from Sir G. M. who chuses to be displeased that the Loch Carron road is to be first surveyed; I have written him today in

---

[1] Hope, 13 March 1805
[2] H. of L. Rickman to Telford, 7 July 1809
[3] H. of L. Rickman to Telford, 9 July 1809
[4] H. of L. Rickman to Hope, 7 October 1809
[5] H. of L. Hope to Rickman, 24 November 1820

such manner, I hope, as to calm his passion.'[1] Telford's eminence as an engineer and his integrity soon came to be widely recognised and accepted, but even he was not entirely immune from the bitterness and indiscretion of Sir George's pen. In a letter to Hope in the autumn of 1805 Sir George made a fierce attack on the Commissioners and all their works, accusing Telford of employing his own friends. Hope's long and spirited letter in reply conveyed to the Convener much that was unpalatable but long overdue, and must, in the writing, have given no little quiet satisfaction to the long-suffering lawyer.[2] But if tempers wore thin and hard words came easily in these early days, calmer reflection brought kindlier thoughts when the heat of battle and dispute had passed, and years later when the roads were almost complete Hope was able to write, 'We know that private accommodation never entered into the heart of anyone concerned.'[3]

In Telford's estimates of the cost of road construction nothing was included for the value of the land. This was in accordance with the fixed policy of the Commissioners, who considered that the benefit to the property over which the roads passed was in itself ample compensation. Few such claims were made, but a small number reached the Commissioners including, strangely, one by that great champion of Highland development Sir John Sinclair.[4] Claims for damage to fences were occasionally allowed, but compensation for the land itself appears to have been consistently refused. 'What is steadily to be kept in mind,' wrote Rickman to Hope in 1809, 'is that we will pay neither directly or indirectly for land without setting up a counter-claim.'[5] Besides the benefits to the estates over which the new roads passed, the Commissioners took into account the large sums paid by them for surveying, advertising and the administrative work of Hope's office, 'which last', observed Hope, concluding a long correspondence with the agent for Macdonald of Kinlochmoidart, 'cannot be supposed trifling if all the Highland proprietors occasion a

[1] H. of L. Rickman to Telford, 28 June 1806
[2] Hope, 18 November 1805
[3] Hope, 13 November 1818
[4] Sir John Sinclair's attitude in this respect seems the more strange because Joseph Mitchell records that in 1794 Sir John had obtained a private Act of Parliament to open up Caithness by means of roads. Owing to the opposition of other heritors in the county the Act remained a dead-letter, one heritor ascribing the proposal to 'personal vanity, because he [Sir John] as a rich man was able to keep a carriage, and wanted the public to make roads to show off his grandeur'. (Mitchell, II, p. 127)
[5] H. of L. Rickman to Hope, 12 July 1809

correspondence equal to that which your client has made necessary'.[1]

With Rickman and the Commissioners stationed in London, Hope in Edinburgh and Telford constantly on the move, the problem of communication between them and with landowners, surveyors and contractors in all parts of the Highlands was not easy. Ordinary letters were difficult enough, but far worse was the unavoidable exchange of plans, surveys, specifications and contracts, documents of a size and weight which made them unsuitable to the postal arrangements of the time or at best chargeable at crippling rates. Here William Kerr, the secretary of the G.P.O. in Edinburgh, and in the later years his successor Godby, came to the help of the Commissioners, accepting without postal dues bulky packages sent to their care. A charge of £3 4s 2d for a package inadvertently sent through the normal channels shows the value of this concession, for which the Commissioners could make no other return than by the dispatch each year to Kerr and Godby of a copy of their Annual Report. A further economy kept down the labour and the postage bill. 'The transparent paper is a fortunate invention for us', wrote Rickman to Hope in July 1809. 'I verily believe that without it our plan copies and the carriage to and from Scotland would ere now have cost us upwards of £2,000 or to avoid the intolerable expense we must have uniformly declined the innumerable alterations which the imperfection of the first surveys or the desire of the contributors seems to impose on us.'[2]

One of the first routes brought to the notice of the Commissioners as suitable for the construction of a new road, was that which leads from the Great Glen through Glenmoriston and Glenshiel to Loch Duich and the Skye ferries. A road on this line was considered to be urgently needed to help the considerable droving traffic from the Islands and the coastal fishing trade, but when plans for its construction were under detailed consideration it was found that serious administrative and financial difficulties stood in the way. The route led partly through Inverness-shire and partly through Ross-shire, and before progress could be made in its construction it was necessary to determine the extent to which each ot these counties was responsible. At this stage it was

[1] Hope, 1 September 1812
[2] H. of L. Rickman to Hope, 2 September 1809

discovered that, though many surveys of small sections of the country existed, the information available was not sufficiently detailed or accurate to allow the county boundaries to be clearly determined.

It so happened that Aaron Arrowsmith was at that time engaged in making a new large map of England, and it was felt by the Commissioners that the opportunity should be taken of having a new map of Scotland prepared, using all the local surveys and any other material available. In the early summer of 1805 Arrowsmith was commissioned to do the work, a task which he took in hand at once with energy and enthusiasm. At that time the most accurate map of Scotland was believed to be that which had been prepared by John Ainslie and first issued in 1789. This map, though a great improvement on any others then believed to exist, was not sufficiently accurate or detailed for the purpose of the Commissioners. The considerable number of local surveys also in existence were very limited in scope and of little use for large-scale road construction. Before Arrowsmith had been long at work it was discovered that there already existed a far more detailed and accurate survey of Scotland than had hitherto been known. The Highland section of this survey had been prepared between 1747 and 1755 on the instructions of the Duke of Cumberland, who had been handicapped by the lack of an accurate map during and immediately after the Rising of 1745. This survey, which subsequently came to be associated with the name of General Roy, who had been largely responsible for the work, had been carried out with great care, and, considering the primitive nature of the surveying instruments then available, remarkable accuracy. Later it was extended to cover the south of Scotland, and in 1793 the whole survey had been deposited in the King's Library where its existence had been completely forgotten. Arrowsmith has recorded how much he was helped in his work on the new map by Roy's survey which in the first place he copied by means of the new transparent paper which was to prove such a boon to the Commissioners.[1] Besides Roy's survey, Arrowsmith had available to him many local surveys made during the last years of the 18th century, some by surveyors later to be employed by the Commissioners under Telford.

Meantime the mistakes in Ainslie's map were causing great

[1] H.R. & B. 3rd Report, 1807, and Memoir

62

trouble to Telford, Rickman and Hope. Recent surveying had shown errors in many parts of it. The position of certain of the Western Isles was incorrectly shown; the outline of Skye and Islay bore little resemblance to the true shapes of these Islands, while in the construction of the map, variations from the magnetic meridian had been ignored. Nowhere were the shortcomings more apparent than in the tracing of the county boundaries, exact knowledge of which had, with the passing of the various County Assessment Acts, become of first importance. In Edinburgh, Hope was searching in the Advocates' Library for old surveys which might be useful, besides examining those made by the Commissioners on the Forfeited Estates. Most of these were too limited in area and too inaccurate to be of much service, though Hope wrote to Rickman in the autumn of 1805 that he was having some of them copied by one of the old surveyors whose perquisite it was to do this work.

Arrowsmith's map was finished in 1809. It had cost the Commissioners over £2,000 in labour and material, while Arrowsmith himself received £300 for his work. The marking of county boundaries which had been the first object had not been overlooked. Alexander Nimmo, the Rector of Inverness Academy, had undertaken this part of the work, and during the summer vacation between June and August 1806 he had investigated the boundaries on foot, accompanied and helped for part of the area by an old man of eighty. Nimmo's work, which was done with great care, proved invaluable, and when it is considered that at that time the old county of Cromarty consisted of twelve or fourteen areas of land scattered irregularly throughout Ross-shire, it is easy to imagine that without it the Commissioners' work would have been still further complicated, and that the £150 paid to Nimmo was money well spent.

5

ROAD-PLANNING AND ROAD-MAKING

AMONG the documents which had been handed over to the Commissioners at the start of their work in July 1803 were a number of surveys of Highland roads, made by George Brown, a competent civil engineer of Elgin. These surveys, prepared between 1790 and 1799, had been commissioned by the Government as the result of persistent pressure by the British Fisheries Society and the Highland Society with the active support of George Dempster of Skibo and Sir John Sinclair, the first President of the new Board of Agriculture. Brown had visited Dempster at Skibo in the course of his work in the early autumn of 1795. 'At present', wrote Dempster after that visit, 'a great part of this immense country is accessible only to goats and garrons. From Inverness to Cape Wrath and Johnny Groat's House a track of 150 miles in length and 60 miles in breadth there are neither roads through the country nor bridges over its rivers nor accommodation at its ferries. To this first step of improvement of roads, bridges and ferries the present plan should be confined. . . . When the Government have provided a fund and an organ for all application and when these lines of roads shall be really made as well as planned it will have done its duty towards the Highlands. The rest is to be done by the proprietors in allowing the Highlanders to cultivate the waste grounds on decent and equitable conditions.'[1] Brown's survey covered the main lines of road north and west of the Great Glen, which he considered to be conducive to 'the no small comfort of the valuable natives and to the wealth of the kingdom at large'.[2] 'It is not easy', wrote Dempster from Skibo on 2 September 1795, 'to say whether Mr Brown's instructions for the surveys have been given with most judgment or the surveys and estimates made with most skill and attention for both do great honour to the parties concerned in them.'[3]

The roads recommended by Brown had included a road from Fort William by Morar to Arisaig—or Loch-na-Gaul as it was

---

[1] Sir John Sinclair's Letters, 2 September 1795 (Thurso. East, MSS; M.P's, fol. 258)
[2] H.R. & B. 1st Report, 1804, Appendix C [3] Sir John Sinclair's Letters, loc. cit.

then called—and by 1803 a sum of over £1,500 had already been spent on it by the local proprietors, while a post office and an inn had been established at Arisaig. The further sum of £4,000 which was believed to be needed to complete the road, was beyond the immediate capacity of the local proprietors, and the first application received by the Commissioners in the Autumn of 1803 was contained in a memorial prepared on behalf of Lord Macdonald, Macdonald of Clanranald, Maclean of Ardgour, Macdonald of Glenaladale and Macdonald of Kinlochmoidart for help in its completion. Telford reported favourably on the project, with a possible extension northward to Loch Nevis and Loch Hourn, as being of benefit not only to the fisheries but to droving traffic to the south.[1] 'The usual intercourse of the country', he had reported, 'with black cattle and sheep will be along this road from various parts of the country.'[2] For the making of this road and the bridges on it at least fifteen offers were received, and in their Second Report the Commissioners were able to write that the offer of a Perth firm of contractors, Messrs Dick and Readdie, had been accepted, though with some misgivings as their offer of £6,900 was £600 below Telford's estimate of the true cost. It was fortunate for the Commissioners that their choice of contractors for this, the first road undertaken under the new Act, had fallen on men who, if lacking in experience, were to show themselves at least honest and reasonably conscientious. Troubles indeed were to come to the Perthshire men, but these were still in the future, and in the autumn of 1804 work had started.

Hard on the heels of the memorial of Lord Macdonald and his friends came another, this time from Colonel Macdonell of Glengarry, urging the construction of a parallel route leading up Glengarry to the head of Loch Hourn.[3] At the beginning of September 1803 Telford and Colonel Macdonell spent three long days examining the line of the proposed road, and a few weeks later Telford, the arduous nature of the expedition evidently fresh in his mind, reported to his Commissioners that the glen, which had lately been made over from cattle to sheep, was rugged and inaccessible, making travel through it 'tedious, difficult and danger-

[1] 'This [road] would prove of great importance to the Fisheries on account of facilitating intelligence which is one of the most necessary steps to promote the success of this Business.' (Telford, *Survey and Report*, 1803)
[2] H.R. & B. 1st Report, 1804, Appendices D and E
[3] H.R. & B. 1st Report, 1804

ous even to those who have been accustomed to the country'.[1] The road, he considered, besides opening up the fishing grounds in Loch Hourn could be connected with Glenmoriston, Glenelg and possibly Loch Arkaig and was thus 'of the utmost importance as a drove road from a very extensive tract of country'. Glengarry was willing to share the cost with the Commissioners, and soon Hope was negotiating with Glengarry's agents in Edinburgh a bond to secure his contribution which the Commissioners had no hesitation in accepting, since it was secured over the estate of Glengarry stretching from Loch Oich to the coast of Knoydart with an annual rental of £6,000 and debts of only £11,000.[2]

Among the fourteen offers received for the Glengarry road was one from Colonel Macdonell himself, who proposed to do the work at the price estimated by Telford, and all Hope's tact was needed in explaining to Colonel Macdonell that his knowledge of Telford's figure could secure him no preference over others who might make lower offers.[3] The Perth firm who were to do the Arisaig road, again proved to be the lowest offerers, and as they had found adequate security for the execution of the contract they were soon at work on the two roads, helped by an advance of £1,000 which the Commissioners had approved.

Meanwhile far to the south, in Argyllshire, more plans were afoot. Many of these were aimed at helping the fishermen of Loch Fyne where, it was said, at least five hundred large herring-boats were employed each year.[4] Hitherto fishermen on the Loch had been handicapped by the lack of quick communications to the south. Herrings for the Glasgow market had to be transported to the Clyde shore by creel or on horseback, while the lack of roads made it difficult to bring salt and casks north to the fishing centres. The fishermen, too, depended on early news of the movements of the herring shoals. The Highland Society reported that in 1802 the Clyde fishermen had failed to find herrings on the fishing grounds of the north-west and that owing to poor communications several weeks had passed before news of the subsequent appearance of the fish reached the Clyde. To meet these needs roads were proposed and in due course put in hand, from Loch Fyne through Glendaruel to Colintraive,[5] by Loch Eck to

[1] H.R. & B. 1st Report, 1804, Appendix G
[2] Hope, 10 February 1804   [3] Hope, 4 April 1804
[4] H.R. & B. 2nd Report, 1805, Appendix G
[5] See Appendix No I

Ardentinny, and through Hell's Glen to the head of Loch Goil.[1]
Ambitious plans were also put forward for roads crossing the high
ground both north and south of Loch Awe, including the improvement of 'that much-frequented path' by which the people of
North Lorn and certain of the Islands had long been accustomed
to take their cattle across the Leckan Muir from Ford on Loch
Awe to Inveraray on their way to the markets of the Lowlands.[2]
Though some of these projects, including the Leckan Muir road,
were later abandoned, they involved Rickman, Telford and Hope
in endless work and correspondence, and the Commissioners in
no little expense.

Landowners in the roadless districts of Morven, Ardnamurchan and Ardgour complained not unreasonably that these
districts were almost entirely cut off from the south, while the
possibility of valuable fishing in Loch Moidart was pleaded in
support.[3] To meet their needs work was soon in hand on a road
from Lochmoidart to Corran Ferry on Loch Linnhe, while to
replace Wade's road over the Corrieyairack Pass, which was
blocked by snow for months each winter, a better route from
Spean Bridge by Loch Laggan to Kingussie was planned and
approved, though long before it was complete the Commissioners
must have felt tempted to regret that the Loch Laggan road had
ever been suggested.[4]

By the end of the 18th century the export of cattle from the
western and north-western Highlands had reached large proportions, and in the early years of the 19th century the cattle
trade, stimulated by the French Wars and the demand for beef
for the services, was rapidly climbing to its peak. Many of these
cattle came from the Islands, brought to the mainland by drovers,
who purchased them in late summer and drove them slowly south
to the great Tryst at Falkirk and on across the Border to the rich
grazings and markets of England. Skye cattle were in particular
demand, and each year large numbers of beasts from that island,
together with many brought across the Minch from the Outer
Isles to Loch Dunvegan, crossed to the mainland at the narrow
ferry at Kyle-Rhea, which in Telford's view would 'always remain
the usual ferry for black cattle from Skye'. Hitherto the only

---

[1] H.R. & B. 2nd Report, 1805, Appendices G, H and I
[2] H.R. & B. 3rd Report, 1807, Appendix L. See Appendix No. II
[3] H.R. & B. 1st Report, 1804, Appendix H. See Appendix No. III
[4] H.R. & B. 2nd Report, 1805, Appendix L. See Appendix No. IV

attempts at road-making in Skye had been by local effort and statute labour, unskilled and totally inadequate, but in the summer of 1804 Lord Macdonald and eleven other proprietors in the island put forward to the Commissioners plans for roads leading from Stein in the extreme north-west, where the British Fisheries Society had established a fishing village, to Ardavasar Bay at the south end of the Sleat Peninsula, with branches to Portree and Kyle-Rhea.[1] Two years later the Skye landowners were again in the field, this time asking for a road from Dunvegan to Portree, 'the line by which the cattle from the Long Island are driven to the market of Portree; . . . it is also of the utmost consequence as forming, when opened, an easy access to the harbours and fishing lochs of Dunvegan Bay, Arnisort, Snizort and Portree, being the principal lochs in the whole Island for the resort of herrings and vessels'.[2]

In Mull the Duke of Argyll asked support for a road from near Bunessan to the head of Loch Don where cattle from Mull, Coll and Tiree were shipped to the mainland, while the cattle-breeding proprietors in Islay and Jura and the fishermen on Loch Roag on the west coast of Lewis were soon numbered among the petitioners. So the list grew, and when at the end of 1806 Rickman set to work to prepare the Commissioners' Third Report, more than thirty roads fell to be included. Many of these were still in the stage of discussion; others were in various stages of construction, while some were already encountering those varied and complex problems which for the next few years were to perplex so sorely the Commissioners and their three hard-driven servants.

The work which had been done on the old military roads during the last quarter of the 18th century had, as the years passed, grown increasingly perfunctory. Inadequate supervision had accustomed contractors and workers alike to feel that careless and slipshod work would be accepted. Now, under Telford, all this was changed in a transition sudden, difficult and painful. The new road specifications which Telford drew have not survived in full detail, but in 1819 when the work was far advanced, the poet Robert Southey toured the Highlands with his friend Rickman, and to Southey and to scattered references in Hope's letters we owe much of what is known of the nature of the roads

[1] H.R. & B. 2nd Report, 1805, Appendix C. See Appendix No V
[2] H.R. & B. 3rd Report, 1807, Appendix F

which Telford made. 'The plan upon which he (Telford) proceeds in road-making', wrote Southey, 'is this—first to level and drain; then, like the Romans, to lay a solid pavement of large stones, the round or broad end downwards, as close as they can be set; the points are then broken off, and a layer of stones broken to about the size of walnuts, laid over them, so that the whole are bound together; over all a little gravel, if it be at hand, but this is not essential; . . . every precaution is taken to make the road firm in all its parts.'[1]

In Telford's work on these Highland roads, nothing marked his engineering skill and foresight more clearly than his attention to their embankments and his careful provision against that great enemy of road construction—water. 'Toward the hill', wrote Southey in his Journal for 1 September 1819, 'there is a low stone line. If the hill be cut away, it is walled a few feet up, then sloped, and the slope turfed; if there be no slope, a shelf must be left, so that no rubbish may come down upon the road. The inclination is toward the hill. The water courses are always under the road, and on the hillside back drains are cut, which are conducted safely into the water courses by walled descents, like those upon the Mount Cenis road, but of course upon a smaller scale. This road is as nearly perfect as possible.' 'The bridges,' he noted in another passage, describing the Fearn road in Ross-shire, 'the walled banks, the steep declivities, and the beautiful turfing on the slope, which is frequently at an angle of forty-five degrees, and sometimes even more acute, form a noble display of skill and power exerted in the best manner for the most beneficial purpose.'[2] It did not need in the autumn of 1819, nor does it need today, the eye or the imagination of an engineer to recognise that here was work of a quality far exceeding anything which had been attempted before.

From the start Telford kept always clearly before him the type of traffic likely to use these Highland roads and, at least in the northern and western parts of the Highlands, cattle rather than wheeled traffic appears to have been uppermost in his mind. A hard or uneven surface, he knew, would hurt the feet of the beasts 'whose accommodation and good condition when brought to

[1] Southey, pp. 54, 97. Southey is hardly accurate in his remarks about the use of gravel on Telford's roads. Hope's letters and other contemporary documents make it clear that, especially on the roads in the northern Highlands, gravel was much used.
[2] loc. cit., p. 97   [3] ibid., p. 143

market is a primary object of all Highland road-making'; so, while the foundation of the road must be firm and solid, he was insistent that the surface must be of gravel. Scattered references in Hope's correspondence with the contractors make it clear that ten and sometimes fourteen inches of gravel was in many cases insisted upon for the centre of the road, with six to eight inches for the sides.[1]

These new roads were in general of a surprising width. Few were to be less than fifteen feet wide, except where cut into rock, when twelve feet was commonly allowed, and in at least one case, in Caithness, a width of twenty-one feet was specified. As Hope explained in a letter to a prospective contractor for the Ardelve road in Kintail, if a road were narrow the feet of the cattle, confined to a restricted area, would do great damage.[2] In crossing peaty ground, as in Skye, where the peat was less than two feet deep this was to be dug away until the firm ground was reached, but in deeper peat a firm foundation was to be established by laying turf, heather or brushwood to support the gravel surface.[3]

One of the strongest arguments which had weighed with the Government in deciding to proceed with Highland road construction and the building of the Caledonian Canal, was that these projects would provide work at a time when many were losing their livelihood as a result of the changes brought about by the break-up of the old clan organisation and the growth of sheep-farming. In the early stages of the new roads, there were times when the Commissioners and the contractors working for them must have felt that the aims of the Government had been only too successfully achieved. Roads and Canal each competed for local labour, casual and seasonal at the best, and the Highland labourer was not slow to sell his labour in the best market, moving from one to another as suited him, with ever a close watch on the peat-cutting, the corn and potato harvest and the fishing which would soon call him home. Wages were by far the largest factor in the cost of road-making, and in the early years, when even Telford and his surveyors tended to err in their reckoning of this item, it

[1] 'The Commissioners do not think that in general metal is required for a Highland road. It is only required where the intercourse ought to be able to make and maintain the road.' (Hope, 23 March 1813)
[2] Under the Highway Act of 1669 and possibly for much the same reason, it was provided that the roads were not to be less than twenty feet broad.
[3] H.R. & B. 3rd Report, 1807

is not surprising that contractors with small experience often went still more widely astray. Of the roads first put in hand it seems that underestimate of labour charges in nearly every case led to the work being undertaken at prices which meant serious loss for the contractor. No exact information as to the wages paid by road contractors for local labour can be found in the contemporary documents which have come down to us, but in the early years on the Canal, one and sixpence a day was the wage fixed by Telford for ordinary labouring work, and it seems probable that on the roads the rates were little different. It was not long before the labourers on the Canal were demanding more, while as early as October 1804 Telford was writing to the unfortunate contractors from Perth who had offered at too low a price for the Glengarry and Arisaig roads, advising them to engage as little local labour as possible 'to convince the people of the Highlands that if necessary the work may be carried on without them. This will soon dissolve any weak combination that may at present exist, and I have no doubt that in a very short time plenty of men will offer for employment.'[1] How successful Messrs Dick and Readdie were in opposing this early trades union movement is not known, but their efforts certainly did not save them from incurring serious loss on these first two road contracts for the Commissioners. During the next few years Telford himself was to experience, on the Canal, the irresistible rise in wages and prices which played havoc with many an estimate and brought ruin to those who made them. To Rickman also, rising costs were a source of growing concern. 'Do we attempt', he wrote to Hope in the autumn of 1809, 'to make Highland Roads more grand than is requisite, or is the price of labour and materials doubled since we commenced our operations?'[2]

The modest wages paid to the workers on roads and Canal alike meant hard living and plain fare for all. Joseph Mitchell, who was to play a leading part in the later stages of the work, served his apprenticeship about this time with the masons working on the Canal near Fort Augustus. The masons were paid at a considerably higher rate than the ordinary labourers. Those with whom Mitchell lived were earning twenty-one shillings a week out of which they paid three and sixpence to four shillings

[1] H.R. & B. 2nd Report, 1805, Appendix A
[2] H. of L. Rickman to Hope, 2 September 1809

a week for their living. The fare was oatmeal, morning, noon and night, cooked as porridge, brose or bannocks, with tea and butter added as a treat on Sundays, and in the autumn some potatoes and herrings brought from Arnisdale on Loch Hourn, which was then a fishing village of some importance.[1] On the Canal the men lived in the comparative luxury of huts, but on the roads there were no such refinements. When Robert Southey made his tour with Rickman ten years later, he found the road workers at Garve in Ross-shire housed in tents with huts of branches for their kitchen, the tents having been purchased by the Commissioners from surplus military stores at the end of the French Wars.[2]

With porridge, brose and bannocks the workmen's staple diet, the provision of oatmeal was clearly the first pre-occupation of the road contractors. In a few cases oatmeal may have been supplied free to the men, but in most cases it would seem to have been sold to them at cost price by the contractor. In any event a plentiful supply of meal was essential, and it was largely to allow for this and for the purchase of tools, that the Commissioners advanced a small proportion of the contract price at the start of the work. As work progressed, further payments were made by Hope in instalments at two-monthly intervals, and generally by means of drafts drawn by the contractors on the Commissioners' account with the Bank of Scotland, which Hope accepted if progress reports were satisfactory. From Hope's letter-book it is clear that these periodical payments were a source of great worry to him. The progress reports which reached him from the road inspectors in the Highlands and from the contractors themselves were often widely at variance. While Hope dared not pay for more than the work completed and must keep in hand a margin to repay the initial advance, he was often in the position of having to nurse a hard-pressed contractor struggling with a losing contract, knowing full well that if the contractor failed the loss would fall not only on the bankrupt, but on his cautioners and above all on his unpaid workmen.

As time passed and the number of roads under construction increased, the provision of large sums for the payment of wages in the remoter parts of the Highlands imposed on the banking system of Scotland a considerable and unaccustomed strain.

[1] Mitchell, VIII, pp. 81-2   [2] Southey, p. 150

Though the number of banks in Scotland was rapidly increasing, many districts in the Highlands were still without them. As the number of banks grew, fierce competition arose among them to get their notes into circulation often by methods hardly consistent with sound banking principles. When in the summer of 1804 Hope had asked the Bank of Scotland to help in financing the work of the Commissioners, he had offered as an inducement to the Bank, to do what he could to see that only notes of the Bank of Scotland should be used for wage payments. The offer was one which the far-seeing directors of that institution were not slow to accept.[1] To make this offer was one thing; to ensure its fulfilment was another. Before many months had passed, contractors in the western Highlands were complaining that lack of cash at Fort William forced them to seek accommodation where they could find it, or to transport large sums from Perth, keeping the money at great risk 'in the miserable huts which form their present habitation', and that even in Inverness the agent of the Bank of Scotland could only produce miscellaneous notes of many banks.[2] The Bank of Scotland denied any failure on their part, reminded Hope of his bargain, and called on him to secure 'the rejection of the underhand solicitations of any other Banking company who have afforded no accommodation either to Government or to the country'.[3] Hope bore the reproaches of both, troubled perhaps by the thought that he had made with the Bank of Scotland a bargain which could not be fulfilled; comforted certainly by the knowledge that what he had done was for the best and in a good cause.[4]

While Hope was doing what he could to acknowledge the help of the Bank of Scotland in a practical fashion, the Commissioners were by no means unappreciative of what the Bank was doing. In the early weeks of 1805, James Fraser, the secretary of the Bank, had told Hope that his directors hoped that the extent of their help would be brought to the notice of the Commissioners. Hope passed on the message to Rickman who wrote in reply, 'I

[1] Hope, 6 October 1804
[2] Hope, 1 March 1805
[3] Bank of Scotland, Letters, 24 July 1805
[4] That Hope did his best to hold to the bargain with the Bank appears from a letter which he wrote to Dick and Readdie, the Perth contractors, in the autumn of 1804 when he pointed out to them that in view of the help which the Bank was giving in the building of Highland roads and bridges it was only right that the notes circulated among the workmen on the roads should be those of the Bank of Scotland. Hope, 6 October 1804

think the Bank of Scotland will have an honourable mention in the annual Report of next session. They seem more eager to forward the projected improvements than could in any reason be expected from any large Company who seldom can be persuaded *collectively* to any exertion except in their own affairs. I cannot but feel singular respect for them on this account.'[1]

The pioneering quality of Telford's work was not confined to problems of engineering. Here indeed he was constantly breaking fresh ground, meeting and solving, especially on the Canal, technical problems which both in their nature and their magnitude were without precedent; but on the administrative side the innovations for which he was responsible were scarcely less important. Hitherto the execution of public works by contract had been virtually unknown, but now, under his guidance, contractors for public works came to be selected as a result of competitive tenders based on carefully drawn specifications from which Telford would allow departure only if he was completely satisfied of the necessity or the advantage. The skill, experience and resources of the contractor were now examined with a care undreamt of before Telford's time, while the system of periodical payments as work progressed, which he applied to all road contracts in the Highlands, was completely new. All this called for constant inspection to ensure that the work which was going on was of good quality and in accordance with the detailed plans, that the contractors were keeping at least reasonably well up to the agreed timetables, and above all that the progress of the work justified the periodical payments for which the contractors were not slow in asking. The surveyors who had helped in the laying out of the routes were not permanent employees of the Commissioners. Their responsibility was in each case limited to planning the individual road and estimating as best they could the cost of the work, and it was soon clear that a permanent staff of paid inspectors was urgently needed. James Donaldson, who had formerly been employed by the Commissioners on the Forfeited Estates to advise on certain of their works in the Fort William district, was appointed in 1804 to act as Chief Inspector on the new roads which were now being built, and on Donaldson's death two years later Telford brought north in his place John Duncombe who had worked with him on the construction

[1] Hope, undated, probably February 1805

of the Ellesmere Canal in Shropshire; but one man alone was not nearly sufficient, and as the work grew, a number of sub-inspectors were appointed, each to be responsible for certain specified roads and ultimately for the six districts of Argyllshire, Lochaber, Badenoch, Ross-shire, Sutherland and Caithness, and Skye, into which the work was divided.

If the building of the Canal and the simultaneous making of the new Highland roads caused an undesirable competition for labour and a general rise in prices, the two projects were in some ways complementary and helpful one to the other. Telford was determined that the roads he built would be of lasting benefit to the Highlands, and though even he underestimated the effect of Highland weather on Highland roads he saw to it that his road plans provided, as Southey later observed, for bridges, drains and retaining walls on a scale which far exceeded anything previously attempted. 'We should deem ourselves to be bad stewards of public expenditure,' wrote the Commissioners at a later stage, 'did we not labour for posterity as well as for the present genera-tion.'[1] It was therefore clear that whoever was responsible for inspecting and supervising the work on behalf of the Commis-sioners must have a good knowledge of mason's work. The work on the Canal had attracted to it a very large number of masons from other parts of Scotland, and it was from them that Telford selected his first road inspectors to work under Duncombe. Many of these masons came from the southern shores of the Moray Firth, and as the work on Canal and roads grew in extent the number of masons about Elgin, Forres and Nairn increased far beyond local needs. The work was mainly seasonal, the men returning to their homes in the autumn to spend the winter, and their accumulated wages, with their families till 'as the spring of the year came round they might be seen in parties of eight or ten wending their way with light burdens of apparel and tools to fulfil their season's engagements in the Western or Northern Highlands'.[2]

Telford had a genius for picking men engaged in one of his many projects and moving them to another where their qualities, knowledge or experience could be used to advantage. He seldom made a mistake, though sometimes a plant taken from the softer climate of the Severn Valley wilted at first in the cold of an

[1] H.R. & B. 8th Report, 1817   [2] Mitchell, p. 35

Inverness-shire winter or the rains of Lochaber. For poor John Duncombe the change seems to have been too great, and less than three years after his move to the Highlands, Telford was writing to Rickman, 'Duncombe seems to be getting into his dotage— there is no getting him to finish things in time. I have for ten weeks stopped his salary and shall pay him only by the mile for what he really does. We can by means of Mitchell and Easton (and some subalterns) who are very active and accurate and good judges manage the inspection and estimations of work done.'[1] Telford's drastic treatment was of no avail and seems only to have precipitated the end, for a few months later he wrote to Rickman from Chester, 'I am vexed about the old fool [Duncombe]—his dying will be no matter of regret; but in a jail at Inverness is shocking.'[2] Of all the letters from Telford which have survived this is the only one which suggests that he was other than a humane and kindly man. It was written at a time when work on the roads and on the Canal was reaching its peak, and it can only be assumed that Telford's enthusiasm for the work, his passion for efficiency and his own great physical strength had made him intolerant of weakness in others and forgetful in the urgency of the moment that he himself had brought about the change of work and scene which had tried his colleague too high.

Among the masons who came from the Morayshire coast each spring to work on the Canal was one John Mitchell of Forres. Mitchell was an able and energetic workman, and he was one of the six masons chosen by Telford as inspectors under Duncombe, responsible for the supervising of the construction of the roads on the side of Loch Ness and in Glen Garry. On Duncombe's death Mitchell was appointed in his place as Chief Inspector, a position which he held until his own death in 1824. When Mitchell first came to Telford's notice he was only a plain working man, but he possessed the qualities of integrity, courage and physical strength which Telford knew were needed for the position he was to fill. Robert Southey who met him a few years later wrote of him, '. . . a remarkable man and well deserving to be remembered. Mr Telford found him a working mason who could scarcely read or write. But his good sense, his good conduct, steadiness and perseverance have been such that he has been gradually raised to be Inspector of all these Highland roads

[1] Telford, 20 October 1809   [2] Telford, 9 June 1810

which we have visited and all which are under the Commissioners' care, an office requiring a rare union of qualities—among others inflexible integrity, a fearless temper and an indefatigable frame. Perhaps no man ever possessed these requisites in greater perfection than John Mitchell. . . . No fear or favour in the course of fifteen years have ever made him swerve from the fair performance of his duty, tho' the lairds with whom he has to deal have omitted no means to make him enter into their views and do things or leave them undone as might suit their humour or interest. They have attempted to cajole and to intimidate him equally in vain. They have repeatedly preferred complaints against him in the hope of getting him removed from his office and a more flexible person appointed in his stead; and they have not unfrequently threatened him with personal violence. Even his life has been menaced; but Mitchell holds right on. In the midst of this most laborious life, he has laboured to improve himself with such success that he has become a good accomptant, makes his estimates with facility and carries on his official correspondence in a respectable and able manner.

'In the execution of his office he travelled last year not less than 8,800 miles and every year he travels as much, nor has this life and exposure to all winds and weathers and the temptations, either of company or of solitude at the houses at which he puts up led him into any irregularities or intemperance; neither has his elevation in the slightest degree inflated him. He is still the same temperate, industrious, modest, unassuming man as when his good qualities first attracted Mr Telford's notice.'[1]

[1] Southey, pp. 251-3

6

IN THE GREAT GLEN

WHILE the project of the new roads was steadily gathering momentum, events in the Great Glen between Inverness and Fort William had been moving fast. Within a few days of the passing of the Act of Parliament which gave birth to the Commission for building the Caledonian Canal, the Commissioners had held their first meeting and Telford had been appointed engineer to the great undertaking. As the whole cost of the work was to be met from public funds, its execution did not, as in the case of the roads, depend primarily on local support; so while on the Canal the technical problems were immensely greater than on the roads, the financial difficulties were in the early stages smaller. The idea of this great waterway connecting east to west through the hills of Inverness-shire, bringing industry and employment to thousands and solving, it seemed, at one blow so many intractable problems, appealed to the imagination of all, and any lingering doubts were swept aside in a flood of public enthusiasm.

Between August and October 1803 Telford was in Scotland. Plans for the new roads claimed part of his time, but much of it was spent on surveying and examining, in collaboration with William Jessop, a fellow engineer, the ground in the Great Glen. Telford had lost no time in consulting both James Watt[1] and John Rennie, who had already reported favourably on the possibility of a Canal, and by the early spring of 1804 he had obtained approval of his detailed plans for the line of the Canal where the first excavations at either end had already started. Meantime inquiries had been put on foot through the Conveners of the northern counties as to the labour and material available. A start was made in building up stores of tools at Inverness and at Corpach near Fort William, where supplies of oatmeal were being accumulated for the use of the men already at work, some of whom, already familiar with Canal work in the south, had

[1] Watt had surveyed the line of the Canal for the Commissioners on the Forfeited Estates in 1773, and though nothing further then came of the matter, the project retained a firm place in the minds and imaginations of many. See Appendix No. VI

78

been brought north to instruct the local labour force. Hopes ran high. The surveys and preliminary excavations had revealed no serious difficulties. Timber and stone were readily available at moderate cost. Local support was assured and it was believed that much of the land needed for the Canal would be given free.

Telford, following his usual practice, sought for and found among his former colleagues men to supervise the work on the Canal at either end. Matthew Davidson had been a master mason at Langholm in Telford's apprenticeship days in Dumfriesshire, and in 1790, when Telford was commissioned to build, near Shrewsbury, his first large bridge, he had taken Davidson south to help him in this and subsequent canal work in the Severn Valley. Now, at Telford's urgent request, he returned north to take over the heavy responsibility of supervising the work at the Inverness end of the Caledonian Canal. For Davidson's opposite number at the western end Telford's choice fell on John Telford, another of his Shropshire colleagues who had worked with him on the Ellesmere Canal. Both men were to receive salaries of £200 per annum with a house and an allowance for a horse. Whether John was any relation of Thomas Telford himself is not certain, though in writing to Thomas to commiserate on the death of John in the late spring of 1807, Hope referred to John as 'your kinsman'.[1] By a happy accident the letter-book kept by John Telford at Corpach has survived the passage of a hundred and fifty years. The book in which he kept the copies of his letters is now little more than a loose pile of leaves barely held together by the tattered leather of the binding, the faded writing in places barely legible against the yellowing paper; but from it and from certain letters which Thomas Telford himself wrote to Rickman in the first eight years of the Canal, something can be learnt of the hard work and harder conditions in the Great Glen in those early years of last century and of the men who faced them day by day.

Matthew Davidson was a man of very different character from his younger colleague at Corpach. Robert Southey, writing from Inverness in his diary for 4 September 1819, describes Davidson, who had recently died after fifteen years service on the Canal, as having been 'a strange cynical humorist . . . who had lived long enough in England to acquire a taste for its comforts and a great contempt for the people among whom he was stationed

---

[1] Hope, 4 May 1807

here; which was not a little increased by the sense of his own superiority in knowledge and talents. Both in person and manners he is said to have very much resembled Doctor Johnson; and he was so fond of books and so well read in them, that he was called the "Walking Library".[1] Though a Scot by birth and upbringing, Davidson had indeed no high opinion of the Highlanders nor of the country or climate in which they lived. John Telford's letters to Davidson, written in surroundings much more hard and primitive than Inverness, reflect the more resilient spirit and tolerant outlook of the younger man, deriving good-natured amusement from the complaints of his colleague. In the late autumn of 1804 John Telford wrote to Davidson who had been ill and in low spirits, describing his own troubles at the western end, assuring him that Inverness was a paradise compared to Lochaber.[2] The summer brought no improvement in Davidson's spirits. 'I had a letter from Davidson yesterday,' writes John Telford, 'where he says his legs and temper improve nothing.'[3] 'The colony in the snowy regions', he wrote in a later letter, 'desire to be remembered to their friends in the milder climate of Inverness'[4]; but Davidson seems to have derived little comfort from the comparison, for a few weeks later John writes to a friend in the south, 'I suppose Mr [Thomas] Telford has given you a particular account of this country, but if you were to compare his account with Mr Davidson's you would find a material difference. Mr Davidson declares he would not accept a seat in Heaven if there were a Scotsman admitted into it.'[5]

If Davidson's troubles were partly of the spirit, John Telford's were material enough. As a shopping centre, Fort William in 1804 left much to be desired, with only two markets a year compared with two a week in Inverness. 'We can hardly get anything for money', wrote John to Davidson. Supplies were always short, and with a growing labour force living on brose and bannocks, oatmeal was a constant worry. 'There is not a pick of oatmeal in Lochaber', wrote John Telford to Davidson in November 1804 envying him the flesh-pots of Inverness. 'Potatoes is all the food at present. Butter sixteen pence a pound. Eggs and milk not to be got for money.'[6] Two months later the oatmeal position was no

[1] Southey, p. 111   [2] J. T., 5 November 1804
[3] J. T., 3 January 1806   [4] J. T., 4 February 1806
[5] J. T., 16 June 1805   [6] J. T., 5 November 1804

better, and on the last day of the year John wrote that none of the
Fort William merchants had any, despite their previous assurance
that the supply question could be safely left to them; but John
had got a supply in Ballachulish after a fruitless journey to Lismore, so the men on the Canal had not gone short.[1] Maintenance
of the supply of oatmeal seems to have been almost an indigenous
problem in the Highlands ·at the start of last century, and two
years later Thomas Telford, his active mind always on problems
ahead, was writing to Rickman suggesting a purchase in bulk as
he feared a failure of both oats and potatoes in the north. The
crisis passed, but in the following year the problem was again
acute, and Hope warned Telford that there was a risk of men
leaving their work on both the Canal and the roads for lack of
meal. 'I fear', he wrote in December 1807, 'that part of the
Highlands will be very ill off indeed, potatoes not lifted; crops
wasted.'[2]

There was good reason for the concern which Davidson and
John Telford felt as to the supply position. The labour force was
growing fast. During the autumn and winter of 1804 only some
one hundred and fifty men were at work, but by the following
year the numbers had grown to nine hundred, of which five
hundred were at work at the Inverness end and four hundred
round Corpach. From now on the average force at work each
year appears to have varied from seven to nine hundred, with the
numbers employed rising to twelve or fourteen hundred during
the summer months and falling to less than half that number in
the winter when, as both John and Thomas Telford repeatedly
complained, the Highlanders were not accustomed to working.[3]
At a later stage, when those responsible for the Canal project
were faced with criticism in press and Parliament, the charge was
made that nearly all the engineers and the workmen were Irish
and that the Highlanders were not benefiting from employment
on the Canal. This seems to have been very far from the truth.
In March 1805 John wrote to Thomas Telford, 'I expect that
men will be dropping in fast from different quarters if the weather
continues open. I expect a considerable quantity from Lismore,
perhaps two hundred or upwards, and about the same quantity
from Skye. I understand that each of these Islands can furnish
more than that number besides what may come from different

[1] J. T., 31 December 1804   [2] Hope, 19 December 1807   [3] C. C., passim.

quarters.'[1] Two months later Telford reported to Rickman that of four hundred men working at the west end the majority came from Kintyre, Lismore, Appin, Skye, Arisaig and Morar while the five hundred at the east end came mostly from Caithness, Ross-shire, Moray and Aberdeenshire, many from land recently enclosed.[2] Fifteen years later, when the Canal was nearing completion, the Commissioners reported that of five hundred and fifty men employed on an average over the preceding year, only one in every sixty was not a Highlander. Perhaps this estimate was put into their Report to meet the criticisms of the Canal project which were then reaching their height, but over the twenty years during which the main work of construction continued, the evidence that the work was largely done by that local labour for which it was intended seems overwhelming.

Each spring saw a great influx of workmen to the Great Glen; each autumn a corresponding exodus, while during the eight months of the effective working year there took place fluctuations which might well try the most placid temper. Seed-time and harvest, fishing, peat-cutting and potato-lifting each in due season made its call and seldom called in vain. John's letters to Thomas Telford during the first year of work on the Canal from November 1804 to October 1805 record the constant ebb and flow of labour, an ebb and flow repeated with little variation in the years to come. The numbers at work, wrote John early in November 1804 were reduced because many had gone home 'to get their little harvest and potato crops and are not yet returned. Indeed many of them do not intend to return before spring never having been used to work in the winter in this Country.'[3] With the coming of spring the numbers at work again rose, but early in June 1805 John wrote that those with families had again gone home for a week or so to plant potatoes and cut peats. If their absence was temporary so was their return, and at the end of July the start of the herring fishing was again drawing them off. The last days of August saw an exodus for the harvest, and not till the end of October could the harassed John report a return to work delayed by a late gathering.

These seasonal fluctuations were a sore trial to those in charge of the Canal, and there is more than a hint that as time passed

[1] J. T., undated   [2] Telford, 26 April 1805
[3] J. T., undated

82

John was perhaps coming to understand Davidson's view of the local inhabitants, though hardly to the point of rejecting the thought of joint occupation with them of the Heavenly Mansions! In the first days of 1806 John wrote to a friend in Inverness reporting a severe gale which had caused great damage at Corpach and had blown off the stocks a vessel on Loch Oich. 'You may assure Mr Davidson', he added, 'that there was not one Highlandman smothered. They understand self-preservation too well. As soon as the gale commenced they took to the open shore with their families for shelter.'[1] Thomas Telford's exasperation at the delays caused by the casual habits of the workmen is reflected in a letter to Rickman written from Inverness at the end of September 1818, when he was doing all he could to complete the work. 'The herring season', he wrote, 'has been most abundant, and the return of the fine weather will enable the indolent Highland creatures to get their plentiful crops and have a glorious spell at the whisky making.'[2]

The peat, the herrings and the harvest were not the only enemies of good time-keeping on the Canal. Fears of French privateers had weighed heavily in the balance in favour of the Canal when its construction was under discussion. Now, the bogey of Napoleon and the calls of the local militia hindered the work. In August 1805 John Telford wrote that 'all Skye men, a large number, have been sent for to do volunteer duty', and five years later, after John's death, Thomas Telford was still complaining to Rickman that 'the permanent duty of some Militia Corps will be a considerable drain'. The press-gangs too were active. In October 1804 the master of the *Caledonia*, a sloop of forty tons which had been built to carry supplies to the Canal, was armed with a letter from John Telford to James Hope, asking Hope to endeavour to arrange for the release of any of the crew who might be pressed for the services.[3]

While nearly all the work on the roads was done by contract, a substantial part of the work on the Canal was done by direct labour employed and paid by the Commissioners. For the payments to the road contractors for which he was responsible, Hope drew on the account with the Bank of Scotland fed from London.

[1] J. T., 3 January 1806
[2] H. of L. Telford to Rickman, 23 September 1818
[3] J. T., 22 October 1804

Thomas Telford was primarily responsible for nearly all payments on the Canal which were made from an account in his
name fed by the Commissioners. For these Canal payments the
arrangements were complex and troublesome, for while Hope
sat in his Edinburgh office within ten minutes walk of the Bank
of Scotland, Telford was constantly on the move, now in London,
now in Shropshire, now in Wales and often on long tours of
inspection in the Highlands. Between 1803 and 1811 his letters
to Rickman in London of which there is a record come from nearly
thirty different addresses. In the early days of the Canal work
Telford's account was kept with Robarts and Company, and
from time to time Messrs Hoare, acting for the Commissioners,
were instructed to sell Exchequer Bills held for them, to feed
Telford's account as required. Telford then drew on the account
and sent the drafts to the superintendents on the Canal to enable
the latter to cash them in Inverness to pay the wages. One of the
earliest records of the operation of this complex system appears
in a letter from Telford to Rickman in October 1803, when Telford reported that a draft for four hundred pounds had been sent
by him to Scotland to enable John to pay for oatmeal purchased
for men working on the Canal.[1]

Telford found the Commissioners to be strict and exacting
taskmasters. To his many responsibilities on the Canal was soon
added the task of preparing for the Commissioners reports on the
emigration problem, on insurance rates for shipping and on
Scotland's trade with the Baltic ports, while constant reports on
the progress of the work, with monthly statements of receipts and
expenditure were both expected and demanded. His original
instructions had been to draw on his account at regular intervals
by means of bills which did not require to be met until the expiry
of forty days. To the Commissioners this no doubt seemed a
sensible plan which would allow them to budget in advance and
give them ample time to provide the necessary funds; but it took
little account of the day to day contingencies involved in the
employment on the Canal of a fluctuating labour force engaged
in a vast and novel undertaking. Before many weeks had passed,
the Commissioners were complaining that Telford's bills were
drawn at irregular intervals and for varying amounts, and that
the money was needed before the expiry of the stipulated forty

[1] Telford, 1 October 1803

days. Telford pleaded, as well he might, that pressure of work prevented him from adhering to rigid rules, that it was impossible for him to meet these payments himself, and that if wages were not regularly and punctually paid the credit of the Commissioners and the work on the Canal would suffer.[1]

By the summer of 1804 the labour force had grown to such an extent that Telford estimated the sum needed for payments on the Canal at four thousand pounds a month, but before many months had passed he was reluctantly forced by the Commissioners to limit the monthly expenditure to fifteen hundred pounds, taking what consolation he could from the fact that if this hindered work on the Canal it would at least leave more labour available for the roads. Telford's was a sanguine temperament and through it all he always hoped for the best. 'With the present Board and Secretary', he wrote to Rickman in May 1809, 'I have no doubt of protection in all that's right—only it is prudent to leave as little as possible to chance when dealing in public matters.'[2] But even he had his bad moments and in the following spring he was writing, 'I begin to dread that the drafts transmitted to answer the payments of this day may be presented at Hoare's before they are provided for.'[3]

At the northern end of the long supply line from London, John Telford and Matthew Davidson waited with real anxiety, and looking between the faded lines of John's letter-book many a sleepless night can be discerned. The 'common labourers' who started work on the Canal towards the end of 1803 were paid at the rate of 1s 6d per day, and 'those habituated to Canal work', 1s 8d to 2s—rates fixed by Thomas Telford as the standard not to be exceeded without express authority.[4] Cutting in the great peat moss near Corpach had been let at a rate of $2\frac{1}{2}$d per yard for the first six feet of depth, while rock blasting was paid at the rate of 2s 6d per cubic yard, the men supplying the powder. Soon, higher rates were demanded, and in the autumn of the following year John reported a disagreeable pay day. The men had refused to accept 1s 6d a day claiming that they knew no English and had not understood the bargain. There had been high words, and John and his assistant had been in fear of their lives.[5] Already the

---

[1] Telford, 18 October 1803   [2] Telford, 21 May 1809
[3] Telford, 3 February 1810   [4] *Life of Telford*, ed. Rickman, p. 310
[5] J. T., 22 and 23 October 1804

daily rate had been largely abandoned, most of the men now being paid on a piece-work basis; but this in its turn led to trouble when John discovered that some of the men had moved the measuring marks to their advantage.[1]

The drafts which Thomas Telford sent north were cashed in Inverness by the Bank of Scotland which had undertaken to provide the necessary funds. Posts were irregular, and with Thomas Telford moving from place to place, his drafts sometimes did not arrive in time for John at the Corpach end of the Canal to send them to Inverness and get back cash for pay day. Fraser, the agent of the Bank of Scotland in Inverness, would not send cash in advance, and not infrequently the Bank itself was short of funds, sending to John miscellaneous notes of many different banks. In the summer of 1805 John had to report that some of the men had refused to work for fear of not being paid and had gone off to the fishing. A few weeks later Fraser was reduced to sending bills which the men would not accept in place of cash, and John was in despair. 'If all the men are not settled within Monday night at furthest,' he wrote to his opposite number Davidson at Inverness, 'I dread the consequences. We are all well here at present; God knows how long we shall remain so if John [his messenger] does not come here with the money on Monday night.'[2]

If labour troubles were the worst of John Telford's problems there were many others. In the records of these early years at the western end of the Canal, John appears in many rôles, now as engineer, now as accountant, often as house-builder and timber merchant and constantly as general dealer. The demand for timber was almost insatiable, first to build huts for the men, workshops and offices, and later to supply the carpenters' shops which made boarding, wheelbarrows, rough tools and the innumerable items needed for the work. The demands of the Navy in these wartime days were soon to limit the supply of good oak needed for the lock-gates, and latterly nearly all the high quality timber needed had to come from the Baltic; but native fir and birch and ash were ready to hand, and soon down the rivers flowing to Loch Oich and Loch Lochy came a stream of timber, in single logs and rafts, as the woods in Glengarry and Lochiel's country met the growing needs.

[1] J. T., 18 November 1804   [2] J. T., 24 August 1805

Some of Thomas Telford's earliest correspondence on Canal business was with Lochiel. 'Fir, Ash and Birch', he wrote early in September 1803, 'are all needed.' A month later the bargain had been made, the timber to be floated down to Loch Lochy when the River Arkaig was full. Soon John, too, was writing to Glengarry for timber to be taken out to Loch Oich, and 31,000 cubic feet had already been measured for purchase.[1] The price varied from tenpence to fourteenpence per cubic foot. Glengarry had asked a shilling a cubic foot for blown timber, but John thought this too dear and Lochiel had offered standing timber round Loch Arkaig for one shilling, and one and threepence for cut timber at Achnacarry.[2] All these purchases, and the cost of floating the timber to the Canal and down the loch to the sawmill on the River Lochy worked by water from the River Loy, meant extra calls for money, and caused those fluctuating drafts which Thomas Telford found so essential and the Commissioners so annoying. John at Corpach made his budgets and laid out his money with all the care and frugality of a good housewife, but time and again his orders, even for essential supplies, had to be placed with only the fervent hope that money would be available to pay the bill. In April 1805 a cargo of coal was daily expected to reach Loch Linnhe, but the till was empty.

Housing for the men and for the Canal offices at Corpach called for plasterwork and slating. Plasterwork required hair and split lath, or alternatively skilled men to split local timber. All these were hard to find. Slate rock was near at hand, and Lochiel offered a free gift of a quarry near Onich on Loch Leven[3]; but in the western Highlands the step from owning a slate quarry to possessing slates is long and troublesome, and slaters for the roof work must in any event come from Oban. Stone quarries had been opened on Loch Ness, near Clachnaharry on the Beauly Firth, and at Fassifern on Loch Eil, but good stone for building was further to seek. John had found granite at Ballachulish and in Glen Nevis, but tests showed this to be too soft, while the Glen Nevis stone would involve a railroad up the glen. The best freestone came from the Cumbraes in the Firth of Clyde and this, shipped in sloops built by the Commissioners, proved the cheapest despite a duty of $33\frac{1}{3}\%$ on deliveries at Fort William. Sheep

[1] J. T., 19 June 1804   [2] J. T., 4 July 1804
[3] Telford, 5 October 1803

Island off Lismore provided limestone to be burned in kilns erected at Corpach, while farms on the Appin shore helped to make up for the deficiencies of the local provision merchants. So John's letter-book grew and with it his worries, while on the coastal sea-lochs and among the islands the *Caledonia* and her sister ships of the little Canal fleet were seldom idle.

As the work progressed, John's needs at Corpach far outgrew the narrow limits of local resources. Contracts for ironwork were placed in Aberdeenshire, Derbyshire and Wales. Rails, wheels and axles for the quarry workings came from Outram and Company at Butterley in Derbyshire, parts for the sawmill from Hull and Glasgow, while bricks and other supplies came from Liverpool in ships which took back kelp and wool. Three steam engines for working the pumps had been supplied by Boulton and Watt of Birmingham. These, said the Commissioners in their Second Report to Parliament, were of the power of thirty-six, twenty and six horses respectively, and lest the value of the purchase might be underestimated, they pointed out that as the engines could be worked for twenty-four hours a day they could do more work than the equivalent number of horses![1] With it all John found time to give thought to the welfare of his men. Cows were kept at Corpach to provide milk on reasonable terms, and hay for them at eightpence a stone appears on the shopping list for 26 November 1804. A brewery too was started in the hope of limiting the amount of whisky drunk, and in February 1805 John wrote that he was waiting for a consignment of hops, with comfortable chairs for the public house.[2]

Despite his enthusiasm for the work and the lively sense of humour which his letters show, John Telford's never-ending worries, the vagaries of the weather and the isolation of Corpach were taking their toll of his health and spirits. The vivid comparisons which he drew in his letters between his life and that of Davidson at Inverness, intended though they clearly were to cheer his colleague, reflected in fact consciousness of, if never real complaint at, his own hard lot. Like Davidson he had turned to reading, but while Davidson had books to hand and was at least in reasonably close touch with the outside world, John Telford had to rely on what reading material and other comforts for mind and body he could get from Inverness. John, his messenger, on

[1] C. C. 2nd Report, 1805   [2] J. T., 4 February 1805

weekly visits to the Bank had many commissions to execute; now
to order newspapers from the south, now to call at the booksellers
for long-awaited volumes,[1] and occasionally to bring back, with
the pay money, small creature comforts unknown in Lochaber.
His own visits to Inverness were few and far between. With all
his responsibilities he could seldom leave Corpach, and even at
that distance from London the grip of the Treasury was tight and
remorseless. A visit to Inverness with his wife had been planned
in the summer of 1805, 'but', he wrote to Davidson, 'I must
return the next day, as my expenses the last time I visited you
were deducted'.[2] Perhaps as with Duncombe, the change from
Shropshire to Lochaber was too sudden, the load too heavy to
bear, for in the spring of 1807 John Telford died, the first of the
responsible officers of the Commission whose life was to be given
for the great work now in hand.

In the four years which had borne so heavily on John Telford
at Corpach, great strides had been made on the Canal. Alexander
Easton, his successor, took up his work at the western end with
energy, and before the Canal project was ten years old Rickman
could record in his Annual Report a measure of progress sufficient
to satisfy even the driving energy of Telford and the high expectations of the Commissioners. Despite the constant rise in wages
caused partly by the competition of roads and bridges in the
labour market, the supply of labour had been satisfactory and at
least as steady as seasonal fluctuations would allow. Labouring
work on the Canal was heavy, and many preferred work on the
roads where this was to be had in the districts from which they
came; but Hope's efforts to meet the banking problem had proved
not unsuccessful, and certainty of getting their pay at the week's
end weighed heavily in the balance in favour of the Canal at a
time when many a Highland workman had already suffered
cruelly from defaulting road contractors. Steady work and steady
pay for men hitherto little accustomed to either had gone far to
justify Telford's words in his First Canal Report in 1804. 'The
people have already with considerable facility fallen into the
necessary modes of employment and will soon, I have no doubt,
acquire habits of industry which will prove a lasting benefit to
themselves and may be expected to improve that part of the

---

[1] J. T., 3 January 1806
[2] J. T., 16 June 1805

United Kingdom and put a final stop to the spirit of emigration.'[1]

Work in these early years had been concentrated mainly at the two ends of the Canal and on the construction of the great basin at Clachnaharry, near Inverness, which was to prove one of Telford's hardest problems and greatest achievements. For the rest, work on the middle sections had been confined to the sinking of borings, though as time passed, short sections of the Canal were excavated at intervals. In their Report of 1806, the Commissioners recorded that on the central section round Loch Oich, little had been done save the extraction of birch wood from Glengarry.

It was early realised that the deepening of Loch Oich would be necessary, and by the summer of 1806 the dredger for use on the loch was ready. A few weeks later Telford reported that it had sunk, a mishap which he accepted without undue concern, since as he reported to Rickman in October of that year, its sinking relieved the Commission of the cost of its upkeep, while it could be readily refloated when required. Telford's philosophical view of the sinking of the dredger was to be justified even more fully than he then realised, for operations on Loch Oich were to be the subject of a long and bitter controversy. The early estimates of the cost of the Canal had assumed that the land to be taken could be acquired at a cost of about £15,000. Entry to the land had been allowed to the Commissioners subject to adjustment, at a later stage, of compensation either by agreement, or failing this by assessment before a jury. Three years after the work had started, the Commissioners reported that many of the claims had been settled, at figures only slightly in excess of the valuation made on their behalf by George Brown of Elgin, and by 1807 they were able to record that settlement had been reached for nearly all the land required. They little knew what lay ahead.

[1] C. C. 1st Report, 1804

7

PROGRESS REPORT

NEARLY every year, in early summer, the two Commissions presented to Parliament an account of their stewardship with a report on the progress during the preceding months of the work on the new roads and the Caledonian Canal. These reports were the work of John Rickman the secretary, and to their preparation he sacrificed his leisure, his sleep and his health. Like Telford and Hope, Rickman took a real pride in being so closely associated with work the value and novelty of which he recognised to the full. Throughout all the years which witnessed the work on roads and Canal, there were few instances of round pegs in square holes, and Rickman with his passion for accuracy, his clear-cut mind and his capacity for marshalling in order bewildering masses of facts and figures, was pre-eminently the right man in the right place. 'Never', wrote a contemporary at the time of Rickman's death, 'was work more energetically carried out by its efficient officer.'[1]

If Rickman's Annual Reports were thus to some extent a labour of love, they were none the less a labour of great magnitude, superimposed as they were on his day to day work as Secretary to the Speaker, the tasks of supervising census returns and cataloguing the Library of the House of Commons and, after 1814, on the heavy responsibilities of Clerk Assistant at the Table of the House of Commons. 'No payment', he wrote to his friend Southey in the summer of 1816, with real feeling if somewhat mixed metaphor, 'can compensate such a tantalising quantity of work; yet from this I cannot escape without the art of brain transfusion could be discovered and all my memory of the subject placed on another man's shoulders. But this cannot be, and for three years more I must drudge on. Yet on the bright side of the subject I ought not to be dis-satisfied at having been the instrument of trying a new experiment which I myself much distrusted originally, and trying it successfully; I speak of the aid given to Highland roads, and of the other affair of the [Caledonian] Canal; I ought not to forget

[1] *Gentleman's Magazine*, April 1841

that it is of unexampled dimensions and consequently of much originality in its details, that my history of it in the Annual Reports is the first regular history of the formation of a Canal, and a history, which with the adaptation of the appendixes, those of *workmen* and of accounts, I do not fear will ever be equalled.'[1]

For all his interest in the work and his high sense of duty, there were times when Rickman found his burden almost intolerable. As early as 1816 he spoke with longing of early retirement, but three years later he was still in the harness where in fact he was to remain for almost another decade. At the beginning of 1820 he was again writing to Southey, '. . . and now I must work hard at a Road and Bridge Report till Parliament meets, and on the Appendices till Easter I suppose. In fact the history of proceedings is more to me than the business itself—a necessary evil however and one of which I now see the termination. Part of life has been well spent perhaps in starting well such a novelty in the government of civilised nations as the half-contribution scheme pursued in the Highland improvements, and on similar occasions, if ever they occur, the managers will perceive that it is possible by care and attention to produce a satisfactory result.'[2]

These Reports on which Rickman laboured so hard have indeed, as he hoped and intended, preserved for later generations a clear picture of the progress of the work. Prepared as they were as a factual record by a man whose genius lay in clear and accurate presentation rather than in literary style, they alone might seem today somewhat arid documents. It may be that Rickman and his Commissioners had the same thought, for added to the Reports are many documents of the time which lighten the picture, while the letters of James Hope, of Telford and even of Rickman himself, with such other contemporary documents as have survived, add colour and human interest to the scene. Rickman's part in the work was not to go unnoticed or unappreciated, for in presenting to Parliament in 1821 their ninth Report on Road and Bridge work, then almost completed, the Commissioners wrote of Rickman's work, 'Considering the great value of the business of the Board being in the hands of a person fully informed of all its proceedings from the commencement, and above all in the hands of one so peculiarly fitted for the duties of that situation,

[1] Rickman to Southey, 22 July 1816, in *Life and Letters of John Rickman*, p. 181
[2] Rickman to Southey, 10 January 1820, ibid., p. 213

from the variety of his knowledge and his unwearied diligence in the discharge of those duties, we are persuaded the greatest public benefits have been derived from his labours both in carrying the views of the Board into execution and in preparing the materials for our successive Reports to Parliament.'[1]

Of all the road projects which reached the Commissioners during the twenty years of active road construction, the great majority came in the end to completion. Some prospered from the start and came by easy paths to early maturity. Others proved weak and fractious children from birth, nursed to manhood by the Commissioners and their servants through many youthful ills and accidents, while relatively few came in the end to nothing. It was not surprising that in the first years of the work the attractions of novelty and early enthusiasm should sometimes outweigh considerations of prudence and practicability, and here and there in the early Reports appear for a time the names of projects which were destined to reappear no more. Of the early casualties, some failed to get the local support on which their original projectors had counted, while others, designed mainly for droving traffic, could only look for the support of interests which proved in the event too distant and too diverse.

The modest beginning which was made in 1804 when the Perthshire contractors started work in Glengarry and on the Road to the Isles by Loch Eil and Loch-na-Gaul, foreshadowed a great development of road work in the next few years, and when in the winter of 1812 Rickman took up his pen to draft the Sixth Report of the Commissioners, a total of nearly forty road contracts were under way or in course of adjustment. A few had already been completed at a cost, to the State, of close on £120,000. In the extreme south of the Highland area, the Cowal roads linking Loch Fyne with the Clyde ports for which the fishermen had asked were far advanced, while in the Lorn district, with the making of a short section of road near Loch Melfort, the communication from Oban south to the Crinan Canal was, if primitive, now at least continuous. South of the Great Glen, the road from Spean Bridge by Loch Laggan was, after many early misfortunes, soon to connect Lochaber with the valley of the upper Spey, while on the line of the Canal new roads were in the making on the north side of Loch Ness and westward from Fort Augustus to Fort

[1] H.R. & B. 9th Report, 1821

William. Branching north-westwards from Loch Linnhe and the Great Glen, the road-makers had already reached the Atlantic coast at Kinlochmoidart, at Arisaig and at the head of Loch Hourn, while up Glenmoriston and over the watershed into Glenshiel the road to Skye was fast being opened. Through the heart of Ross-shire, men were at work on the road which would link Dingwall with Loch Carron and Loch Alsh, and up the north-east coast the road from Dingwall to Wick and on to Thurso was well advanced. The needs of the Islands had not been forgotten. In Arran, roads from Brodick would soon reach to the southern and western shores of the island, while drovers from the south of Islay crossing to Jura could now bring their cattle by the new roads to the ferries on the Sound of Jura. Projects in Mull hung fire—'I should not be much surprised if there were still a blow up', wrote Hope in prophetic vein to Telford in September 1812 after months of negotiation over the Mull roads,—but in Skye, Portree was being linked southward to Broadford, Kyleakin and Sleat and north-westward to the Trotternish Peninsula.[1]

The road projects for Arran, Islay and Jura were the most southerly of the works undertaken by the Commissioners, and in Central Scotland only a few petitions reached Rickman's office from landowners south of Loch Tay. Of these few, the most promising was a plan put forward in 1807 by Lord Breadalbane for a road from Ardeonaig on the south side of Loch Tay to cross the watershed to Comrie and to continue southwards by Glen Lichorn to Dunblane.[2] Telford had long regarded the farms on the loch side with their mixture of sheep, cattle and arable ground as a particularly favourable type of Highland farming, and plans for a road to help the transport of coal and lime northward and farming produce southward had his warm approval. The cost of the road had been estimated at about £300 a mile, but no offer under £600 a mile was received, while some were more than five times the amount of the estimate. 'This great disproportion', wrote Hope to Rickman in the summer of 1811, 'between the estimate and the offers is beyond anything we have hitherto experienced. . . . I am persuaded there has been a concert among the offerers and that unaccustomed to slump offers upon so large a scale they have wisely guessed in a way safe to themselves.' The contributors would not increase their offers; the contractors

---

[1] H.R. & B. 6th Report, 1813, passim   [2] See Appendix No. VII

would not reduce theirs. Protracted correspondence was productive of little but exasperation, and when in the autumn of 1811 Rickman reported to Abbot the 'probable extinction of the business', the Chairman endorsed on the Secretary's letter the pencilled comment, 'I do not regret it.'

The progress which the Commissioners were able to report to Parliament in that summer of 1813 had not been achieved without trial and tribulation for the contractors, and no less for Telford, Rickman and Hope. As time passed bringing with it experience and fuller knowledge the way grew smoother, but the early years were full of trouble. 'In works of this kind,' wrote Telford to Rickman in the autumn of 1808, 'widespread, executed by contractors indiscriminately employed and amongst a people just emerging from barbarism, misunderstanding and interruptions must be expected.'[1] Some contracts seemed to move continuously under an evil star. The Perthshire partners Dick and Readdie at work on the Glengarry and Arisaig roads were soon in the toils. Their offer, as Telford had feared, was much too low. Even Telford himself for all his experience and foresight sometimes reckoned too little with the rainfall of the west, and the partners had fallen even more deeply into the same error. Both men were honest and did their best, but lack of experience of Highland work and Highland workmen, bad weather and the knowledge that they laboured on losing contracts, weighed heavily against them. Readdie was slow to learn. 'The honesty, sobriety and diligence of Mr Readdie', wrote one of the inspectors, 'are unexceptionable but he is very positive and will do things his own way, however wrong or to his own disadvantage, and I doubt he will suffer by it in the end.'[2] Hope described him more tersely as 'a man bereft of common worldly sense'.[3] In terms of the contract the Glengarry road was to be finished by 1806, but long after this date he was still struggling on. His funds were running low. 'The state of public confidence at Perth', wrote Hope, 'is so much affected at present that he cannot get the accommodation there which he could formerly have commanded.' To make matters worse the priest at Arisaig had spread a rumour that Readdie was bankrupt.[4] The rumour was untrue—or at least not quite true. The priest, wrote

[1] Telford, 30 November 1808
[2] H. of L. Report by Charles Gowrie, 1 March 1809
[3] Hope, 17 September 1812
[4] H. of L. Report by Charles Gowrie, loc. cit.

95

Hope, was known to be 'worthless and unprincipled'[1]; but the damage had been done. All Readdie's men left him, and in despair he threw up the contract leaving it for the guarantors and the Commissioners to complete as best they could.

Rickman meantime was having a difficult correspondence with Colonel Macdonell of Glengarry, one of the chief contributors to the Glengarry road. His contribution was much in arrear. Hope with his usual tact had, as Glengarry admitted, already asked for payment 'in the handsomest manner', and when Rickman pressed for settlement, Glengarry replied that he was waiting for a large compensation payment from the Canal Commissioners. His estate, he explained, was large; but ready money could only be raised by bonds over it, and the raising of money in these wartime days, as Readdie too was finding, was difficult.[2] It was suggested by Glengarry's Edinburgh lawyer that in the circumstances the Road Commissioners should take over in settlement his claim against the Canal, and Rickman and Hope were at pains to point out that the two Commissions were entirely separate bodies, transactions with one having no relation to transactions with the other.

While Readdie struggled in Glengarry, his partner Dick fared little better on the Arisaig road. 'The good intentions and honest ideas of Mr Dick the acting contractor cannot be exceeded,' wrote John Mitchell, 'but the method he has in conducting his work and the manner he has in setting his men to it and even the authority he has over them cannot be recommended.'[3] Fate had a further blow in store, for crossing the hills from Glengarry to Arisaig Dick was killed.[4] It was not till 1812 that the Commissioners could report that the two roads were virtually complete. Time and, in the case of the Arisaig road, money had been spent far in excess of expectations; but two much-needed roads had at last been opened, while already the Glengarry road was in constant use by cattle drovers from Skye and for timber traffic to the Caledonian Canal.[5]

---

[1] Hope, 19 May 1809
[2] H. of L. Glengarry to Rickman, 13 June 1808
[3] H. of L. Report by John Mitchell, 28 February 1809
[4] 'Poor Dick's death is melancholy, the more so as he seems to have struggled nearly through the difficulties of an incompetent contract price.' H. of L. Rickman to Hope, 6 January 1810
[5] The troubles of the Commissioners over the Loch-na-Gaul road did not end with its completion in 1812. Three years later Hope was still in correspondence with

On the north-west side of Loch Ness a road by Invermoriston to Fort Augustus had been asked for, surveyed and let to contract. In the early stages all went well, and by the autumn of 1805 James Livingstone, a Fort William contractor, was already at work with Sir John Campbell of Ardnamurchan as his guarantor; but the early promises of a smooth passage were deceptive and by the summer of 1807 Hope was warning Sir John's agent of troubles ahead. Livingstone was proving 'languid and inattentive'. A good overseer was urgently needed, such as Milne who had been employed 'in the prolongation of Princes Street',[1] a sub-contractor had not been paid and was now in jail for debt, while Livingstone himself was 'in hiding somewhere and scarce a workman to be seen on the road'.[2] The Commissioners had no concern with sub-contracts, and Hope could only write to Rickman suggesting that in this case they might stretch a point. The substance of the guarantor was beyond doubt. Sir John's estate, Hope had ascertained, was worth three thousand pounds a year and was not entailed. 'His woods are a-cutting which will give him about six thousand pounds and pay a new house he is building.'[3] Sir John was heedless of warnings. 'Really Sir,' wrote Hope to him in the summer of 1807, 'I fear, nay I am confident, that you are misinformed; there will be a heavy loss upon the road and there is not the faintest possibility that the Roads and Bridges Commissioners can or will give you the least relief. Nothing has been done on the road for a long time. What has been done is going to wreck.'[4] Rickman too was fully alive to the dangers. 'If Sir John Campbell persists', he wrote at a later date to Hope, 'in trusting these delinquents, the Livingstones, in repairing their own misdeeds and perfecting the road, no good result can be expected from such infatuation.'[5] Hope's fears were all too well founded and by the end of 1808 Livingstone had abandoned the contract, leaving Sir John as guarantor to complete it at his own expense. From the subsequent correspondence it appears that the full extent of Sir John Campbell's loss was £2,000, and in reporting the final completion of the road in 1813 the Commissioners wrote,

[1] Hope, 17 August 1807   [2] Hope, November 1807
[3] Hope, 19 December 1807   [4] Hope, 8 December 1807
[5] H. of L. Rickman to Hope, 27 July 1809

the agent for Macdonald of Clanranald endeavouring to get payment of Clanranald's share of the cost which had been secured by his bond, but had not yet been paid.

'With respect to Sir John Campbell it would be an injustice not to state that, though suffering under the hardship which he sustained from his misplaced confidence in Livingstone, he has caused no unreasonable trouble to us or our agents and has always manifested an intention to complete the contract in that satisfactory manner in which it has now been accomplished.'[1]

From an early stage a road from Dingwall by Achnasheen to Loch Carron had been in contemplation. The adoption by Ross-shire of a system of road assessments payable by the whole county eased the problem of finance, and in due course the contracts were let; but nothing prospered with the work. Cumming, the surveyor, was slack and dilatory. 'Surely,' wrote Hope to him in exasperation, 'since October last [1807] you might have found time if necessary to perambulate the 10th Division of the road ten times over and to clear up the small inconsistencies in your Report which prevent my proceeding.' Two successive contractors on the eastern section of the road, and their guarantors, proved little better than men of straw. 'I have not been inattentive', wrote Hope, 'to the importance of bringing to a close the discussion with the Cautioner for the Bankrupt Contractor of the Achnasheen Road and for these six months past I have been occupied with it, at intervals. . . . The result is that all the parties are bankrupt except Mr Andrew Davidson, Advocate, Aberdeen . . . and Mr Hector one of the supplementary securities.'[2] The sternest letters which Hope could write—and some were very stern—had no effect and, as he wrote to Rickman, 'we should gain nothing by putting them in prison'.[3] Progress was at a standstill, and for long it seemed that the road which wrecked Lady Seaforth's carriage by Loch Achanalt in the last years of the 18th century was fated to see no better days. At the western end, too, work on the road by Loch Carron to Strome Ferry was for long held up, the Ross-shire proprietors, who seldom spoke with one voice, failing to agree about a proposal by Hugh Innes of Lochalsh that a route through Glen Udalain to the south of Loch Carron should be preferred to a road on the north shore. Telford fretted at the delay, and even Hope's endless patience wore thin. 'Time presses,' he wrote to Innes in July 1812, 'the days get short and if the advertisements are long delayed the season may be

[1] H. R. & B. 6th Report
[2] H. of L. Hope to Rickman, 22 November 1820   [3] Hope, 22 October 1813

lost.'[1] But another year was to pass before the northern route was chosen and the work could be put in hand, Mr Mackenzie of Applecross becoming responsible for the road work and Mr (later Sir Hugh) Innes of Balmacara for the construction of the piers at Strome. Not till 1819, ten years after its commencement, was Rickman able to report the completion of the road by Achnasheen to Strome Ferry, leaving behind it in the records a tale of bankruptcy, frustration and weariness.

While the road by Achnasheen to the west coast moved by slow and painful stages to completion, another Ross-shire project had come and gone. In the early years of last century, communications with the Island of Lewis passed almost solely through the tiny port of Poolewe near the western end of Loch Maree. Here, too, came cattle shipped from the Islands to join the drove roads which led eastward to the great cattle tryst at Muir of Ord in Easter Ross-shire. The plans for a road from east to west by way of Achnasheen not unnaturally turned the thoughts of local landowners to the advantages of a connecting road from Achnasheen by Glen Docherty to the head of Loch Maree, whence the journey to Poolewe could be virtually completed by boat. In the early weeks of 1811 James Hope was in correspondence with Sir Hector Mackenzie of Gairloch as to a survey of the road, and by April of that year a survey had been ordered by the Commissioners, the road to be on a narrow scale but sufficient to take wheel carriages.[2] By the end of September the road had been surveyed, the Commissioners estimating the cost of a fifteen-foot road at £4,385. The winter of 1812 had come before Hope could report that the local contributions had been paid into the Bank of Scotland, and Mitchell had been instructed to delay preparing detailed plans as the days were short, there was nowhere for the surveyors to stay, while despite the efforts on the road through Strathbran, a horse could get no further West than Contin.[3] In the following spring offers were invited for more than $11\frac{1}{2}$ miles of road from Achnasheen to 'the small bay of Ruarroar on the south side of Loch Maree', while the specification which Mitchell and Telford had prepared had been lodged with the innkeeper at Kinlochewe.[4] Three offers were received, and as each of these was for a sum in the region of £7,000, the Com-

---

[1] Hope, 31 July 1812   [2] Hope, 1 April 1811
[3] Hope, 15 December 1812   [4] Hope, March 1813

missioners concluded that, as with so many of their early estimates, their reckoning had been too low.[1] A gap occurs in Hope's letter-books about this date, so it is uncertain whether the Commissioners or the local contributors drew back; perhaps both shrank from the rising cost. In the late spring of 1816 the contributions of the proprietors were repaid, the plans were abandoned, and the Loch Maree road—for a time at least—took its place in the inconsiderable list of projects which failed.

Each year Telford paid two visits to Scotland, in spring and again in autumn. His lodgings for the few days he was in Edinburgh were at the Turf Coffee House in South St Andrew Street, where the London Mail Coach called. It is not difficult to imagine with what eagerness Hope waited for Telford's arrival, and what long and anxious consultations took place between the two men at Hope's Office, first in Princes Street and later at the west end of Queen Street. But Telford's time was ever too short for all he had to do, and soon he was on his way north to the Canal and the roads. From the time he left Edinburgh for the north, Telford was almost continuously on the move. John Telford and Davidson had a host of problems waiting for solution at Corpach and Inverness, technical, administrative, financial and domestic. Work completed must be inspected in detail and plans laid for the coming months. Receipts for expenditure must be examined, wage rates considered and budgets prepared, for the Commissioners kept a close watch on finance and disliked fluctuating or sudden demands for funds. The daily records of wind and weather must be scrutinised, for in the early years of the Canal work the fear was never entirely absent that adverse winds, blowing for long periods up or down the Great Glen, would hamper sail traffic in the lochs from east or west. Added to all this, Telford was mainly responsible for negotiations with local proprietors for acquisition of land, for opening of quarries and for purchase of timber.

With the Canal problems disposed of, Telford set out on long tours of inspection of roads, completed, in progress, or still only under consideration. Surveyors, contractors, local proprietors and County Road Committees all had their problems, their petitions and their grievances. Telford's repute as an engineer, and no less as a man of scrupulous fairness and honour, is nowhere shown more clearly than in the readiness with which his views on

[1] Hope, 5 October 1813

all technical matters and his decisions in disputes were accepted by all concerned. Contractors aggrieved at an inspector's report on their work; local contributors at variance with contractors as to the responsibility for a fallen bridge; private owners seeking deviation of a route for the benefit of their property; County Road Committees unable to agree among themselves; all accepted Telford's verdict, and accepted it without question. When roads made at the joint expense of the Commissioners, the counties or local proprietors had been reported by the inspectors as complete, a final inspection had to be made in the presence of all parties concerned before the road could be taken off the hands of the contractor and a final accounting concluded. Telford personally represented the Commissioners at most, if not all, of these inspections, which were lengthy and often controversial. If the weather of a Highland autumn often added to the hardships of Telford's journeys, there were occasions when he had reason to bless the rain. An inspection of roads in west Inverness-shire in the autumn of 1818 which threatened to be long and tedious seems to have been a case in point. 'The Equinoctial Gales', wrote Telford to Rickman, 'met us and helped the inspection.'[1]

All this meant constant travelling in all weather, on foot or in the saddle, over rough roads and tracks and often through untracked moor and glen. The Commissioners were strict guardians of the public purse, and if the three guineas a day which Telford was paid for his time may not have been ungenerous by the standards of the day, the one and sixpence a mile allowed to him for travelling costs was little enough to cover the cost of horses, gigs where he could use them, board and lodging, even in days when a good breakfast at an inn could be had for two shillings, dinner for two and sixpence and a bed for the same price.[2] It is clear that Telford himself found it so, for a note on an account of expense rendered to the Commissioners in 1813 records that on Telford's representation the rate was raised from May of that year to two shillings.[3]

Telford loved his work, but as he set out on his journeys he had no illusion as to their probable length and their certain discomfort. 'Tomorrow', he writes to Rickman from Glasgow in

[1] H. of L. Telford to Rickman, 23 September 1818
[2] As the accounts of the two Commissions were kept entirely separate, Telford's fees and expenses were scrupulously apportioned between the two.
[3] Public Record Office, T.861, Voucher H

September 1809, 'I set out across the abominable ferries to the Argyllshire roads',[1] and a little later he asks that a letter be sent to Edinburgh, 'where I propose going first, then returning to the Isle of Arran and passing thro' Argyllshire to Corpach, thence to Inverness and to Mickwell and down the eastern side of the Island thro' Aberdeenshire: all this with traverses not a few.'[2] 'I hope you are safely arrived at home,' wrote Hope to Telford at Shrewsbury at the end of one such journey in the autumn of 1805, 'If a person who moves about so much can be considered as having one.'[3] Telford's journeys were not confined to these islands. In the spring of 1808 he had been invited by Count von Platen to advise on the construction of the Gotha Canal in Sweden, and for over twenty years Telford was closely associated with the project. This entailed periodical visits to Sweden, and Hope, on whom this placed an added burden of responsibility in Scotland, viewed with little enthusiasm Telford's overseas adventures. 'I long for his return', he wrote to Rickman, harassed by road and Canal problems in the autumn of 1813.[4]

If the progress of the Commissioners' work was bringing a rapid transformation to Highland roads, it could do little to lessen the hardships of a winter journey, and a few years later Telford was writing from Edinburgh to his friend Andrew Little, 'In the re-survey of the Glasgow and Carlisle Road your neighbour Mr Easton and I have had to weather the late storm of snow. I have yet to repass the Grampians and travel from Inverness through Argyllshire, a very promising expedition previous to Christmas.'[5] The passing years brought no lightening of the burden, and in the late summer of 1823 Telford was still 'continually posting with all possible dispatch between the eastern and western shores of our magnificent island', with visits to Wales, Norfolk and Ireland. 'When these little matters have been accomplished I must turn my face towards the stormy north in the month of October.'[6]

Through it all Telford managed to find time to deal with letters and papers which followed him or awaited him at the few fixed points where his correspondents knew he would call. 'Voluminous and some of it a little perplexing', as he wrote of one batch in the early summer of 1807.[7] How this was achieved with

[1] Telford, 27 September 1809
[2] Telford, 7 July 1811
[3] Hope, 29 October 1805
[4] Hope, 18 September 1813
[5] Telford to Little, 24 November 1816
[6] H. of L. Telford to Rickman, 1 August 1823
[7] Telford, 15 June 1807

the postal arrangements of the times is a matter for wonder; but achieved it was. 'A rainy day in Argyllshire may afford you time for considering them', wrote Hope, forwarding a package of papers in October 1811.[1] Strong man though Telford was, he was not immune to the weather. 'I remain here only this day and to-morrow,' he wrote to Rickman from Edinburgh in the spring of 1820, 'and then proceed on the proposed lines of roads if health and weather permit; but at present neither are very flattering.'[2] Considerations of personal health indeed weighed lightly with him. In the late autumn of 1825 Hope wrote to Rickman re-porting that Telford had cholera,[3] but only nine days later Telford himself wrote to Rickman that a satisfactory inspection of the Canal and other works had restored his health[4]—an episode which would seem to say much for the strength of Telford's constitution or little for the standard of contemporary diagnosis.

Rickman's visits to Scotland were relatively few, but in the late summer of 1819 he and his family made, with Telford and Robert Southey, the extended tour of the roads and the Canal which are so graphically described in Southey's *Journal*. A hardened traveller, Telford had good reason to foresee that this tour, to which he himself looked forward with great pleasure, might have in store for his less experienced friends some unwel-come surprises. 'I have', he wrote to Rickman from Ellesmere on 30 July, 'this day requested Rob Roy Macgregor to take you under his powerful protection when you reach his Capital. I trust the Northern Ocean will smooth his rugged features and your watery way. Experience obliges me to confess he is some-what wayward. He can enchant with delight or toss you about with abundant incivility.'[5]

At that time much work was in progress on harbour works partly financed by Government funds arising from the restoration to their owners of certain of the Highland estates forfeited after the Rising of 1745. These works, too, were under the supervision of the Commissioners with Telford as engineer, and the route of Rick-man's party to the north took them up the east coast and along the south shore of the Moray Firth, where certain harbour works were

[1] Hope, 24 October 1811
[2] H. of L. Telford to Rickman, 7 April 1820
[3] H. of L. Hope to Rickman, 12 November 1825
[4] H. of L. Telford to Rickman, 21 November 1825
[5] H. of L. Telford to Rickman, 30 July 1819

under way, to Inverness. From Inverness they continued north to the boundary of Caithness, admiring as they passed the new stone bridge over the Beauly, the iron bridge at Bonar and the great Fleet Mound devised and planned by Telford which had lately been completed by Lord Gower. Turning south again, they took the new road by Garve and Achnasheen, and came to the Western Sea at Strome Ferry. Piers on both sides of Strome Ferry had been built by the Commissioners to link the new road on the north side of Loch Carron with those through Kintail to Glenshiel and Glenmoriston, and Sir Hugh Innes of Balmacara had agreed to provide a ferry boat; but when the party reached the ferry no boat was to be found and, like many a party since, they were forced to return to Inverness by the way they had come and so down the Great Glen to Fort William and on by Glencoe and the Moor of Rannoch to Dalmally, Inveraray and the south. Southey found much to admire in the great works on which Telford and his colleagues were engaged, and no less in the beauty of the Highlands in early autumn, when, as he wrote in his journal of a September morning on Loch Carron, 'the mountains and the vallies and the streams were drest with sunshine'.[1]

The tour proved a happy venture for all three men, and, thanks to Southey's pen, no less so for posterity. Telford charmed his companions. 'This parting company', wrote Southey on the last page of his *Journal*, 'after the thorough intimacy which a long journey produces between fellow-travellers who like each other, is a melancholy thing. A man more heartily to be liked, more worthy to be esteemed and admired, I have never fallen in with; and therefore it is painful to think how little likely it is that I shall ever see much of him again—how certain that I shall never see *so* much.'[2]

Hope's work grew heavier year by year. In the summer of 1803 when he was appointed Law Agent to the Commissioners, his duties and responsibilities were to all appearances limited; but

[1] Southey, p. 163. Southey had always a keen eye for natural beauty. Of the view from Ballachulish he wrote: 'The evening was glorious. To the West the Linnhe Loch lay before us, bounded by the mountains of Morvern. Between those two huge mountains, which are of the finest outline, there is a dip somewhat resembling a pointed arch inverted; and just behind that dip the sun, which had not been visible during the day, sunk in serene beauty, without a cloud; first with a saffron, then with a rosey light, which embued the mountains and was reflected upon the still water up to the very shore beneath the window at which we stood, delighted in beholding it.' Southey, p. 226
[2] Southey, p. 269

Plate 5   Loch Fyne

Canal Office Ellesmere
30. July 1819 —?

My dear Sir

The Pay Bills and Prospective Accounts accompany this.

We yesterday had a very full and agreeable Canal meeting, for in addition to the good humour which our Chairman Lord Bridgewater never fails to inspire, the Revenue was Reported more than £6000 above that of the preceding 12 Months. —

I shall this Evening proceed towards Yorkshire, so that for a couple of days you may if necessary write to the Post Office Boro. Bridge afterwards to the Post Office Carlisle.

I have this day requested Rob Roy Macgregor to take you under his powerful protection, when you reach his Capital. —

I trust the northern Ocean will smooth his

Plate 6 Letter from Thomas Telford to John Rickman, 30 July 1819

his rugged features, and ~~crossed out~~ your watery way. — Experience obliges me to confess, he is somewhat wayward. he can enchant with delight, or toss you about with abundant incivility. ——

The weather here has consisted of local and pretty heavy Thunder Storms, it is still very hot — Crops abundant, and Harvest on the verge of commencement. —

from am Yours very truly

Thos. Telfer

Plate 7   Princes Street, looking to the south west, about 1814

like many members of his profession before and since he was quickly to learn that a lawyer's work deals with much besides the Law. Rickman four hundred miles away and Telford always on the move could give him only limited help, and like a local commander far in advance of headquarters he was compelled to take a growing responsibility and to carry an increasing burden. His letter-books grew and multiplied, the copies transcribed, sometimes in his own hand, more often in those of others, as more and more of his staff were drawn into the work. A few bear the marks of haste, while the standard of legibility often varies; but as volume succeeds volume the extent and diversity of his work becomes ever more clear. Colleagues in the Law, landowners and their local agents, surveyors and inspectors, county conveners, contractors and their guarantors were among his many correspondents. To Rickman he sent progress reports, estimates, draft contracts and constant reports on finance, while with Telford he carried on a correspondence which as time passed grew increasingly detailed, complex and technical.

While Hope's work for the Commissioners thus grew steadily heavier he had many other preoccupations. Scotland in these wartime days was by no means exempt from the fears of French invasion, and the early weeks of 1804 had seen in Edinburgh a muster of the working classes armed with spades to break up the roads should Napoleon come. Hope, since 1803, had held a commission as Lieutenant Colonel in the Royal Edinburgh Volunteers, and for several years to come military duties made heavy and increasing calls on his time. Even after the threat of invasion had passed, drills and parades went on, and as late as the summer of 1811 he wrote to Sir Patrick Murray, 'We are on duty at present and drill mornings and evenings so that those times must be avoided.'[1] The French War brought no cessation of political warfare and the work of the Commissioners suffered. 'The Commissioners have still a good deal to do concerning letters of mine from September to December', Hope wrote to Telford in the early spring of 1807. 'The Election Committees must be a vile interruption of the other business.'[2] As agent for the Conservative Party in the Lothians, Hope himself was deeply involved. 'The dissolution [of Parliament] renews all my plagues', he wrote to Telford in May, 'and will make me a worse correspondent for

---

[1] Hope, 17 July 1811   [2] Hope, 5 February 1807

a while', but three weeks later he was able to report, 'I am happy to tell you all my Election business was over on 26th curt, and *well* over. You have been much better employed.'[1]

Hope with his extensive legal practice in Edinburgh was in close touch with a number of Highland proprietors either directly or through their Edinburgh agents, many of whom were his personal friends. He was, therefore, exceptionally well placed to forward the business of the Road and Bridge Commission which he served. For all that, his path was seldom smooth and there were many times when it was uphill going. Once the novelty of the half-contribution system had worn off, and with it the first enthusiasm, Highland proprietors showed a marked inclination to leave to the Commission and its servants an unfair share of the work. Many were the times when Hope and Rickman had to remind them in forceful terms that if the Government were to pay half the cost of road construction and the whole cost of surveying and engineering, they too were expected to show some degree of energy. Hope had devised and arranged with the Bank of Scotland the system whereby advances to proprietors were made against their bills. The execution of these bills and the actual discounting of them by the Bank were matters for the attention of the proprietors or their agents; but time and again Hope found himself left to arrange the whole transaction, which he could do only out of goodwill and not as agent for the Commissioners. A meeting of proprietors at the Bank of Scotland, arranged in June 1805 to discuss the financing of the proposed road from Strachur on Loch Fyne to Ardentinny, is typical. Of all those to attend only Hope himself appeared. 'You will now be able', he wrote to MacLachlan of MacLachlan, 'to form a slight idea of the pushing I have of four folks to do their own business.'[2] Yet, disheartened as he must have felt at times, Hope had the never-failing consolation of knowing that he was helping in a great work for the Highlands. 'There is plenty to do', he wrote to Rickman in May 1809, 'to keep all right among the contributors, contractors, surveyors and inspectors; but the improvement to the Country is incalculable.'[3]

Of the many varied problems which the Commissioners and their servants had to face in the early days of their work, the great

[1] Hope, 4 and 28 May 1807   [2] Hope, 21 June 1805
[3] Telford, 21 May 1809

majority arose less from its inherent difficulties, great as these were, than from the ignorance of most of the parties to the contracts. Despite the best precautions Hope could take, many of the early contracts fell to men with little experience and small substance, while many of the guarantors were in little better case. Many contractors were entirely ignorant of what lay ahead of them or of the conditions under which the works must be carried out. Many, too, were poor hands at measurement and calculation, and as the contracts were awarded on the basis of lump sum offers for an entire stretch of road and not at a rate per mile, any error of under-calculation fell on the contractor. Records of weather and rainfall were not available, with the result that too little allowance was made for one of the major contingencies of work in the northern and western Highlands. To make matters still worse, the main work of road construction covered a period of steadily rising costs and wages. In the nine years from 1803 to 1812 the average day's wage of a labourer—on the Canal and almost certainly on the roads also—rose from 1s 6d to nearly 2s 6d, while the price of meal rose from 20s to 36s a boll.[1] For such contingencies the terms of the contracts made no allowance. So it was that in all but a very few of the contracts for which they were responsible Telford, Rickman and Hope were dealing with men desperately struggling against heavy odds.

Bad bargains meant trouble for all. The contractor in many cases failed, leaving his workmen unpaid and his guarantors forced to complete the work and share as best they could the inevitable loss. Sometimes, as in the case of the road to Achnasheen, the resources of the guarantors proved to be insufficient, and Hope faced the weary task of advertising the work anew, while the unfinished road lay at the mercy of the weather. Even where actual failure was averted, the temptation for a man who had little hope of profit to skimp the work was almost irresistible. So the inspectors had to be always vigilant, till as time passed the Commissioners found themselves able to report that the contractors 'are at length convinced that though all reasonable indulgence will be allowed to them, the specifications annexed to the Contracts must be strictly fulfilled in justice both to the contributors and to the public'.[2] 'I do not think', wrote Rickman to Hope in the

---

[1] C. C. 11th Report, 1814. A boll contains 140 lbs.
[2] H. R. & B. 3rd Report, 1807

autumn of 1809, 'that the Commissioners acting for the public can ... deviate from the plain rule of seeing the public money well spent—and that by the only means in their power, Mr Telford's eyes.'[1] If Telford was satisfied that more expenditure was required on bridges and embankments than the first survey had suggested, additions to the contract price might be allowed, but these cases were closely scrutinised and grudgingly approved. More often the contractor was held closely to his bargain with no relief.

Amid so many pitfalls Hope had to move cautiously, steering a wary course between the Scylla of a bankrupt contractor and the Charybdis of over-generous payment for ill-completed work. Each contract presented its own special problems, and each as it progressed added slowly and painfully to Hope's knowledge, his judgment and his sureness of touch. In Moidart stern measures were soon called for. Halkett the contractor proved a rogue. 'He is a specious clever fellow', wrote Hope to Colonel Maclean. 'He wishes to do us up if he can and you have no idea how artfully he has corresponded with me'.[2] Neither Halkett nor his partner Kidd gave personal attention to the work, which they left to unsatisfactory sub-contractors for whom the Commissioners were not responsible. 'I cannot blame our surveyor for declining to be whipper-in of a number of different sub-contractors', wrote Hope to Halkett in the autumn of 1805.[3] The contract was finally abandoned, the road still unfinished. Halkett claimed no less than £3,143 from the Commissioners, largely for extra work done outside the contract price, and after an infinity of trouble the claim was settled by arbitration, Halkett being awarded sixty one pounds. In their Fifth Report the Commissioners expressed the hope that the outcome 'will operate as an example to deter other contractors from making exorbitant demands'.[4]

Still worse trouble was to come on the road by Loch Laggan to Upper Speyside. The cost of the whole stretch of forty-two miles of road had been much underestimated at less than ten thousand pounds. Of the four offers received, one was more than double the estimate. With some misgivings the lowest was accepted. Livingstone, the offerer—the same who was later to

[1] H. of L. Rickman to Hope, 2 September 1809
[2] Hope, 30 March 1809   [3] Hope, 6 November 1805
[4] Hope's answers to the contractors' claim alone extended to 116 pages of manuscript.

fail on the Invermoriston road—was reported to be 'A feeble and nerveless workman without anything to lose'.[1] Hope demanded ample security which, fortunately, Livingstone could not then produce. A new estimate revealed the gross error in the old. 'The amount of the estimate will stagger the Board,' wrote Hope, 'but it is certainly fortunate that no contractor appeared at the amount of the old estimate'[2], and it became necessary to let the work as two separate contracts. The cost of the western section 'seemed to elude all calculation', and it was only after much negotiation that new offers were at last accepted; but nothing prospered on the Laggan Road. Clark, the contractor for the western section, went bankrupt and his guarantor proved to be already ruined by his obligations for Faichney, the bad mathematician in trouble in Skye.[3] Meantime Clark was 'at Perth in hiding till the wrath against him is over', though Hope still hoped that matters might be 'so soldered up as to permit of his going on with the road'.[4] The hope was vain and in the last days of December 1813 Hope had to report 'Clark is now in Edinburgh in the sanctuary of the Abbey.[5] . . . His workmen have been most cruelly treated.' Not till 1818, thirteen years after the first survey, was the whole road complete at a total cost of £23,300. Of John Davidson, the contractor who finally completed the troublesome western section, Southey reported that he was 'an honest, plain, and contented man, who works with his workmen, places all his pride and pleasure in performing his work well, and has lost by several of his contracts'.[6]

[1] Hope, 15 October 1805   [2] Hope, 1 June 1809
[3] Hope, 4 September 1812   [4] Hope, 8 and 13 December 1813
[5] Hope, 22 December 1813: The right of sanctuary at Holyrood probably dates from a charter of David I and continued in existence far into the 19th century. Indeed the privilege of sanctuary has never been repealed by Act of Parliament. After imprisonment for debt was virtually abolished in 1880 the need for sanctuary came to an end, but in the 18th and early 19th centuries many debtors availed themselves of it. In 1816 three years before Clark's failure the number of refugees in the sanctuary was 116. The area covered by the sanctuary stretched from the foot of the Canongate to Duddingston Loch and included the whole of the King's Park and Arthur's Seat. At one time refugees in the sanctuary, or 'Abbey Lairds' as they were popularly called, took up regular residence. Lodgings and taverns abounded and in the early 19th century a decent room could be rented in houses mostly to the east of the Palace itself for 3s to 6s a week. Refugees in the sanctuary had the privilege of leaving it each week from 12 p.m. on Saturday till 12 p.m. on Sunday, during which time they were immune from arrest. De Quincey's name figures in the list of the 7,000 or 8,000 people who are believed to have enjoyed the shelter of the sanctuary during the last 200 years of its activity, and though Sir Walter Scott never entered it as a refugee there was a period in 1827 when he believed he might be forced to do so. (Hugh Hannan, *Book of the Old Edinburgh Club*, vol. 15, April 1927)   [6] Southey, p. 211

The Skye roads added their quota to the mounting troubles. Lord Macdonald and nine other local landowners had joined forces to contribute to the cost of making a road from Broadford to Sligachan and on to Portree, posing for Hope a formidable problem of administration and finance. 'From the number of the other proprietors who are to contribute . . .', he wrote to Telford in the spring of 1805, 'I foresee a thousand obstacles to the forwarding of the business. You can hardly form an idea of the difficulty in getting even two or three proprietors to come forward together or the *pushing* it requires.'[1] Contractors too were difficult to find for the island roads. 'We are all aware', Hope wrote to Telford at a later stage, 'that the Isle of Skye does not hold out flattering prospects to contractors and of course we cannot expect much choice.'[2] Even on the mainland, news of the losses suffered on other roads had made contractors more cautious, while the cessation of payments to unsuccessful offerers still further restricted the bidding.

Despite the error in his offer Faichney was entrusted with the Skye roads, but before long he was in trouble. 'I am suspicious', wrote Hope, 'Faichney is engaging in other speculations. . . . Of late he has married in the Island a clergyman's daughter and I have heard that he has begun to traffic in meat.'[3] Faichney's ventures—in commerce at least—proved unsuccessful. The contract was abandoned and the roads had to be completed at a cost to the contributors of £3,500. 'The loss is grievous', wrote Hope, 'and the Cautioners stript of the greater part of their means.' John Grant and John Bayne, Oban merchants who had backed Faichney, were all but ruined. When Bayne died shortly after, his affairs were found to be in hopeless confusion and his widow likely to be in dire need. In her interests the Commissioners agreed to give up what at the best must have been an almost worthless claim against Bayne's estate.

Bankrupt contractors and their creditors soon led Hope into paths seldom trodden by the feet of a respectable family lawyer. All payments for work done on the roads passed through his hands, and he thus found himself acting as guardian not only of public money but of the funds of local contributors. In such a position it was his clear and inescapable duty to ensure by all

[1] Hope, 23 May 1805   [2] Hope, 13 November 1815
[3] Hope, 22 May 1809

means in his power that, except where an advance was made for essential tools and supplies at the start of a contract, payments to a contractor never exceeded the value of the work already done. For this he must rely chiefly on the reports of the inspectors. Here Telford's care in their choice stood him in good stead, and on men like John Mitchell in the north and Robert Garrow and Alexander Martin in the west, Hope could place every confidence. So, relying on their reports, on his growing knowledge of the contractors and on his own native caution, Hope made his payments from the joint fund in the knowledge that so far as care could ensure it the balance remained always in favour of the payers. A letter of 31 July 1815, dealing with a troublesome stretch of road near Dunbeath in Caithness, is typical of his perplexities and his policy. 'Receiving as I do', he wrote to William Munro of Achany, 'most contradictory letters from four individuals, I am left no alternative but that of caution.'[1] When the troubles over the Achnasheen road were at their height, he had written to Rickman, 'My payments are conducted as cautiously as possible. It is certain that the Contractor has a ruinous bargain and that his Cautioners must suffer for it; and they are not so able as others; so that I am aware of the importance of the advance being as little beyond the work as possible.'[2] From this policy he never deviated, and when at length the completion of the Achnasheen road had been achieved Hope could report to Rickman, 'Amidst all the vexation which the Achnasheen road occasioned to me, as well as to the Inspector and Mr Telford, we had always the consolation that in the work done there was more value than had been paid by the Public.'[3]

Few items of news in the commercial world travel faster than news of an impending bankruptcy. Many of those who failed on the roads had no assets except such parts of the contract price as remained still unpaid in Hope's hands, and on these assets, sometimes real, more often imaginary, the creditors quickly descended. Some claims came from ordinary creditors for meal and general supplies and some from guarantors; but behind all these, more helpless but still more needy, were the unpaid workmen on the road. Many of these worked only for sub-contractors and for them there was no hope; but for others something might be done.

[1] Hope, 31 July 1815   [2] Hope, 27 August 1811
[3] H. of L. Hope to Rickman, 22 November 1820

Hope was a kindly man, and amidst all the work and worry which came to him from failures and broken contracts, his first thought was always for the workmen. 'The misery is', he wrote after one of the many failures on the Achnasheen road, 'that all this is at the expense of the poor workmen.' 'I confess myself not very skilful in that branch of our practice', he wrote in the winter of 1813, hoping to deter a colleague who sought to get, for a guarantor, preference over the workmen;[1] but there is more than a little evidence to show that in this too his skill was not deficient, and that where he could he used it for those who needed it most.

While Hope's work for the Commissioners was involving him in legal and financial problems of growing complexity, another problem of a more personal and much more embarrassing kind was troubling him. When Hope was appointed Law Agent to the Commissioners in the summer of 1803 it is probable that little thought had been given to the amount of work which he would be called on to do, and it is certain that no-one did or could foresee that before many months had passed his share of the burden would at least equal that borne by Telford and Rickman. Hope was sensitive and, for all his ability, extremely diffident, and a private letter which he wrote to Rickman in July 1804 must have cost him much anxious thought. 'I have been a good deal embarrassed in making out my account. According to the usual practice of this place among the respectable part of my profession there is only charged in account Law Deeds or Writings properly so called, while at the end of the account there is left a blank to be filled up by the employer for trouble in the management independent of such Legal Deeds, for correspondence and the like to which in general the employer has access to be well acquainted. This mode I understand to be unknown to you.

'In regard to the concerns of the Board, correspondence and meetings have hitherto formed the chief part of my duty and as that has not been confined to nor under the eye of the Board they could form no estimate of the extent of it. On mentioning my embarrassment to the Lord Advocate he suggested that I should make an account in the Scots form with a blank at the end for correspondence and other trouble and attendance, and another account according to the form which we understand to be the practice with you in which correspondence is charged separately,

[1] Hope, 8 December 1813

and that the Board should take whichever account they choose.

'I have, therefore, sent you two accounts, number one in the usual Scots form, number two in which the articles are separately charged and I shall take it as very obliging if you will have the goodness to present to the Board the one which you think they will most approve of. I value my own time and labour and the remuneration for it like others; but I value a thousand times more the approbation of your Board and am extremely anxious that my account shall be such as to preclude the most remote possibility of it being faulty.'[1] Rickman's letter in reply has not survived, but Hope's tactful approach to an embarrassing subject was evidently well received, and from now on his business accounts to the Commissioners showed in detail the work done.

Hope's tact and frankness had taken him over one difficult obstacle, but soon another loomed ahead. As road work progressed and contract payments started, a steady flow of financial transactions passed each year through his hands. On the receipt side came funds from the Commissioners for the credit of the account with the Bank of Scotland and payments by local proprietors which had been secured by bonds over their estates or by bills discounted by the Bank. The payments included all sums due to the contractors for roads and bridges. These payments were made by means of drafts on the Commissioners' account with the Bank of Scotland, and as that account stood in the names of Rickman and Hope, a supply of drafts for varying sums were periodically signed by Rickman in advance and sent to Hope so that he could complete and use them as required. As the volume of the road and bridge work increased so did the calls on the bank account of the Commissioners. As time passed and early contracts neared completion, payments tended to exceed receipts, and Hope was hard put to it to keep the account in funds. Local contributions secured only by heritable bonds or county assessments were slow in reaching the Commissioners' account with the Bank, and the time had not yet come when Hope could write to Rickman as he did at a later stage, 'You need put yourself to no inconvenience in regard to a supply of cash, as the Bank of Scotland will cheerfully allow us to draw whatever is wanted.'[2]

All this placed on Hope a heavy burden of work and respon-

---

[1] Hope, 14 July 1804
[2] H. of L. Hope to Rickman, 18 October 1816

sibility, while the keeping of separate accounts in his office for each of the many road contracts meant much involved book-keeping.[1] His remuneration, though now based on the more liberal arrangement made in the summer of 1804, took no account of financial work and responsibility; and this was growing fast. Once again, in July 1807, Hope wrote privately to Rickman enclosing his professional account for the past year. 'The accompanying account would have amounted to the same sum though none of the money transactions of the Board had passed through my hands and the payments had not been made by me. It is usual to make a charge in one shape or another for money trans-actions. No Banker would do the business without his com-mission unless he were indemnified by the funds lying in his hands or some other advantage—and it is certainly the part of the business which is attended with most responsibility and anxiety. I shall be obliged by your thinking of this. I would be very un-willing to state to the Board any matter, though usual and reason-able, that might have to them a contrary appearance, for I have had the greatest pleasure in the business in being concerned in measures which are to be so highly useful.'[2]

Rickman put the matter before the Commissioners who con-sulted Archibald Colquhoun the Lord Advocate as to who in Scotland should be asked to advise on Hope's proposition. At Colquhoun's suggestion the matter was referred to the Auditor of the Court of Session who in turn reported that Hope's pro-fessional account did not cover the financial work involved and that additional remuneration was appropriate. The details of Hope's subsequent remuneration for this part of the work do not appear, but looking today at the modest payments to him for professional work carried out for the Commissioners during all the years he was their agent, it is apparent that he found much of his reward in the knowledge of useful work well done, and that when in their Report for 1821 the Commissioners wrote, 'Mr Hope's charges have been as moderate as his conduct has been

---

[1] The security measures which the Commissioners felt themselves obliged to take were not confined to the contractors and local contributors. Hope himself was required in the early years to find security to the extent of £4,000 to cover the public funds from time to time in his hands, offering as one of his guarantors his brother Thomas, the Professor of Chemistry at Edinburgh University, and at a later date when he became responsible for heavy payments for road upkeep and repair the sum was increased to £10,000. H. of L. Hope to Rickman, 29 August 1820

[2] Hope, 28 July 1807

exemplary in punctuality and incessant diligence', their praise
was indeed well earned.[1]

While the great bulk of the money for which James Hope was
responsible reached the Commissioners' account with the Bank
of Scotland in the form of remittances from the Commissioners in
London or payments of road contributions from Highland
proprietors, there was one item of a different nature which caused
him no little trouble. When in 1784 it was decided to return to
their owners certain of the estates which had been forfeited after
the Rising of 1745, the restoration of these lands was made condi-
tional on the repayment by the owners to the Government of the
large amount of debt secured on the properties which had been
cleared off during their long and efficient administration by the
Commissioners on the Forfeited Estates. The debts so repaid
amounted in all to over £90,000, and accordingly when the Forfeited Estates Commission came to an end and the estates were
handed back, this sum became available for future use in Scotland.
Part of it was used for the completion of public works, including
the building of the Register House in Edinburgh, while £50,000
was advanced as a loan towards the building of the Forth and
Clyde Canal. On the repayment of this loan, £25,000 was lent to
the proprietors of the Crinan Canal, while the remainder was lent
to the City of Edinburgh to help in the enlarging of Leith Harbour.[2]

Shortly after the setting up of the Commission for Highland
Roads and Bridges it had been decided to entrust to the Commissioners the administration of these funds, and in 1807 Hope
received instructions to arrange for the transfer of the Edinburgh
loan into the Commissioners' names.[3] With the road commit-
ments of the Commissioners steadily rising, capital rather than
income was becoming their principal need. In the autumn of
1807, therefore, Hope was in communication with the City with a
view to the repayment of the loan; but the City were unwilling
to repay and the matter was not then pressed.[4] Two years later a
further application for payment was made with no more success.
'I have to report', wrote Hope to Rickman in May 1809, 'that
the City of Edinburgh are not more able now than they were at

[1] H. R. & B. 9th Report
[2] Report of the Committee on the Funds of the Forfeited Estates in Scotland, 1806
[3] Hope, 6 July 1807
[4] Hope, 12 October 1807

the time of my former communication to meet the payment of any part of their Bonds. The works on which they are engaged at the Harbour of Leith are not terminated; they even require to raise more money for the purpose. I find that the City is very anxious that the Commissioners should continue to be their creditors, as, if the debt came into the hands of others, payment after a lapse of any stipulated period might be enforced to their embarrassment and distress.'[1] Interest rates in these wartime days were high. Those with money to invest had little difficulty in lending it on their own terms and, as Hope pointed out, if the Commissioners decided to transfer the loan to anyone else this could only be done on terms which would expose the City to the imminent risk of demand for early repayment by the new creditor.

It had been suggested that the bond be made over to certain Highland proprietors, who, having carried out road contracts for themselves, looked to the Commissioners for repayment, 'but', wrote Hope, 'this alternative would be earnestly petitioned against by the City especially as they could expect no aid from the Public Banks, each of which had made them considerable advances at the commencement of the New Docks under the assurance that repayment was not to be demanded'.[2]

Five years later the matter again threatened to reach a crisis. Arrangements for the making of the harbour at Banff were under discussion, and the Banff contributors had offered to put up half the cost (£7,000) in return for a transfer, or assignation as the lawyers call it, of the Edinburgh Bond to that extent, their share of the Bond to be repaid on an agreed date. Charles Cunningham, the Town Clerk of Edinburgh, pleaded the Town's case with the Commissioners. Work on the Leith Docks had been going on for fourteen years and already £200,000 had been spent; but a further £60,000 was still needed to complete the work and the Treasury had refused a further advance. 'In the circumstances,' he wrote, 'the Town have earnestly to entreat the protection of the Commissioners against the consequences that could result from such a demand being insisted on at this time.'[3]

The deadlock seemed complete. The Commissioners shrank from extreme measures, and it may be that Hope's influence was

[1] Hope, 13 May 1809
[2] ibid.
[3] H. of L. Hope to Rickman, 23 September 1814

used on the side of indulgence to his native city. Whatever decided the issue, no more appears in Hope's correspondence till the autumn of 1817 when the city was sternly and finally warned that the Commissioners proposed to make over the loan to other less considerate creditors unless the City availed itself of the easier money conditions which peace had brought to make repayment. In November of that year Hope could at last report that repayment had been agreed.[1]

[1] Hope, 14 and 24 November 1817

8

BRIDGE-BUILDING AND ITS PROBLEMS

When Telford made his survey of the Highlands for the Government in the autumn of 1802, the lack of bridges over the principal rivers was one of the greatest weaknesses of Highland communications. 'Previous to the year 1742', he reported, 'the roads were merely the tracks of Black Cattle and Horses, intersected by numerous rapid streams, which being frequently swoln into torrents by heavy rains, rendered them dangerous or impassable. The Military Roads, which were formed about this time, having been laid out with other views than promoting Commerce and Industry are generally in such directions and so inconveniently steep as to be nearly unfit for the purposes of Civil Life; and in those parts where they are tolerably accessible, or where Roads have since been formed by the inhabitants, the use of them is very much circumscribed for the want of Bridges over some of the principal Rivers.' General Wade's work in the Highlands had included the making of thirty or forty bridges but, with the exception of his great bridge over the Tay at Aberfeldy and the High Bridge over the Spean, the bridges he made were almost all comparatively small. In particular the Spey and the Tay remained unbridged in their lower courses, while the Conon, the Beauly and many other rivers of some size could still be crossed only by ferry. Each year these ferries took their steady toll of human life, while adding to the hazards of the cattle-droving traffic to the south, which in the latter half of the 18th century was the chief export trade of the Highlands. Bridges over the lower Spey and Tay were much-needed links in the communications between Inverness and the south by way of Aberdeen or Drumochter Pass, while those over the Beauly and the Conon were, as Telford reported, 'the roots from which a great number of branches of road are to proceed which are necessary for the improvement of the Country and the extension of the Fisheries'.[1]

The lack of a bridge over the Spey at Fochabers had long been a handicap on the road from Inverness through Morayshire to

[1] H.R. & B. Telford's *Survey and Report*, 1803

118

Aberdeen, and when the Commissioners started their work some progress had already been made towards bridging the river, at the expense of the Duke of Gordon and other local proprietors; but it was clear that without Government help the completion of the task would be long delayed. The Act which set up the Roads and Bridges Commission made no reference to expenditure which had already been incurred, but in their First Report in 1804 the Commissioners offered all assistance possible in the completion of the Spey Bridge as it was then called. Subsequently a special grant was made by Parliament, and though for this reason the bridge at Fochabers formed no part of the work done by the Commissioners for Highland Roads and Bridges, the completion of the Spey Bridge figured in their Third Report as the forerunner of the great works on which they were engaged.

While the building of the Spey Bridge at Fochabers was rapidly being completed, the bridging of the Tay at Dunkeld was progressing with nearly equal speed. Telford in his first Survey had reported on a plan for a bridge at Dunkeld, where up till then travellers on the road from Perth to Inverness crossed the Tay by ferry at a point guarded from danger of ice by shallow water nearly opposite the mouth of the River Bran. The problem of finance was not serious, for the Duke of Atholl had offered to pay one half of the estimated cost of £15,000, giving up his interest in the two ferries which then existed, in return for a toll on the bridge which would repay his contribution and provide some annual income for repairs.[1] The work was soon in hand, made easier, according to Southey's subsequent account, by the fact that the River Bran had brought down so much gravel that the old bed of the Tay was filled up, allowing the bridge to be built over the dry channel into which, on completion of the work, the river was again diverted.[2] On 29 March 1809 Hope was able to report to Telford that the bridge was complete and ready for final inspection. 'A considerable object was thus attained, Dunkeld being as it were the portal of the Central Highlands, and more remotely the access to all the Northern Roads.'[3]

In their bridge-building as in all their work, the Commissioners, with the Treasury at their elbow, exercised throughout the greatest economy, the scale of their expenditure in nearly every

[1] ibid.   [2] Southey, p. 46
[3] H.R. & B. 9th Report, 1821

case being dictated solely by considerations of strict utility. 'Farthing-wisdom' Southey called it, as he looked in vain for some ornamentation on Telford's great bridge at Craigellachie. This rule was relaxed only in the case of the bridges at Fochabers and Dunkeld where, in deference to the close connection of the Dukes of Gordon and Atholl, some decoration was introduced into the plans; but even for this the Dukes paid, so the concession of the Exchequer was more apparent than real.

If the building of these two large bridges followed a smooth and comparatively uneventful course, the story of the smaller river crossings was much less happy. Telford designed his roads to last, and the contracts based on his specifications provided for mason and bridge work on a scale far in excess of anything hitherto attempted. Two bridges to a mile of road came to be looked on as a general average, but on some roads particularly in the west this was far exceeded. Experienced bridge-builders were even more scarce than ordinary road-builders, and wooden bridges were seldom accepted as sufficient. Experience in the building of large arches was particularly deficient, and in many of the early road contracts this was proving the biggest obstacle. On the Glengarry and Arisaig roads, Dick and Readdie were in trouble, and in the autumn of 1805 Telford had reported that two bridges, one of them a large one over the Garry, had fallen just after the arches had been turned[1]; but there was no short or easy path to success in bridge-building, and only time and growing knowledge would supply the answer. James Hope did what he could to nourish and hearten the unfortunate contractors, but he had no illusions as to the hard path they must tread. 'I hope', he wrote to Rickman, 'that dear-bought experience will improve their skill.'[2] In the early days of the Commissioners' work, where a stretch of road involved many bridges, separate contracts were made for their construction, but it was soon found that this led to trouble, since the road-builder objected to his road being used during bridge construction, while the bridge-builder prevented the use of his bridge until it had been accepted and taken off his hands. So the Commissioners found it more satisfactory in their later work to include in the road contracts all but the larger bridges, preferring the possible lack of experience of one man to the quarrels of two.

[1] Hope, 3 October 1805   [2] Ibid.

While many of the troubles which overtook the Commissioners' early efforts in bridge-building could fairly be laid at the door of ignorant contractors, there were others for which the contractors were in no way to blame. Nearly forty years before the Commissioners started their work, certain proprietors in Ross-shire had been engaged in trying to link the port of Poolewe with Dingwall and Inverness. Their project entailed the bridging of the River Orrin which joins the Lower Conon opposite Brahan Castle; but funds were lacking for a bridge.[1] When the Commissioners started their work the river was still unbridged, and almost the first application to the Commissioners in the autumn of 1803 was for the building of Orrin Bridge.[2] James Hope's successful negotiations with the Bank of Scotland and the decision of Ross-shire to levy a county assessment had to all appearance solved the difficulty of local contributions, and for a time it seemed that the bridging of the Orrin might be among the first of the Commissioners' works to be completed; but disillusionment was soon to follow. In the county assessments the local proprietors saw a prospect of delaying their personal contributions, and to Hope fell the disagreeable task of warning Sir George Mackenzie of Coul, the County Convener, that the Bank would not lend money against bills payable at a more distant date than two years, and that meantime the Commissioners would not advance the whole cost of the work.[3] Until all these difficulties were resolved the bridge could not be advertised for contract. Months passed in fruitless negotiation and the river remained unbridged. 'I am heartily sick', wrote Rickman to Telford in May 1806, 'of Sir G. M. and his bridge, which has cost more trouble than all the roads now making in Scotland.'[4] A site was at length chosen and an offer for the work accepted, but still no agreement had been reached about financing the building, and even the question of a site became again the subject of disagreement.[5] Tired of the delay the contractor claimed damages for loss, while Rickman lost all patience with 'the infinite mutability of Ross-shire intentions'. 'It is impossible', he wrote to Telford in July 1809, 'to avoid disgust with the undeserved ill-usage which we meet in attempting to benefit Ross-shire . . .', and two months later to Hope, 'I now

---

[1] Dunlop, *The British Fisheries Society*   [2] H.R. & B. 1st Report, 1804
[3] Hope, 10 October 1805   [4] H. of L. Rickman to Telford, 26 May 1806
[5] Hope, 4 January 1809

learn from Mr Davidson that seven persons have perished in fording the Orrin. A melancholy confirmation of the want of a bridge there and which will furnish no very pleasant reflection to those who have so unreasonably delayed that improvement for three or four years last passed.'[1] Hope too was deeply involved and no less exasperated. His correspondence with the County Convener, on this as on other subjects, grew heated, and to Telford he relieved his feelings in a letter in the summer of 1809. 'I am quite confounded at the haste with which Sir George Mackenzie changes his opinions; and yet he is keen for the prevalent one at the time.'[2] Three years passed. The contractor's claim for damages had been referred to Telford as arbiter, and in the autumn of 1812 the contractor was awarded £241 'for expense labour and disappointment'[3]; the project disappeared from the Annual Reports of the Commissioners—and Orrin remained unbridged.

The general lack of experience in road-building had made it necessary for the Commissioners to insist on guarantors that the contractors' work would be adequately carried out. Of those who came forward to offer security many were in the end to rue their bargains, but optimism was not lacking, and in the early days of road-making under the Commissioners the problem lay less in the finding of willing guarantors than in the elimination of those whose means were inadequate for the risks they offered to take. For bridge-building the problem was still more complex. Here the lack of good bridge-builders forced the Commissioners to redouble their care and precautions. The quality of the work on a road could be readily assessed during its progress, and as soon as it had been completed and inspected it was taken off the contractor's hands to the relief of him and his guarantors; but a bridge must prove that it could stand the test of winter storms and floods before it could be accepted.

Among the many innovations introduced by Telford in his work for the Commissioners of Highland Roads and Bridges was the provision in bridge contracts for a clause binding the contractor to maintain the bridge for a specified period. It had been the original intention of the Commissioners on Telford's advice that the new bridges should be maintained by the contractors and

[1] H. of L. Rickman to Hope, 13 September 1809
[2] Hope, 15 June 1809   [3] Hope, 26 November 1812

guaranteed by them and their cautioners against virtually all risks save earthquakes for five years. This period was soon recognised as excessive, and before long had been reduced to three years. Even a three-year guarantee presented difficulty, for even if men of substance could be found to accept the risk, both they and the contractor were to this extent debarred from further ventures till the end of the period of guarantee had released them and their resources from potential claims. Hope was, as always, solicitous for the interests of all parties to the contracts. It was not in his nature to encourage those whom he knew to be ignorant of the extent of their indiscretion, whether as contractors or cautioners, and before all was done there were very many in Scotland who must have blessed the name of that honest, kindly lawyer. His correspondence with the Reverend Hugh Taylor in the autumn of 1807 is typical of his dealings with those who sought his advice. Taylor had written to him inquiring as to the risk involved for those who acted as guarantors, and Hope's reply lacked nothing in frankness. Those who offered security for a road contract, he explained, took only a limited risk, obvious as the work progressed and to a great extent calculable; but not so those who guaranteed a bridge, 'as the work may be annihilated at the moment of its being nearly accomplished'.[1] For bridge work, as he wrote in a subsequent letter to William Fraser Tytler, the only real security lay in the skill and experience of the contractor. In the spring of that year Hope had written to Rickman asking him to explore the possibility of having the bridges insured, and he himself asked the Sun Insurance Company to quote a premium for the insurance of the bridges for three or five years.[2] The records now available do not show what came of these inquiries, but it is not hard to imagine the difficulties involved in Hope's proposal, and there is no evidence in the later letters to suggest that insurance proved possible.

Telford, too, was alive to the dangers from the start, for even he was learning that Highland rains and melting snow could bring down floods far beyond his early calculations. In Cowal and Moidart, Glengarry and Easter Ross the early years of the work had seen the fall of many a new bridge. Some, like that on the Lochgoil Road which fell five times, were ill-built,[3] but

---

[1] Hope, 2 October 1807   [2] Hope, 10 May 1807
[3] Hope, 16 March 1811

many failed from underestimate of the floods which winter storms would pour beneath them. Telford's respect for Highland floods had lately been increased by two salutary lessons. Mackintosh, the contractor for the eastern section of the road to Achnasheen, was having an uphill struggle, getting from Hope the utmost help the Commissioners' lawyer could give him, and from his own worthless guarantors no help which they could avoid giving; but the Achnasheen road moved ever under an evil star, and a great flood in the spring of 1811 destroyed the newly-built bridge over the Contin. The contractor pleaded that he was not liable, since in Telford's plan to which he had worked, the water-way was too small. Hope thought him liable. 'I sincerely lament the business', he wrote to Telford on 9 March. 'The poor man has a ruinous contract and I fear he will lose all heart'[1]; but Telford, ever ready to bear the blame where the blame was his, reported that the fault lay not in bad work but in bad planning, and Contin Bridge was replanned and rebuilt at the expense of the Commissioners. Before many months had passed, the fate of a bridge on the River Arkaig was to provide a still more striking example of the power of a Highland river in flood. Here a bridge had recently been built to Telford's specifications by one of the most reliable firms of contractors employed by the Commissioners. The contractors had considered that Telford's plan provided for a quite unduly ample water-way, but it chanced that they had available what the engineers call 'centering' for making arches on a larger scale than that specified. This for convenience they chose to use, thus constructing a bridge with an even larger water-way than Telford had intended; but even this was not enough, and in a flood in the autumn of 1811 the new bridge was so far damaged that it had to be rebuilt.[2]

By the end of 1811 Telford's attitude to Highland weather had grown almost fatalistic. Writing to Rickman in the autumn of that year Hope referred to a letter received from Telford in which the latter expressed the somewhat startling view that it was useless to attempt to build bridges 'proof against any quantity of water which the storms may bring down'.[3] It was more economical, he thought, to repair and rebuild them occasionally. 'In Highland rivers,' he wrote to the Commissioners in 1812, 'where

[1] Hope, 9 March 1811   [2] H.R. & B. 6th Report, 1813
[3] Hope, 12 November 1811

in general the stream has not before been noticed with any correctness it is only by degrees that the proper dimensions of bridges can be ascertained; that is in rainy seasons only and by continuing the observations through a succession of these seasons. The bridges now built will serve for a scale of measurement each for its own river, and we have already found that the water-way which at the time of building was supposed to be unnecessarily ample has experimentally proved to be too small.'[1]

The number and extent of these early bridge disasters made it increasingly apparent that to call on contractors and their guarantors to make good the damage would in many instances be quite unfair, while it would make almost impossible the already difficult task of finding experienced and reputable bridge-builders willing to contract with the Commissioners. So considerations of expediency and fair dealing pointed alike to the same conclusions, and in their later bridge work damage due to abnormal floods or faulty plans was made good in part or in whole at the Commissioners' expense; but the definition of an abnormal flood left much room for controversy in the years to come, and it was left for James Hope, apprehensive of trouble over bridges on the Spean, to recommend to Telford in 1817 that marks should be placed on the river banks above which, if the river rose so high, the contractor would not be held liable.[2]

Of the hazards to which the bridges were exposed, water was the most natural but not, as it proved, in itself the most serious. The caustic comments on the treeless aspect of Scotland, which had for centuries been made by early travellers through the land, were indeed well merited for much of the country through which they passed; but for centuries past natural forests had grown undisturbed and almost unnoticed in many parts of the central and western Highlands. In particular, wide areas of natural woodland of great age and of great potential value stretched along the Spey and its tributaries and beside the middle course of the Findhorn where the forest of Darnaway was thus described by writers of the mid-19th century: 'Few know what Tarnaway was in those days—almost untrodden except by the deer, the roe, the foxes, and the pine martens, its green dells filled with lilies of the valley, its banks covered with wild hyacinths, primroses and pyrolas and its deep thickets clothed with every species of wood-

[1] H.R. & B. 6th Report, 1813   [2] Hope, 28 February 1817

land luxuriance, in blossoms, grass, moss, and timber of every kind, growing with the magnificence and solitude of an aboriginal wilderness, a world of unknown beauty and silent loneliness, broken only by the sough of the pines, the hum of the water, the hoarse bell of the buck, the long wild cry of the fox, the shriek of the heron or the strange mysterious tap of the northern wood-pecker. For ten years we knew every dell and bank and thicket.'[1]

For long these great woodlands had been looked on as in-accessible and almost valueless. Before the great agricultural revival, demand for timber on Scotland's farms was small, while even at the sea ports the fishing and trading vessels were largely built with timber from across the North Sea. With the 18th century came renewed interest in and need for timber, and Scottish traders and landowners turned their eyes at last to the great forests which had for so many hundreds of years grown, flourished, decayed and fallen in almost primeval solitude. One of the earliest ventures in the cutting of the old forests had been started shortly after the '15, when the York Buildings Company had purchased from the Commissioners on the Forfeited Estates a great area of valuable Scots pine at Abernethy on Speyside,[2] and here on the woodland streams running down to the Spey the timber cutters first put into practice the technique which, nearly a century later, was to bring trouble to Telford's bridge-builders. As the 18th century wore on, the demand for timber rose steadily, while another use of the old woods had arisen. At a few places in the Highlands, charcoal had long been burned for fuel, but with the increasing smelting of iron, charcoal took on a new importance, and soon the woods of Argyllshire and parts of Inverness-shire were coming under the woodman's axe to provide the charcoal which, before the advent of plentiful supplies of coal, could alone provide the high and steady heat required for the smelting works on Loch Etive, Loch Fyne and in Stirlingshire. The great iron works at Carron on the Forth soon abandoned the use of charcoal for the more accessible coal at its very door, but at Bonawe on Loch Etive charcoal continued to be used well into the 19th century.[3]

To meet these growing needs for timber, the rivers and lochs

[1] J. Sobieski and C. E. Stuart, *Lays of the Deer Forest*, II, p. 255
[2] Murray, *The York Buildings Company*, p. 57
[3] Macadam, 'Notes on the Ancient Iron Industry of Scotland,' *Proc. Soc. Ant. Scot. 1886-7*, 9, New Series, p. 90

of the Highlands had, in days before roads, come to serve a new purpose. When the timber cutters on Speyside employed by the York Buildings Company started in 1723 the practice of floating the cut trees in rafts on the Spey and its tributaries, they had introduced almost a new industry, and long before the century ended the great rivers of the Highlands were carrying on their waters cut timber to the saw-millers and the charcoal-burners on their lower reaches. In the forests of Speyside, systematic cutting of timber had come to be recognised as a valuable part of the management of a Highland estate, and when Elizabeth Grant wrote of the timber cutters' work during her childhood at the Doune of Rothiemurchus, she was describing a process which was well understood and well organised. Here the timber, cut and dragged during the autumn and winter to the tributary streams, was floated to the Spey on the flood waters from the melting snows, helped by artificial floods sent down from dams built far upstream. Where the streams entered the Spey, the descending logs were caught and built into rough rafts for their final journey down the river to the saw-mills or to the Moray Firth.[1] In the Great Glen too, spring floods on the Arkaig, the Garry and the Moriston were bringing to the line of the Canal the timber for which the new work called incessantly, but had Telford been able to foresee the troubles in store, he would perhaps have bartered this easy form of transport for freedom from the worries awaiting him.

The first hint of danger came from Deeside. Here in the spring of 1809 the making of a new bridge at Ballater[2] was already far advanced, when news came that a great sale of timber had taken place about Invercauld and Abergeldy and that the floating of logs on the river would soon begin. Hope wrote in March to the agents for Lord Fife and Gordon of Abergeldy, asking that the floating be suspended while the arches of the bridge were being completed; but at first with little success. The sale of the Invercauld trees was already complete. The market for timber was good and nearly nine thousand trees, many of them big logs suitable for use as masts, had been put into the river ready for floating. The Commissioners and Simpson, the bridge contractor, were considering interdict proceedings before the Court, but Hope was nervous lest success in the Courts would open the way for claims

---

[1] Elizabeth Grant of Rothiemurchus, *Memoirs of a Highland Lady*, pp. 217-30
[2] See Appendix No. VIII

by the proprietors for loss of sales. Several anxious weeks passed with the issue in the balance, and not till the end of May was final agreement reached that the Commissioners, the proprietors and the contractors would share the cost of guarding the bridge till the floating timber had passed down stream.[1]

Ballater Bridge had been saved by a narrow margin, though the contractor lost £1,300 on his contract, but the full extent of the danger from floating timber had not yet been realised, and a sharper lesson was still to come. Towards the end of 1811, William Minto, a competent and reliable contractor who had already done good work for the Commissioners in Aberdeenshire, had contracted to build a bridge over the Dee at Potarch near Kincardine O'Neil, where the existing ford was liable to frequent interruption in winter from floods and floating ice.[2] The bridge was to be finished in 1813 at a cost of £3,500, and in the autumn of 1812 two of the arches had already been turned and work was proceeding on the last arch. In view of the disaster which had been so narrowly averted at Ballater three years before, notice had been given to the proprietors of the woods upstream to suspend floating for the short time required till the arch was complete. The warning was ignored. Timber, not in the form of rafts but in single logs, heavy and uncontrollable, came down the stream, and in a few hours poor Minto saw the work of months ruined. Hope's first impression was that the flood had been so heavy that it had carried away logs on the river side not intended for floating, but in a subsequent letter to Telford he reported that the damage had been caused by timber which Farquharson of Monaltrie had sold to Aberdeen merchants who refused to stop floating while the bridge was being built.[3] Minto claimed, and was awarded by the Courts, damages for negligence against the timber merchants, while a sum of £283 raised by local subscription and a similar contribution by the Commissioners went far to reduce the loss of eight hundred pounds which he had suffered by the accident.[4] Potarch Bridge was rebuilt and completed in 1813 and the disaster had at last brought home to the Commissioners and the Government the need for legislation to guard against a repetition. An Act passed in July of that year prohibited, during the working months of March to November each year, the floating of

---

[1] Hope, 14 March, 22 April and 29 May 1809   [2] See Appendix No. IX
[3] Hope, 23 October and 3 November 1812   [4] H.R. & B. 6th Report

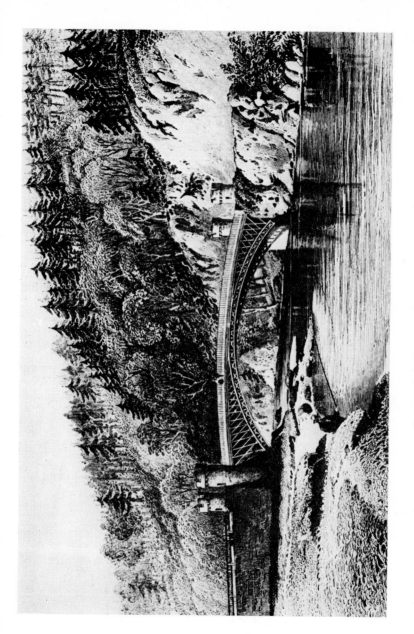

Plate 8 Craigellachie Bridge, River Spey

Plate 9 Loch Eil and the entrance to the Caledonian Canal

timber under bridges in course of erection or under repair, except in the form of rafts under the control of a floater, and made the owners of timber liable for any damage caused by contravention of the regulations.[1]

While Minto was in trouble at Potarch, George Burn at work on the new Lovat Bridge over the Beauly was faring ill from the same cause. Here the service bridge, built by the contractor for the carriage of material for the work, had already been broken four times by floating timber. In February 1813 Hope wrote to William Fraser Tytler, Convener of Inverness-shire, suggesting that Chisholm, the largest owner of timber upstream, should be approached, while Burn's foreman was warned of the danger of using on such a river slender centering no stronger than 'spectacle-rims'. A few days later Hope wrote himself to Chisholm of the need to ensure in the contractor's interest that 'A thousand battering-rams were not to be brought into play against him. . . . Plain it is', he added, 'that no bridge can be built over the Beaulie with the ordinary centres unless the floating of single trees is suspended during its progress.'[2] Chisholm was at first unco-operative. The Act providing for the use of rafts was not yet in force, and in any event the falls on the Beauly would make their use almost impossible, and some form of boom defence for the bridge was under consideration. Burn was urged to advertise in press and pulpit the dates on which timber floating should be suspended; but at the end of April Hope was able to report to Rickman that Chisholm had agreed that men should be employed to see the timber safely past the bridge.[3] By the autumn of 1813 the bridge was well on towards completion helped by a dry season. 'Burn', wrote Hope, 'has had a season propitious to him beyond all reasonable expectation.'[4]

The Act of 1813 referred only to bridges under construction or repair and gave no protection to those completed and in use.

[1] 53 George III, ch, 117
[2] Hope, 8 March 1813
[3] Hope, 27 April 1813. Timber operations on the Beauly about this time seem to have been of considerable proportions, for five years later Southey recorded in his *Journal* that timber to the value of £200,000 had been sawn in the mills on the river.
[4] Hope, 24 September 1813. The completion of the contractor's work did not end the worries of the Commissioners over Lovat Bridge. The total cost of the bridge was £8,800 for half of which sum Lord Lovat as contributor was liable, but two years after its completion the Commissioners were still pressing him for payment, though he appears to have retained for the purpose his county assessments to the extent of £3,250.

Time passed without serious mishap for which the floaters could
be blamed, but in the autumn of 1825 trouble again threatened,
and Ballater Bridge which had so narrowly escaped in 1809 was
again the danger point. A great sale of timber had taken place for
Lord Marr's creditors at a price of twenty shillings a tree, and
Hope warned Rickman that sixty to seventy thousand trees were
soon to be cut and floated down the Dee.[1] Sellers and purchasers
were warned of the danger, in the hope, as Hope later wrote to
Farquharson of Whitehouse that 'they may be staggered by undefined responsibility'. That danger too passed. Ballater Bridge
survived, only to fall in the disaster which was to bring ruin to so
much of the Commissioners' work in the great floods of 1829.

While the bridges on Deeside were under attack from the
battering-rams sent down from the wood-cutters on the upper
reaches of the river, others further to the north were faring little
better. The weather during the winter of 1817 had been more
than usually severe and indeed far into the spring of 1818 snow
lay deep in the Highlands. Early in the New Year news reached
Edinburgh of a great flood immediately north and south of the
Great Glen. 'I am truly sorry', wrote Hope to Mitchell in the last
week of January, 'to receive what I fear is only the commencement
of your accounts of the injury sustained by our different works. . . .
I almost fear to receive the next accounts as I observe the Inverness papers mention the rise in the Ness to have been very great'.[2]
Hope's fears were well founded. John Mitchell had gone south
to Dunkeld on an inspection of the Perthshire roads when news
reached him of great damage in Inverness-shire. The road up
Glen Garry and over Drumochter Pass was blocked by snow, but
through drifts in places six to twelve feet deep he made what speed
he could back to the north. The new bridge over the Spey at
Laggan and that at Drumnadrochit on the north side of Loch
Ness had been badly damaged. At Torgoyle, the bridge over the
River Moriston on the new road to Loch Duich and the Skye
Ferries had been completely destroyed. Four thousand birch logs,
cut and ready for floating on the river bank had been swept away
by the height of the flood.[3] These birch logs, destined for con-
version into herring barrel staves for the fisheries of the north-
east coast, were much smaller than the great logs which ruined

---

[1] Hope, 10 October 1825   [2] Hope, 22 January 1818
[3] H.R. & B. 5th Report (Repair), 1818

Minto's work at Potarch, but caught in the narrow waters of an impetuous river they had proved too much for the bridge, the ruins of which greeted the tired inspector. To keep open the road to Skye a temporary wooden bridge was built, the men working for long spells in four feet of water in frosty weather to drive the piles for the piers, and it was left for John Mitchell's son five years later to design a new stone bridge as one of his first major works for the Commissioners.

Far to the north, on the north-eastern border of Ross-shire and in Sutherland, plans were afoot for improving the road to Wick and Thurso. For the important droving traffic southward bound to the great tryst at Muir of Ord near Beauly, the crossing of Loch Fleet and the dangerous Meikle Ferry over the Dornoch Firth had for long been formidable hazards for men and beasts. Where the small River Fleet flows into the narrow sea-loch, Telford's plan was to construct an earthen mound nearly 1,000 yards long which would carry a road across the junction of loch and river, at the same time damming back the sea-water and re-claiming some 400 acres previously covered at high tide. The plan entailed the construction of flood-gates which, while holding back the sea-water as the tide rose, would allow the passage out-wards of the fresh water of the river as the tide fell. Offers for the construction of this large and unusual work were slow in coming, but finally Lord Gower, who stood to benefit from the improve-ment more than any other single proprietor, undertook the work, which was completed in 1818 at a cost of £8,000 shared by the County of Sutherland, Lord Gower himself and the Commissioners.

Five years before the Fleet Mound was complete, Telford had already bridged the upper part of the Dornoch Firth at what is now called Bonar Bridge. Southey, who passed that way in the early autumn of 1819, records that trouble with the foundations caused serious alteration in the plan at an advanced stage of the work, but by the autumn of 1812 Simpson and Cargil, the Shrop-shire bridge-builders who had already done good work for Telford in the Severn Valley, had successfully spanned the Firth with iron-work cast on the Welsh Borders, which a local inhabitant des-cribed as 'a spider's web in the air . . . the finest thing that ever was made by God or man'.[1] The strength of the new bridge was soon to be tested. The winter of 1813/14 in the north-east was

[1] Southey, pp. 128-9

long and severe, and before the spring came, a great accumulation of ice had built up above the bridge. 'A large number of fir logs which had been rolled into the River Carron in readiness to be floated by the first flood came down altogether fixed irregularly in a mass of ice which was thus converted into a formidable instrument of destruction. Those logs, which were in an upright position, struck the iron arch with such violence that the crash of the timber was heard at considerable distance; but the Bridge stood firm without suffering either crack or flaw from this violent collision. So favourable a result was the more satisfactory to us, because another Iron Bridge on the model of this at Bonar had already been commenced at Craigellachie on the River Spey.'[1] Four years later Bonar Bridge was tested from the seaward side. A schooner, caught in a strong tide, was drifted under the bridge. The schooner lost two masts, but the bridge stood firm.[2]

While the Shrewsbury contractors were at work at Bonar Bridge, plans were in the making for a new bridge over the Spey. From above Grantown to Fochabers no bridge at that time spanned the river, and the ferries were often unusable for weeks on end. An earlier plan for a bridge at the ferry of Boat of Bridge eight miles from Fochabers had been turned down by the Commissioners on the ground that this was too near Fochabers to serve a useful purpose. In place of this the local landowners now proposed a site at Craigellachie. Telford had reported favourably on the plan, estimating the cost at £8,000 and the Commissioners had given their approval, subject to the usual contribution by local landowners of half the cost. In the autumn of 1812 a printed broadsheet was lodged with Coutts and Co. and Sir William Forbes and Co., the London and Edinburgh Bankers, with Messrs Mackenzie and Innes, the Edinburgh Writers to the Signet, with the Editor of the *Inverness Journal* and with many others interested, appealing for subscriptions. 'The building of the bridge', wrote its advocates, 'must be an object of considerable and lively interest to travellers whether for business or pleasure, to the Merchant, the Manufacturer and especially to all dealers in Cattle and Sheep. To the philanthropic and benevolent,' added the promoters, never prone to understate their case, 'to all interested in the cause of humanity it affords a favourable and noble opportunity of snatching from a watery and untimely grave

[1] H.R. & B. 7th Report 1815   [2] H.R. & B. 9th Report, 1821

hundreds of their fellow creatures, for the number of lives which are annually sacrificed in the passage of this rapid and impetuous river exceed all belief.'[1] The eloquence of the promoters served its purpose. The half share of Telford's estimate was raised, and only Hope's prudent advice dissuaded the local landowners from the indiscretion of undertaking the work themselves.

On Hope's suggestion Simpson, at work on Bonar Bridge, was invited to become the contractor, an invitation which he accepted, the iron-work to be provided by Hazeldine of Shrewsbury at a cost of £2,891 and to be maintained by him for three years. Telford was in Sweden visiting the Gotha Canal. His plan for the bridge had provided for the iron arch to be placed on abutments seven feet above low water, but at a meeting at Craigellachie on 26 July 1813 Simpson readily accepted the evidence of the local people that the Spey rose in flood nearly twelve feet, and to that height the abutments were raised. A land arch too was added to provide for flood water in the adjoining meadow land.[2] By 1815 Simpson's work was complete. Telford's graceful arch spanned the river, and years later when he saw the narrow margin by which it had survived the great floods of August 1829, Telford must have felt no little gratitude to the local knowledge without which Craigellachie Bridge would surely have gone.

[1] H. of L. October 1812
[2] H. of L. 26 July 1813

9

NEARING COMPLETION

THE fund at the disposal of the Roads and Bridges Commission was provided by Parliament, and depended for its replenishment on periodical grants by the House of Commons. The amount of these grants had originally been based on an estimate made by George Brown in the last years of the 18th century, when he had reported on the lines of road most urgently required in the Highlands. Brown had reported that about 1,000 miles of road were needed at a total cost of £150,000. Added to this were the four great bridges over the Spey, the Tay, the Beauly and the Conon, and on the assumption that the local proprietors would contribute half the cost it was at that time concluded that a sum of £20,000 for each of the first three years and £12,000 for the next three would be sufficient for the completion of the work spread over six years.[1] The rise in wages and prices in the early years of last century resulted in Brown's estimate of total cost being much exceeded, and in fact from the date when the Roads and Bridges Commission took the work in hand annual grants varying from £10,000 to £20,000 were made over a period of seventeen years.

In the summer of 1816, though the sums which were being paid out each year to the contractors were not far short of their peak, it was apparent that, with the completion of the large number of contracts then in hand and already far advanced, the work of the Commission would be nearing its end. Rickman gave evidence in June of that year before a Committee which subsequently reported that three further grants of £20,000 each would suffice.[2] An Argyllshire Assessment Bill then before Parliament had been drafted on the assumption that large, though undefined, grants would be obtained from the Commissioners, and it was decided that the time had come to set a term to their work and their expenditure, a decision which, it may reasonably be conjectured, was not unconnected with the presence

[1] Telford's *Survey and Report*, 1803
[2] Report of Committee on Estimate for H.R. & B., June 1816

on the Commission of Nicholas Vansittart, the Chancellor of the Exchequer.

The subsequent announcement that no further applications for assistance in Road and Bridge building would be considered, proved not surprisingly to be the signal for renewed local enthusiasm for road planning, and a total of about £80,000 was offered as local contributions for further road schemes in Sutherland, Ross-shire and Caithness. If this tardy recognition of the value of their work was gratifying to the Commissioners, their resolution was proof against such flattery, and no further applications were accepted. 'The cry for retrenchment prevails', wrote Southey regretfully in his diary three years later.[1] Many contracts were, of course, still not complete and in fact construction work continued until 1821, after which new work on Roads and Bridges virtually came to an end.

In the eighteen years which had passed since the start of the Commissioners' work, a great transformation had taken place. It had for long been the custom of the Commissioners to attach to each Report a print of Arrowsmith's Map of Scotland, on which the roads completed or under contract were marked in red, those still under consideration being shown in green. Year by year in spite of all the problems and obstacles the red lines spread, and as Rickman compared the latest map with the earliest he must have felt no little pride. The thirty contracts reported in 1806 had grown to a total of a hundred and twenty, and James Hope could claim a large share of the credit for the fact that despite all the complexities caused by incompetence, insolvency and dishonesty, all had up to that date been accomplished without litigation. More than £450,000 had been expended, just over £200,000 having been provided by local contributions and the remainder by the Commissioners, the difference between the two sums representing the cost to the Commissioners of surveying, planning, inspecting and the endless office work both in London and Edinburgh. Eight hundred and seventy five miles of road had up to then been made and eleven large bridges had been built, besides many hundreds of smaller ones included in the road contracts.[2] Year by year the average number of men employed on

[1] Southey, p. 142
[2] H.R. & B. 9th Report, 1821. The Commission for Highland Roads and Bridges was to remain in existence for many years to come, but after 1821 its work was confined to repair

road-making and repairing was 2,700, with a maximum number in one year of over 3,500.[1]

These results had not been achieved without grievous loss to many, and as Rickman worked at the last of the constructional reports, much that was distressing must have come to his mind. Bankrupt contractors, unpaid workmen and undischarged debts filled the pages of the earlier reports. For these, ignorance, incompetence and rising prices were largely the cause. Many of the losses could be looked on as the everyday risks of business at a time when conditions of life were harsher than they are today; but there were other losses equally disastrous, and even harder to bear for those on whom they fell. These were the losses of the guarantors who, from varying but often entirely laudable and disinterested motives, had backed the contractors to carry out their work. Some may indeed have hoped for profit and prestige from their financial support, but many, it seems clear, aimed at nothing but the good of the community and the early completion of much-needed improvements. Some were totally ruined in the fall of the men whom they had helped and many lost the savings of a lifetime. As the years went by, many appeals for relief in such cases reached the Commissioners to whom they were a source of no little embarrassment. It had long been apparent that many of the estimates of cost prepared by Telford and his surveyors in the early years of the work, such as those at Arisaig and Glengarry, in Skye and on the north side of Loch Ness, had been totally inadequate. These estimates were confidential and at least in theory should have had no bearing on the offers by the contractors. In practice, the official estimates became in many cases widely known, and in the circumstances the Commissioners may well have felt some degree of responsibility for having misled offerers and and their cautioners into error and loss.[2] Final decision on these appeals for relief was deferred until the whole work of road and bridge building was completed and the full tale of loss was known; but when all was finished the Commissioners could only report with real regret their inability to give any relief

[1] These figures included some employed on harbour work under the Commissioners

[2] Despite the fact that the official estimates of the cost of road work became in some cases known to offerers, the efforts of the Commissioners to keep their estimate private seems to have been fully justified, for in 1817 they were able to report that in the road work done up to that date the one-half share of road expenditure contributed by the Commissioners had fallen short of their official estimates by nearly £8,000

in losses which were known to amount to over £34,000, and which were, they believed, in reality double that sum.[1]

If there were times when the Commissioners and their servants must have felt that their task was thankless and their work un-appreciated, there was, in fact, no lack of signs that as the years passed their aims were indeed being achieved. Long before the last road contract was complete and the last bridge built, men, cattle and goods were passing along roads already made, while even on parts of the unfinished Canal vessels were already on the move. Telford and Mitchell on their constant journeys were noting with pride the vast improvement. 'The Highland Roads are a luxury in travelling', wrote Telford to Rickman in 1817, comparing them with the 'execrable roads' in the Lowlands.[2] Rickman and Hope, too, on their rarer ventures north gave the same report, while Southey was high in his praise of the opening of the country. 'Ours was the first carriage which had ever reached the Ferry,' he wrote from Strome in 1819, 'and the road on the southern shore, up which we walked, had never yet been travelled by one.'[3] Telford, Rickman and Hope—and even Southey as Rickman's friend—were perhaps hardly disinterested witnesses, but others more impartial told the same tale. 'From Edinburgh to John o' Groat's House', reported the *Inverness Courier* in the spring of 1818, 'it is now possible to travel without crossing a ferry or fording a river or even encountering a descent where the necessity of drag chains is required',[4] while William Larkin after touring the Highlands in the same year wrote in sweeping commendation, 'In the Highlands of Scotland, where within the memory of man neither a good road nor a good inn were to be found, the roads are now among the best and the inns among the most convenient and comfortable in the whole world.'[5] The road through Glengarry was already carrying an embarrass-ing amount of cattle and timber, while about Contin in Easter Ross-shire the new road was in danger of damage from constant traffic. The quality of the contractors' work had been steadily rising. Hope, writing to Rickman in the autumn of 1817, referred

[1] H.R. & B. 9th Report, 1821
[2] H. of L. Telford to Rickman, 18 November 1817
[3] Southey, p. 156
[4] *Inverness Courier*, April 1818. Barron, *The Northern Highlands in the 19th Century*, vol. 1, p. 140
[5] Larkin, *A Tour in the Highlands*, 1818, p. 24

to the excellent workmanship of the later contracts. Higher standards of road work, too, were now expected by the contributors. 'The fact is', wrote Hope to Mitchell in 1818, 'that general improvement opens the eyes of men and they become dissatisfied with those things which in its earlier stages they most value.'[1]

The benefits of the new roads were showing themselves in many parts and in many ways. Ten years earlier the first stage-coaches had started to run regularly between Inverness, Perth and Aberdeen, and now in 1821 seven coaches passed daily to and from Inverness, where post-chaises, private coaches and gigs were becoming a common sight. A regular coach now ran between Inveraray and Oban, while letters went three times a week from Dingwall to Skye, where the London Sunday paper could be delivered on the following Thursday.[2] On the farms, too, the new communications with the south were having their effect. Cultivation was no longer confined to a narrow strip round the coast. A Ross-shire farm, where in 1798 sixteen oxen and twenty-four garrons were needed, was now worked by three pairs of horses drawing the improved ploughs, and the old *cas chrom* or foot plough had become so rare that in their Ninth Report the Commissioners thought it well to include a diagram and description of its use 'lest it fall into entire oblivion'.[3] From Easter Ross came reports of large increases in wheat-growing and improved livestock, with growing exports of whisky, salt pork and bacon from Cromarty and Invergordon. In Sutherland, too, farming production was rising, while in Caithness in the year 1826 one farmer was reported to have sold off his own land grain to the value of £2,000. A few years after the work of road construction had come to an end, Joseph Mitchell, then Chief Inspector of Roads, reported to Lord Colchester the former Chairman of the Roads and Bridges Commission, that since the start of their work in 1803 the Commissioners had 'succeeded in effecting a change in the state of the Highlands, perhaps unparalleled in the same space of time in the history of any country'. In the course of this report he referred to a letter from a correspondent in Sutherland which read as follows:

'When I came to the Highlands in 1809, the whole of Suther-

[1] Hope, 30 December 1818
[2] Joseph Mitchell, *Notices of the Improved State of the Highlands of Scotland*, 1828
[3] H.R. & B. 9th Report, 1821

land and Caithness was nearly destitute of Roads. This county imported corn and meal in return for the small value of Highland kyloes [cattle], which formed its almost sole export. The people lay scattered in inaccessible straths and spots among the mountains, where they lived in family with their pigs and kyloes, in turf cabins of the most miserable description; spoke only Gaelic; and spent the whole of their time in indolence and sloth. Thus they had gone on from father to son, with little change except what the introduction of illicit distillation had wrought (and this evil was then chiefly confined to the vicinity of Caithness); and making little or no export from the country beyond the few lean kyloes, which paid the rent, and produced wherewithal to pay for the oatmeal imported. But about this time the country was begun to be opened up by the Parliamentary Roads—by one Road, from Novar to Tongue through the barren mountains of which that district is composed, and by another passing along the east shore towards Wick. Certainly, a more striking example of what Roads do effect—and effect too in an extremely poor country—has rarely been seen; such a quick exhibition of what natural wealth lay latent in such a country, is unexampled. Your Roads were opened when the agricultural distresses were just beginning. In the face of that distress we now annually export from the barren district about 80,000 fleeces of wool, and 20,000 Cheviot sheep; and from the sea-coast several cargoes of grain, the produce of three considerable distilleries of Highland whisky, a good many droves of well-fed cattle, and from 30,000 to 40,000 barrels of herrings, besides cod, ling etc. But the most happy result, in my opinion, is its effect upon the people. The fathers of the present generation of young men, were a great many of them brought by compulsion to the Coast; others after they came to substitute carts and wheels for their former rude contrivances, have drawn down to the Road-side of themselves. The effects of society upon human nature exhibit themselves; the pigs and cattle are treated to a separate table; the dunghill is turned to the outside of the house; the Tartan tatters have given place to the produce of Huddersfield and Manchester, Glasgow and Paisley; the Gaelic to the English; and few young persons are to be found who cannot both read and write'.[1]

If the Commissioners and their servants had at times to bear

[1] Joseph Mitchell, op. cit.

abuse and hard words in the course of their work, these were uttered hastily and in the heat of controversy, and there were few who in their hearts doubted the value of the work. If the inhabitants of Middlesex did on one occasion question the benefit they were deriving from the expenditure of public money on roads in Sutherland, their solitary voice served only to give added significance to the all but universal approval of what was being done. John Macculloch it is true, recording an uncomfortable crossing of the River Halladale in the course of a tour in the second decade of the century, had written in his Journal, 'I wish their Honours, the Commissioners, would make Highland roads on the ground and not on paper; that they would forebear at least to entice their friends into such traps as this by their pretty little lying parallel lines'.[1] But even he had noted the general improvement of Highland roads, and his grumble at the lack of a bridge would indicate a criticism of the slow progress of the work rather than of its value. There were some, too, who held with some apparent justice that improved roads, by opening the Highlands to southern capital and southern competition, had stimulated rather than checked emigration; but the ills from which the Highlands suffered in 1803 were, in the judgment of many, such as must be worse before they could be better; and who today would doubt the broad wisdom of the long-term remedy prescribed? With the grumblers rather than with the serious critics went Stewart Mackenzie of Brahan. In a circular letter to the heritors of Ross-shire in April 1827 he had protested that planned improvements on the road from Inverness to Perth should wait, while the Orrin remained unbridged and the road to Poolewe unbuilt. 'I have', he wrote, 'within the last three days with difficulty and at the risk of my health and life scrambled up from Lewis to attend the Circuit Court at Inverness, but arrived too late to do my duties as Juror owing to the want of a road from Poolewe to Achnasheen. . . .'[2] The heritors of Ross-shire were indeed the right recipients of a complaint about the unbridged Orrin, while the Poolewe road surveyed, planned and advertised by the Commissioners, had at length, and after an infinity of trouble, been abandoned owing to the probable cost.

In one instance, and one only, had the Commissioners failed

---

[1] Macculloch, *The Highlands and Western Islands of Scotland*, II, p. 460
[2] H. of L. Stewart Mackenzie, 26 April 1827

to bring to completion a project close to their own hearts. From the start Telford had aimed at helping the important cattle-droving traffic from the far north and the Islands. Much of this came from Skye and the Outer Hebrides, through Kintail and down Glengarry, to reach the Lowlands by way of Corrieyairack and Drumochter Pass or across the Moor of Rannoch to the head of Loch Tay. He had long cherished a hope of improving the drovers' route across Rannoch Moor, and as early as 1811 Nimmo, the Inverness schoolmaster, had on Telford's instructions, surveyed for the Commissioners a route along Loch Treig to cross the Moor by Loch Ossian and Loch Lydoch and to reach Killin by way of the head of Glen Lyon. The new route would, it was claimed, save fifteen miles for the droves compared with the existing route by Ballachulish and Tyndrum, and would result in a total saving for the drovers of £12,000 per annum.[1] In successive reports the Commissioners pressed the project, offering full support, an offer, which if not speedily accepted would be withdrawn and not repeated. Rickman, too, had lent a hand. 'The Commissioners of Highland Roads and Bridges', he wrote in 1814, 'would encourage with their utmost effort any endeavour to accomplish so important an object as the Rannoch Road, by which a considerable portion of the four great counties of Ross, of Inverness, of Argyll and of Perth would be benefited and improved; and he would deserve well of the Highlands who would endeavour to methodise and combine the exertions of his countrymen for the accomplishment of this most important line of Highland intercourse, which if effected through his activity and influence would leave to a traditional remembrance the Ferry of Ballachulish, the Pass of Glencoe and the other dangers which are unavoidable on the military roads through these districts.'[2] The urgings of the Commissioners fell on deaf ears, or at least on ears too distant and too scattered, and the plan failed. Telford seldom erred; but looking today at the green line of the proposed route on Arrowsmith's map, it is impossible not to feel doubt whether even Telford's genius would have sufficed to make and

[1] H.R. & B. 5th Report, 1811, Appendix K. In the course of his tour in the autumn of 1819 Southey was told by a farmer in Glen Spean 'that if the road which has been talked of for that part of the country should be made, he should consider it as saving him a shilling per head on each of his sheep, or, adding that to their value, by the facility of taking them to market, or opening a way for customers.' Southey, p. 238

[2] Rickman, *Statement respecting Origin and Future Repair of Highland Roads*, 1814

maintain a sound road over those miles of peat and bog; whether all Hope's tact and legal skill could have welded into one effective body of supporters, proprietors and cattle-dealers scattered over the four northern counties and all the Hebrides and whether, had these miracles been performed, the drovers would not, as so often, have preferred the old ways.

In the Great Glen, the fourteen years which had passed since the death of John Telford had brought great changes to the scene, and now in the spring of 1821, when Rickman was reviewing the all but completed work on the roads, it seemed that the twin projects were running a neck and neck race. As on the roads traffic was moving in Glengarry and in Easter Ross long before the whole of the road work was complete, so in the Great Glen ships were navigating the eastern end of the Canal and sailing up Loch Ness many years before the whole water-way was open for traffic. In this, the little fleet which had been built by the Commissioners for the transport of stone and timber and other supplies for the work had shown the way, demonstrating that on Loch Ness the winds and currents and winter storms were not the fatal obstacles which some had feared,[1] and that the waters of Loch Linnhe and Loch Eil were indeed the sheltered approach to the western end which had been claimed for them. The sea lock at Clachnaharry, where the Canal met the waters of the Beauly Firth, with the Great Basin beyond it, and the locks giving access to Loch Ness, had presented to Telford formidable problems. The work had been long and costly, but by 1818 ships from the Moray Firth could enter Loch Ness, and on 28 May of that year the *Inverness Courier* was able to report, 'Loch Ness is now enlivened by a number of small vessels passing to and from Fort Augustus where the operations of the Canal are in the greatest activity. During the last week eight sloops were on the Lake at one time.' From now on a steady trickle of traffic made its way into the Loch, anxiously watched by Davidson and promptly reported by him to Telford eager for news of the progress of his great work.

A few years after the start of the work on the Canal the value

[1] When in the summer of 1803 Telford's Report on plans for a canal were before the Parliamentary Committee which examined them, one of the arguments which impressed the Committee was that of the six Government galleys which had been in use for military transport on Loch Ness since Wade's time, none had been lost. 3rd Report of Parliamentary Committee, 1803

of export and import trade, excluding purely coastal traffic, which might be expected to benefit from the completion of the Canal had been estimated at no less than £2,600,000 each year.[1] It may be that even at that time, when hopes were high, this was regarded by many as wishful thinking, but none the less before many years had passed, the trade passing in and out, especially at the Inverness end, though still small in volume was already showing a highly satisfactory variety. Inwards came oatmeal and tar, coal and lime, while outwards went timber and wool, with staves for herring barrels and 'burnwood' for kippering.[2] At the end of August 1818, Telford on his way to the north was able to write to Rickman from Edinburgh quoting a cheering letter from Davidson at Inverness. 'Vessels for various purposes', wrote Davidson, 'continue to navigate the Canal and Loch. A vessel from Leith is at present discharging butter and tar for sheep smearing at Fort Augustus and takes in wool. A Sunderland vessel is lying at Bona Ferry for the above-mentioned purposes and two more have come into the Basin this morning in the wool trade.'[3] That season a total of one hundred and fifty voyages by coasting vessels varying in size from forty to seventy tons was reported, and soon a steam packet was regularly plying between Inverness and Fort Augustus where the improved transport had reduced the price of coal from 40s 6d to 22s 6d a ton.[4]

As time passed, the fishing industry of the north-east coast was coming to play an increasingly important part in the youthful life of the Canal. For years past herring shoals had made their appearance from July to September off the coast of Caithness, and the harbour at Wick, or Pulteneytown as it was then called, which Telford had engineered for the British Fisheries Society, saw a growing traffic. Boats came from Inverness and the Moray Firth as well as from the fishing villages on the coasts of Ross-shire, Sutherland and Caithness, and by 1805 the fishing season saw three hundred boats at work. Two years later boats were coming regularly from the Firth of Forth, and soon Wales, the Isle of Man and Shetland had added their quota. 'Along the Eastern coast of Caithness alone', wrote Sir John Sinclair a few years later, 'no less than fifteen hundred boats go out in an evening to carry

---

[1] C. C. 4th Report   [2] C. C. 16th Report
[3] H. of L. Telford to Rickman, 31 August 1818
[4] C. C. 16th Report

on the fishery and above one hundred decked vessels have been seen in the Harbour at once, besides twenty or thirty at anchor in the Bay. Above two hundred thousand barrels are caught in the Season. . . .[1] To meet the needs of this growing industry, increasing numbers of small coastal boats and larger sloops carried to the Caithness coast birch timber for barrel staves and brushwood for kippering from Glengarry and Glenmoriston. During the summer and autumn of 1822 Davidson had been able to report that twenty-six cargoes of herring barrel staves had gone from the Glengarry saw-mills to Caithness and the Moray coast, while other boats had loaded pit-props from the side of Loch Ness.[2] As the Canal became available to through traffic, herrings for the Glasgow market and for Ireland began to pass along it. In the late autumn of 1823 Andrew May, the hard-worked assistant of John Mitchell at Inverness, reported to Telford that four brigs and three sloops—in all five hundred and thirty-two tons—had entered the Canal loaded with herrings from the Moray Firth for the Irish ports. 'I am sorry', he wrote, 'you was not here to witness the gratifying scene.'[3]

By 1821 the number of ships using the Canal from May to October had grown to two hundred and eighteen. Westward went grain to Liverpool and general cargoes to Glasgow, while from the Irish ports came hemp and flax, some for Aberdeen, but more for Dundee where since the end of the French Wars these imports had grown from 3,000 to 9,000 tons each year. 'The current of trade and intercourse', wrote Telford in a Memorandum on the Navigation of the Canal in 1823, 'is already turning from the eastern to the western coasts; Glasgow and Gourock will undersell London. . . .'[4] In the same year insurance rates over ships and cargoes passing along the sixty-two miles of the Canal were believed to be twenty-five per cent less than those for ships on passage by the Pentland Firth.[5] With the completion of the main construction work grass, broom and whin seed had been sown on the banks of the Canal and half a million

[1] Quoted by Sir Alexander Gibb in *The Story of Telford*
[2] The demand for barrel staves at this time was bringing under the axe other natural woodlands in the north-east. Southey during his tour in 1819 had noted that round Strathpeffer birchwood was being cut down for this purpose 'to the sad deterioration of many a beautiful scene'. Southey, pp. 146-7
[3] H. of L. May to Telford, 31 October 1823
[4] H. of L. Notes by Telford, 25 October 1823
[5] H. of L. Notes by Telford, loc. cit.

Plate 10   Loch Oich

Plate 11   Colonel Alastair Macdonell of Glengarry (1771-1828)

young trees had been planted, some grown from the seed of Norway Pines sent to Telford from Sweden by his friend Count von Platen.[1]

Freight rates for Canal traffic had been fixed low—some thought unduly low—though shipowners using Loch Ness and the eastern end complained that the rate charged on bulky but cheap cargo like small timber and 'burnwood' was too high compared with that charged on more valuable goods like wool and slate. The low rates were alarming the proprietors of the Forth and Clyde Canal who hoped to get the Caledonian Canal rates raised. Telford noted with satisfaction the tendency of competitors 'to exchange former contempt into alarm respecting the Caledonian Canal'.[2] The raising of the Caledonian Canal dues, would in the view of its local supporters 'in its infancy destroy the flattering prospect of its ultimately becoming a great national as well as a local benefit'.[3]

Yet despite the encouraging reports sent to Telford by his loyal employees in the Great Glen, all was not well with the Canal— and in his heart Telford knew it. 'I contempt all silly praise', he wrote to Rickman at a later date.[4] Great technical problems like the construction of the sea lock at Clachnaharry were being solved, but the date for final completion was ever tending to recede, while the cost of the whole undertaking was rising alarmingly. Between 1803 and 1812 the wages of an ordinary labourer on the Canal had risen from 1s 6d to nearly 2s 6d a day, while the rate for piece work had increased by fifty per cent. During these years the labour force on the Canal had steadily risen till it reached its peak in the summer of 1811 when 1,400 men were at work, many of them masons who had been thrown out of work by unemployment in Glasgow. Within the same period the price of oatmeal had almost doubled.[5] Fir, ash and birch timber had been bought from Lochiel in 1803 for from 10d to 14d per cubic foot, but eight years later similar timber cost 3s 6d a cubic foot. As the needs of the Canal cut deeper and deeper into the woodlands on the Lochiel and Glengarry estates and in Glenmoriston, the supply of suitable wood dwindled, and more and more had to be imported

[1] H. of L. Telford to Rickman, 11 November 1818
[2] H. of L. Telford to Rickman, 19 October 1823
[3] H. of L. Anderson to Grant, 1 September 1823
[4] H. of L. Telford to Rickman, 16 October 1824
[5] C. C. 11th Report

at greatly increased rates.[1] Fodder too, for horses was growing scarce and dear. This not only added to the current weekly bills, but threatened to raise a problem for the future so long as the use of the Canal depended partially upon towing, though plenty of horses were reported to be available for tracking where required at a rate of two miles per hour.

In a debate in the House of Commons in 1819 on a motion for a further grant of £50,000 for the Canal, the critics, ignoring the general rise in prices which had taken place, fiercely attacked the fourfold increase in the estimate of the total cost of the Canal since 1803, while the old charge that the benefits of employment had gone chiefly to Irish labourers was again heard.[2] The improvement which had taken place in conditions in the Highlands since 1803 had, they claimed, been due not to work on the roads and the Canal, but to the growth of education and the general progress of civilisation. The friends of the Canal counter-claimed that the payment of £800,000 in wages had had much to do with the improved conditions, and that a considerable part of the workmen's savings had gone on the purchase of boats, fishing tackle and trading vessels, and in the establishment of handicraft industry.[3]

The original plan for the Canal had provided for a minimum depth of twenty feet, with locks of sufficient size to allow passage for the thirty-two gun frigates of the Navy; but as costs rose, the shadow of Napoleon passed, and growing public criticism gave added urgency to the completion of the Canal for civilian use, the depth aimed at was progressively lowered, despite Telford's fears that this would mean a serious loss of traffic. The problem of securing an adequate depth was greatly complicated by the dredging of the shallow Loch Oich, where, as Joseph Mitchell later recorded, excavation was most difficult 'from the vast number of oak trees

[1] Ten years after the opening of the Canal one of the largest tenants on the Glengarry estate told Hope that 'there was now not a birch twig on all Glengarry Estate and that the family had drawn fully £20,000 for their birch wood'. Hope adds the comment, 'Roads and Canal!' H. of L. Hope to Smith, 21 December 1831

[2] 'It is a common error that the Highlanders were found such bad labourers that it was necessary to engage Irishmen by whom it is said the greater part of the excavations and other works were made. We have now before us a detailed account of the number and proportion of labourers employed on the Canal, from which it appears that not above 1 in 60 of the whole were other than natives of the Highlands. . . . The masons were chiefly from Morayshire and the blacksmiths and carpenters principally from the neighbourhood of Inverness with a few from England and Wales.' *Inverness Courier*, 17 February 1841 Barron, II, p. 297

[3] Hansard XXXIX, col. 1119, and *Blackwood's Magazine*, May and July 1820

of great size, some of them 10 ft or 12 ft diameter, that had in the course of ages been carried down by the river and were embedded in the bottom of the lake, forming as it were a net-work of trees and branches most difficult to penetrate',[1] and before the Canal was finally open to traffic the minimum depth had dwindled to twelve feet. Despite the tightening grip of the Treasury the hope was still cherished that a further deepening of the Canal would be allowed. In the autumn of 1823 Davidson reported that many inquiries had come in from owners of ships of deeper draught, and in the same month the Canal Commissioners had optimistically asked Telford for an estimate of the cost of increasing the Canal depth from 12 to 15 and even to 20 feet.[2]

In December 1820, Telford wrote from Edinburgh to Rickman, 'I am taking every practicable measure to get it [the Canal] navigable all thro' by the latter end of next Season',[3] but nearly two years later the goal was still not reached. 'I am sorry to say', wrote Rickman to Southey in the Spring of 1822, 'that the Caledonian Canal is a tender subject at present. It has come to the birth but whether strength will be afforded in this economical year to bring it forth—to open it throughout—I am not confident, so that I am ill at ease on any allusion to a subject which, but for this, ought to be most pleasing to me'.[4] Rickman's fears proved groundless, and before the year ended the Canal had been formally opened for public use. Much still remained to be done Many problems lay ahead, and with the reduced depth the traffic despite its early promise, remained sadly limited; but at least— and at last—the Canal was open.

In the last days of October 1822 the weather had been very bad. In three days Loch Oich had risen seven feet, and by the twenty-third of the month Davidson reported that its level was five feet six inches above 'top level'. That day an official party, including Mr Charles Grant, one of the Commissioners, embarked at the east end of Loch Ness on a steamship which took them to Fort Augustus and through the whole length of the Canal to Fort William reached after twelve hours, returning later to Inverness. Despite the weather and the very high water there were no mis-

[1] Mitchell, p. 25. It seems probable that Mitchell was referring to the circumference rather than to the diameter of the trees.
[2] H. of L. H. M. Treasury to Rickman, 15 October 1823
[3] H. of L. Telford to Rickman, 7 December 1820
[4] Rickman to Southey, 30 April 1822

haps and only one episode to cheer what, for all its novelty, must have been a somewhat tedious expedition. Colonel Macdonell of Glengarry, who had long been at war with the Commissioners over his claim to the exclusive rights of navigation on Loch Oich, had planned to preserve his position by joining the party before they entered the Loch. An early start by the official party upset his plan and their boat had passed Glengarry House before he came aboard, expressing to Charles Grant much concern lest his late arrival might in some way prejudice his claim for compensation. Grant's reply was non-committal and placatory, and Glengarry so far unbent as to own to him that, 'in the present deplorable state of the tenantry of that Country he could not but acknowledge that a speedy settlement would be very convenient to him'.[1]

The encounter which enlivened the voyage of the inaugural party on that autumn day of 1822 was little more than a skirmish in a long campaign, which had, with varying degrees of intensity, been going on since 1804, and which was only now moving towards a climax and a conclusion. The wave of public enthusiasm which had greeted the launching of the project for the Caledonian Canal, had swept certain of the proprietors in the Great Glen into offers of support which, on more mature consideration, may have seemed to some of them a trifle over-generous. The First Report of the Commissioners in 1804 had referred to the expectation that the expense of the land to be acquired for the Canal would not be great, but four years later claims to a total of £14,700 for compensation and for land acquired had already been settled. This sum excluded the highly controversial middle section, and in 1824 shortly after the opening of the Canal, Rickman referred to a total of about £50,000 having been paid for all the land so far taken and occupied.[2] The total included the large payment to Colonel Macdonell on which he had relied to enable him to meet his obligations for the Glengarry road ten years earlier. Settlement with Glengarry had been hard to reach. For the Commissioners, George Brown of Elgin who had made some of the very early surveys had in 1813 assessed the extent of Glengarry's claim at £6,665 and the Commissioners had made a formal offer of £7,000; but Glengarry was not satisfied—'His expectations are very great', wrote Hope to Rickman in September of that

---

[1] H. of L. Grant to Rickman, 30 December 1822
[2] H. of L. Rickman to Hope, 12 November 1824

year—and settlement of the claim had been referred to a jury.[1]

Mr Cockburn, Advocate, who as Lord Cockburn was to delight future generations with his *Memorials of his Time*, had been retained by the Commissioners to argue their case before the jury, and on the evening of 2 September 1814, he, Telford and James Hope met in Inverness to prepare for battle. The jury, drawn partly from the eastern and partly from the western districts, had been summoned for the 5th, and by agreement with Glengarry's advisers it was arranged that the hearing should take place at Fort Augustus so that the whole jury could take part in the inspection of the ground affected by Glengarry's claims. Besides George Brown, the Commissioners had as their witnesses the factor on the Grant estate in Glenurquhart, Colonel Cameron of Achnasoul and Mr Stewart of Ballachulish. All these had valued at figures much below the Commissioners' offer the claim made by Glengarry, which Mr Stewart had described as 'a conspiracy formed against the public purse'.

On the morning of 6 September the whole party set off to inspect the ground; it is hardly surprising to learn that it was raining in torrents. Hope's previous correspondence with Glengarry had been acrimonious, and in view of this and of his prudent refusal to disclose to Glengarry the details of Brown's valuation, Hope anticipated a day of some embarrassment; but Glengarry had, at least for this occasion, learned to curb his temper, and greeted Hope civilly, while Telford he welcomed as 'a friend whom he had always found liberal and a gentleman'. Next morning Glengarry submitted to the jury details of the items claimed for, though with no reference to the sum asked. Glengarry's nine witnesses, mostly from the west coast, then gave evidence assessing the land at an annual value of four to five guineas an acre. Mr Cockburn considered that no purpose could be served by cross-examination of Glengarry's witnesses, and contented himself with submitting the Commissioners' offer supported by the evidence of their four witnesses. The proof lasted till midday, after which the jury retired for four hours to consider their verdict which was to the effect that Glengarry was entitled to a payment of £9,997. The jury had valued the land at 38s per annum per acre and had capitalised this on the basis of thirty years' purchase. 'Tho' the verdict is for a sum beyond the tender made to Glen-

[1] H. of L. Hope to Rickman, 24 September 1813

garry', wrote Hope subsequently to Rickman, 'and subjects the public to the payment of costs, it is but reasonable to state that there are many good men who think that Glengarry has not got a great deal too much. The general opinion, however, is that he has been overpaid; but had the value which his witnesses made out been recognised by the Jury, the sum awarded could not have been less than £18,000 or £19,000.'[1] The cost of the hearing, which the Commissioners had to pay, amounted to £903 16s 10d, but Hope reported that Glengarry was not at all satisfied with the result of the proceedings. 'Upon the whole,' wrote Hope, 'considering the nature of the whole transaction and the circumstances of the parties the public has got off as well as could be expected. The connection which an individual like Glengarry must have in the Country, with the opportunities our forms afford of previous knowledge of the whole Assize cannot be expected to be without its consequences.'[2]

In settling for the value of land taken from him, Glengarry had reserved his claims for disturbance to fishing, for loss of amenity and for the navigation of Loch Oich, and it was soon clear that serious trouble still lay ahead. Glengarry was no mean opponent. Many years later Joseph Mitchell in his *Reminiscences* described him as 'a man of excitable disposition, desirous to be considered the type of an old chief, absolute in his commands, litigious and sometimes hurried by his ungovernable temper into acts of the most serious nature'.[3] Hope's correspondence with him had been strained and difficult. 'He is', wrote Hope to Rickman in 1816, 'a person who would delight in petty warfare. I should be sorry to commence it with him.'[4] In May of the following year Glengarry warned the engineer in charge that the dredging barge which was ready for launching on Loch Oich could not be put into the loch until an offer had been made to him in respect of his claim for damages, and a few months later Glengarry had used force to prevent work on Loch Oich, where of the whole labour force only a man and a boy had the courage to remain. The main difficulty lay in the fact that under the Act of 1803, claimants did not require to specify or value their claims within any stated time, with the result that the Commissioners

---

[1] H. of L. Hope to Rickman, 4 March 1815   [2] ibid
[3] Mitchell, p. 73
[4] H. of L. Hope to Rickman, 27 May 1816

seemed likely for an indefinite period to remain under the shadow of impending but imponderable claims. Hope, writing to Rickman in 1819, expressed the view that Glengarry might accept five thousand pounds for his Loch Oich claims, 'but he is a bold man who would answer for Glengarry'.[1]

It was known that other claims for loss of amenity and damage to fishing rights in other parts of the Great Glen were being held in abeyance until Glengarry's claim, and a large claim by Lochiel, had been disposed of, and it was daily becoming more clear that, for the Commissioners, an intolerable position had arisen. In a long and angry letter written to Hope from Portsmouth in November 1824 Rickman gave vent to his fears and his determination to end the deadlock. It was essential, he considered, that some method be devised of forcing possible claimants to define, value and submit their claims within a limited period. Until that could be done the Commissioners had no way of ridding themselves of potential claims, except by making to the claimant an offer—or 'tender' as the lawyers call it—the amount of which must at best be a matter of guesswork. As the law then stood, the claimant could, if he chose, refer such an offer to a jury in the knowledge that should he be awarded one penny more than the offer, the whole expense of the inquiry would fall on the Commissioners. Since an offer by the Commissioners was most unlikely to be regarded by a jury as too high, the sum fixed would almost certainly be greater than the offer. Thus, reasoned Rickman, the Commissioners would be left to pay both the sum awarded by the jury and the cost of the inquiry, and further claims would appear 'like Hydra Heads' when it became known 'that every person who lives within sight of the Canal, or whose supposed rights or property are ever so remotely or contingently affected by the influence of the Canal operations on the waters of the lochs and rivers—that every such person may attack the Commissioners with impunity and armed with an unbounded power of extortion. . . . No surveyor, no Civil Engineer', continued Rickman's letter, 'can tell, much less value in money, the feelings of a Highland Proprietor, so that the Commissioners are left without rule of conduct yet loaded with the responsibility of burdening the Public to an infinite extent. . . . I do not see why a Million Sterling should eventually suffice to liberate the Canal from all the de-

[1] H. of L. Hope to Rickman, 31 July 1819

mands which will never cease to be made against it. My own opinion, therefore, is, and I assure you I have arrived at it not without pain, that unless all claims can be definitely limited as to time and as to specification and estimate, the Commissioners may justly require to be discharged of the Superintendence of the Canal affairs and the Canal itself be advisedly left to gradual ruin. I wish you to think on this and not to forget in looking at the future what will happen (for instance) on the first award of damages to any salmon fishery. Property of that kind on the Ness alone is divided, I believe, into 14 or 15 coble rights and every one of these rights of keeping a coble boat is further divisible and often divided. Again if any person can procure an award, however small, because a Lake is proved to the mind of any Jury to be higher or lower or kept nearer an average height than before— here is another infinite source of claim.

'It is hardly possible to expect to find a Jury many of whom are not prospectively interested in the success of such wide claims as these, so that nothing short of a limitation of time (say one year) during which all process to be suspended and dormant can insure the Public a cessation of growing claims none of which would be unsuccessful. . . . I have omitted to state the necessity of limiting absolutely the costs of any Jury; Parliament would be surprised if the proposed limit was £500, because in England a tenth part of the sum would usually suffice for the cost of a valuation Jury, yet by what I hear of the number and profession and rank of persons summoned and applied to for evidence in the pending case of the Glengarry Jury I do not see why it should not cost five times £500.'[1]

The logic of Rickman's reasoning convinced the Commissioners and the Government that action must be taken, and in 1825 an Act of Parliament was passed which provided that detailed claims must be lodged before 1 February 1826, and that if the sum finally awarded were less than the claim the claimant must pay the expenses of the Inquiry. By the Act of 1825 the Hydra Heads which, as Rickman feared had been ready to spring up, were forced to reveal themselves. Now at last the Commissioners would know the worst, and before 1 February 1826 claims totalling more than £20,000 had been intimated, in addition to Glengarry's large, if somewhat vague, claim in respect of Loch

[1] H. of L. Rickman to Hope, 12 November 1824

Oich, which had already found its way to the Court of Session.

Many of the claimants now forced into the open based their claims on damage to fishing rights. Duff of Muirtown claimed £3,430 on the ground that the width of the Canal at its mouth drew fish into the Canal and locks to die; that in the spring the Canal was alive with descending smolts most of which would also die; that shipping and steam vessels would 'terrify fish from their haunts and deter them from settling to breed', and that the water at the Mouth of the Ness was 'dirtied and muddied and so disgusting the fish away'. John Stevenson of Fortrose assessed at £1,600 the loss in value of his fishing rights on the River Ness owing to the destruction in the Canal of 'foul fish' and fry returning to the sea, and the loss of spawning beds covered by mud thrown out of the Canal. Evan Baillie of Dochfour claimed £445 on the ground that his fishing tenant on Loch Dochfour could no longer supply to Baillie's family the salmon and sea-trout stipulated in the lease, and that the tenant had abandoned his tenancy, while the Canal had interfered with the floating of timber on the loch. Lady Saltoun of Ness Castle claimed £5,547 for damage to net fishing and the loss of value of meal, barley and saw-mills from shortage of water, while at the western end of the Canal, Lochiel's claim of £8,784 was based partly on interference with the passage of fish from Loch Linnhe to Loch Lochy and Loch Arkaig.[1] Matthew Davidson at Clachnaharry considered the claims to be much overstated. In his view the mouth of the Canal interfered little with fish ascending the river; the few salmon which entered the Canal passed safely through the locks, and though smolts and fry were numerous in the spring their only risk of injury was from 'idle persons' at the locks. Some damage, he considered, had been done to two netting stations at the entrance to Loch Dochfour and Loch Ness, but in general he blamed poaching and the taking of fish out of season for any deterioration in the fishing.[2]

The subsequent history of these claims against the Canal Commissioners is not made clear in the correspondence and other documents now available, but it would seem that the Act of 1825 served very adequately the purpose for which it had been designed. Seven years after its passing Hope, writing to Samuel Smith who had succeeded Rickman as Secretary to the Commissioners,

[1] H. of L. Note of Claims, 1825   [2] H. of L. Notes by Davidson, 1826

mentioned that the outstanding claims were still little nearer settlement, and that little effort had been made even to investigate them.[1] It may well be that the remaining claimants hesitated to press matters to an issue in the knowledge that this might result in reduced awards with expenses against them, while counter-claims might also be made by the Commissioners. On the Commissioners' side, there was little inducement to hurry matters, particularly in the case of claims for deterioration of fishing which, if Davidson's information could be relied on, were unlikely to be strengthened and might well be weakened by delay.

While settlement of the claims against the Commissioners for damage to fishing rights at each end of the Canal made little progress, Glengarry's claims on Loch Oich came at last and by devious paths to conclusion. Neither side to the dispute felt itself on firm ground and the early months passed in manoeuvring for position. Glengarry claimed the exclusive ownership of Loch Oich on the grounds that all the land surrounding it had either belonged to him and his ancestors for generations or had been acquired by more recent purchase. As exclusive owner of the loch he had, he asserted, 'an entire domestic retirement and seclusion from the inroad of strangers and the public which he always deemed of the utmost value', but which since the start of work on the Canal had been interrupted by 'the rude and un-ceremonious visits of strangers and the public at large'. Loch Oich, he maintained, could not be regarded as a navigable water-way open to the public, since they could not approach it save over his land, while even the floating to the loch of timber from Lochiel's land round Loch Quoich at the head-waters of the Garry was impossible owing to the nature of the river. Glengarry's original fear of damage had, he claimed, been dispelled by the assurance of Telford that Canal traffic would be confined to the south side of the Loch and separated from it by an embankment. The shallowness of Loch Oich caused this plan to be abandoned in favour of a navigation line nearer the north side and so nearer to Glengarry House. The introduction of steam boats further increased the threat to amenity, and Glengarry feared that he would be forced to abandon Glengarry House and build a new residence. On these grounds Glengarry's case, at first stated in broad and general terms, was built up into a formidable claim

[1] H. of L. Hope to Smith, January 1832

for compensation for loss of amenity, damage to fishing rights and compensation for acquisition and deepening by the Canal Commissioners of a stretch of water belonging exclusively to him.

Hope and the Law Officers in Edinburgh were perplexed and far from confident. In the summer of 1814 work on the Canal had been seriously affected by the action of Mr Baillie of Dochfour who had sought, and for a time obtained, an interdict against the continued use by the Commissioners of an essential quarry which they had opened on his land. Hope was furious. Baillie's application to the Sheriff was entirely unfounded, and Hope was considering an action for damages against him. This bitter experience now made the Commissioners' legal advisers doubly wary in dealing with the Loch Oich claim. A token offer of compensation was made to Glengarry to avoid risk of similar interruption of work on the Canal, and for a time it seemed that Glengarry's claim must be admitted in principle and referred to a jury for assessment. Hope, who knew only too well that this might mean a crippling award in Glengarry's favour, bent all his energies to resisting the claim. An earlier sale to the Commissioners by Glengarry, of land at either end of Loch Oich threw doubts on Glengarry's claim to exclusive ownership. This in turn raised issues with which neither the sheriff nor a jury could competently deal, and Glengarry was forced to press his claim, not as he had hoped before the sheriff and a local jury, but in the Court of Session where the whole action quickly became entangled and confused in a maze of those declarators, advocations, issues and answers where contemporary lawyers were seldom at a loss and in which not a few of their Highland clients revelled.

Before the case reached its final stages Glengarry died, leaving his widow and his heir to fight on. At this point long delay in procedure caused the case, in the words of the lawyers, to 'fall asleep', only to be 'reawakened' as the legal phrase went 'by great avizandum'. Lord Justice Clerk Boyle and his colleagues of the Second Division of the Court of Session to whom the case was at length referred found the issues by no means clear. Lord Cringletie likened Loch Oich to Loch Ness, a public waterway in which no private rights could be claimed, but Lord Glenlee and Lord Pitmilly had doubts and seemed inclined to favour Glengarry's contention that he owned the loch and could even, if he were so minded, drain it. On 5 June 1830 the long case reached its end, the Court holding that while Loch Oich did in fact belong to Glengarry the Act of Parliament which authorised the building of the Caledonian Canal gave him no right to claim compensation for navigation rights or for loss of privacy or amenity, but only for actual damage to the banks of the Loch or to the fishing, if damage had in fact been sustained. Such damage Glengarry could not prove, so while his claim to ownership had been established, his claim for compensation had in effect been defeated, and what had at one time been looked on as a real threat to the future of the Canal had been finally removed.

Troublesome though Glengarry proved in this and nearly all his dealings with the Commissioners, it is difficult not to feel some measure of sympathy with him. To his eyes and to his way of thinking, the prospect of a public water-way through what had hitherto been a remote Highland fastness must have seemed like a mortal blow to an old way of life. Yet, had he lived to see the outcome, the vindication of his claim to own Loch Oich might perhaps have gone some way to make up for the defeat of his claims for compensation. At least he and his family could look back on more than a decade of legal argument, years which, in a litigious age and to a litigious people, were doubtless not without their moments of satisfaction.[1]

[1] Macdonell and Others v. C. C. Commissioners. 1830 8 Shaw 881 Session Papers Signet Library Collection Nos. 416-37

10

FAIR WEAR AND TEAR

THE rapid decay of the military roads and of Mackenzie's road to Ullapool had shown all too clearly what Highland weather could do to Highland roads. With these lessons so fresh in their minds, it might reasonably have been expected that those responsible for the setting up of the Commission for Highland Roads and Bridges in 1803 would not have failed to make provision for maintenance. Telford, in his surveys of 1801 and 1802, had drawn attention to the question of maintaining the new roads, and in the first draft of the Act of 1803 some provision for maintenance by tolls or local assessment had been included. It may be that the Government foresaw in this risks of controversy and disagreement which would delay the passing of an urgent measure, and that for this reason it suffered the fate of many a wise provision. Whatever the reason, the Act of 1803 came to the Statute Book lacking any reference to the upkeep of the new roads. In the early enthusiasm for the work of the Commissioners, this serious weakness in their powers was at first overlooked, but it was not long before it began to make itself increasingly apparent. The inexperience of Highland road work from which the surveyors and even Telford himself suffered, left its mark on the early roads built under the Act of 1803, while the financial troubles of contractors, contributors and guarantors did nothing to help. As the years passed, Telford and his colleagues grew acutely conscious of the defects of their early efforts. 'I know not', wrote Rickman to Hope years later of one of the early Cowal roads, 'that we have much right to expect that a road made so early in our operations should be much better than the Military Roads.'[1]

On the Arisaig road, where the Commissioners had made their first start, the new road was soon showing the effect of increasing traffic. In Glengarry too, Readdie's work was suffering from the passage of droves from Skye and the carting of bark and of timber needed for work on the Canal,[2] while in one week three hundred

---

[1] H. of L. Rickman to Hope, 28 January 1820
[2] H. of L. Easton to Hope, 15 May 1810

tons of birchwood for barrel staves had passed down the glen bound for the east coast fisheries. In Ross-shire, the eastern section of the ill-fated Achnasheen road was suffering from heavy local traffic, while in Sutherland the Dunrobin road was soon under repair at the high cost of £12 a mile. All this could be looked on as fair wear and tear and was to that extent a measure of the usefulness of the new roads, if also a sad commentary on their quality; but it was soon apparent that Highland weather was an even greater danger than heavy traffic. On many of the roads in the north and west, the closing stages of the construction work saw a race by the contractor to get the work taken off his hands before deterioration set in, and it was small wonder that contractors, well aware of the poor quality of their work, sought to keep traffic off the roads until their responsibility had ended. To the Commissioners the problem was fast becoming increasingly apparent. 'We are far from being without anxiety', they wrote in their Fourth Report, 'respecting the future repair of the roads when taken off the hands of the contractors. The frequency of rainy seasons and of mountain torrents in the Highlands makes the roads more than commonly liable to ruin and decay; and unless effectual means of vigilance and timely repair are provided we cannot venture to calculate on the permanency of the improvements now making with the aid of the liberality of the Legislature. We have not yet been able to devise any mode which appears unobjectionable.'[1]

So matters remained until 1810, when the first tentative and timid step was taken towards solving the problem. By an Act of that year, the Commissioners of Supply of each of the Highland counties were empowered to levy local assessments on owners of land in those districts where expenditure on road repair and maintenance was required, and to see to the proper application of the money. The Act of 1810, however, left the initiative entirely in the hands of local interests, and almost before it was passed it was evident that it would prove ineffective. Soon after its passing, Robert Brown, formerly factor for Clanranald, after returning from a tour of inspection of roads in west Inverness-shire, wrote to James Hope that if the roads were left to the local proprietors alone every shilling expended on them would be lost, 'as the jarring interests and narrow views of some of these individuals

[1] H.R. & B. 4th Report, 1809

will, when the novelty of the thing wears off, prevent their uniting in any common measure however beneficial'.[1]

Meantime the state of the old military roads had been going from bad to worse. The annual grants made by Parliament from 1770 onwards had kept in some sort of repair the hundreds of miles of the old military system on which General Mackay had reported so ill in 1784, but the money spent did little more than retard the progressive decay of roads ill-planned, ill-constructed and now little suited to the needs of the times. As the 18th century drew to a close, the expenditure of public money on these military roads came to be viewed with increasing disfavour. In 1798 the discontinuance of the annual grant had been recommended by a Committee of the House of Commons, which is reported to have placed the upkeep of the military roads in the same category as the establishment of the Mint in Scotland—as a means of giving salaries to people with no functions. The suggestion that the grant should end was greeted with dismay in Scotland. Poor though the military roads were, they were then almost the sole means of communication throughout much of the Highlands. The traffic using them was quite insufficient to provide for their upkeep by any system of tolls. The sparse population of much of the country through which they passed could not possibly maintain them by means of statute labour, and without Government help their speedy decay was certain. Colonel Anstruther, who was Inspector of Military Roads in the Highlands from 1797 to 1814, strongly opposed their abandonment by the Government, stating his opinion that, 'if Government should withdraw the allowance granted for keeping in repair the Roads and Bridges in the Highlands the progress made in Civilisation, Fisheries, Manufactures and Improvements of every kind will soon be lost and the Highlanders will in a few years relapse into their former ignorance or desert their Country'. These arguments prevailed, and though a few stretches of road were allowed to fall into complete disrepair, nearly six hundred miles of military road continued for another fifteen years in bare and unsatisfactory existence.

By the end of 1813 an almost intolerable position had arisen. Despite the continued annual grants, the surviving military roads were fast disintegrating, while public and local funds were being poured out by the Commissioners on the new system of Parlia-

[1] H.R. & B. 6th Report, 1813, Appendix A

mentary roads, now moving fast to completion and almost as fast to decay. Faced with this double crisis the Government at last took effective action. The upkeep of the remaining military roads, now reduced to little more than three hundred miles, was, with that of the new Parliamentary roads, placed under the Commissioners for Highland Roads and Bridges, who thus became responsible for the maintenance of over twelve hundred miles of road—a total to be still further increased as the last of the contracts placed by Telford and his colleagues reached completion. As a contribution towards the cost of maintenance, the Government made an annual grant of £5,000, the balance to be raised by county assessment.[1]

When Telford in 1814 selected John Mitchell, the Morayshire mason, to replace the unfortunate Duncombe, the transfer to the Commission of the responsibility for the upkeep of the old and the new roads had only recently taken place. So, while Mitchell, as senior inspector became responsible for supervising the work on contracts not yet complete, an increasing amount of his time during the next ten years was spent on the upkeep and repair of roads and bridges. Mitchell had under him a number of sub-inspectors, most if not all masons, each responsible for one of the six districts into which the work was divided. These men had been appointed shortly before Duncombe's death, when the poor state of the Ullapool road had brought home to Telford and his Commissioners the folly of accepting a low standard of work. No provision had at that time been made for the upkeep of the new roads, but the importance of seeing that the construction work was well done had at least been realised. The new inspectors fulfilled this purpose and, after 1814, performed the additional function of keeping in repair both the old and the new roads.

As guardians of the public purse and with the Chancellor of the Exchequer among their number, the Commissioners were frugal paymasters. John Mitchell, after the responsibility of road upkeep was added to his other duties, received a total salary of £250. Andrew May, his clerk at Inverness, got £40 a year, and even this was reduced for a time to £30 when funds were low. In January 1823 Hope forwarded to Rickman a letter from May

[1] From the records available it appears that the annual cost of maintenance averaged £5 a mile in the case of the old military roads and £4 a mile in the case of the roads built by the Commissioners.

in which the latter expressed the hope that the reduction might soon be made up 'as I have a large young family to keep quiet'. The remuneration of the local inspectors, too, was far from generous. Robert Garrow, the senior among them, who was responsible for the Argyllshire roads, received thirty-six shillings a week, but the pay of the others varied from twenty-five shillings to twenty-two shillings a week. Mitchell was allowed eleven shillings a day as personal expenses during the spring, summer and autumn months and an allowance of eightpence a mile for travelling. Garrow was allowed twenty-five shillings a week for travelling and subsistence, but the others only twenty shillings.

The distance covered by these men in the course of the working season is remarkable. Shortage of funds soon forced the Commissioners to limit to 7,000 miles a year the mileage for which Mitchell could claim travelling allowance,[1] but the correspondence shows that each year the actual distance covered by him averaged nearly 9,500 miles. Southey in his *Journal* described Mitchell as being so hardened by constant riding 'that if his horse's hide and his own were tanned, it may be doubted which would make the thickest and toughest leather'. The mileage covered by the sub-inspectors can only be conjectured, but when in 1829 Robert Garrow, the Argyllshire inspector, was considering retirement after nineteen years' service, he wrote to Rickman that during that time he reckoned that he had walked over one hundred thousand miles.[2] 'Garrow is a philosopher of the first water,' wrote Hope to Rickman that autumn, 'peripatetic besides, in a degree almost incredible.'[3] Rickman thought that Garrow at the age of fifty-six was far too young to retire. Telford, he pointed out, was still in harness at seventy-two, and with the promise of some help from his son the inspector agreed to carry on.

For many years Mitchell alone was given an allowance for a horse. The others like Garrow walked, and when in 1833 the Commissioners proposed to make an allowance for ponies for the sub-inspectors, Garrow, still through Telford's persuasion in the Commissioners' service, preferred to continue his work on foot. Constantly exposed as these men were to the weather, always on the move and sleeping in poor cottages or at the best in inns which

[1] It seems that this figure was fixed as being the distance which could be covered by two horses in the course of the working season.
[2] H. of L. Garrow to Rickman, September 1829
[3] Hope, 8 October 1829

too often offered little comfort, many of them fell early victims to rheumatism. Rickman in the course of his tour with Southey and Telford in the autumn of 1819 noticed their sufferings, and on his return to London he arranged for a supply of waterproof cloth to be sent north. This proved such a boon that each year a regular supply was sent for the inspectors at an annual cost of £29. Six years later a further step was taken to improve conditions for the men employed on the roads, this time for those employed by the contractors engaged in repair work. The contractor working on part of the roads in north Argyllshire had complained that the wretched accommodation and poor food often meant that the men abandoned their work, and he suggested that caravans be provided. 'The object they have in view', wrote Hope to Rickman, 'of securing a more certain accommodation to the workmen is highly interesting and if we may even allow for a little exaggeration in the inconveniences which are at present experienced, still there must be much real distress and hardship which it would be very gratifying to contribute to remove. The extent of the speculation is not great and if the Commissioners are inclined to contribute to the extent of £10 per annum, Mr Mitchell says they would have the value in the superior execution of the work and I would say in the moderation of future estimates and the readiness of the workmen to embark in the Service.'[1] Telford, too, supported the suggestion and caravans were purchased at a price of £20 each, the contractors paying half the cost and maintaining the vehicles. Among the records which have survived are parts of the journals kept by John Mitchell's road inspectors. Written as they were by plain working men with little education, it was hardly to be expected that the journals would contain more than the bare records of work and weather. The latter was a subject for constant, and almost always unfavourable, comment and Garrow on the Argyllshire roads must indeed have needed all his philosophy.

If Mitchell and his inspectors at all seasons, and Telford during his spring and autumn tours of inspection, were those most directly affected by the weather, they were not the only ones to whom it brought anxiety. The farmer and the forester listening by their firesides to the beat of the rain and the roar of the gale picture in their troubled minds the ruin of precious crops or the

---

[1] H. of L. Hope to Rickman, 3 March 1824

fall of noble trees. To James Hope the passing years had brought a feeling almost of affection for the new roads and bridges over which, if only on paper, he had laboured so long and so hard. So, as tidings came of Lammas floods, of autumn rainstorms or of sudden spring thaws, Hope looking out from his Queen Street office, far over the new buildings of Heriot Row and far beyond the hills of Fife, could picture to himself the swelling streams of Lochaber, Badenoch and Ross-shire bringing ruin to many a bridge and many a road the making of which had come to fill so much of his life. To Rickman in London he wrote of his fears and his anxieties, and with him he shared the ill tidings as they reached him from the Highlands. 'In the West of Scotland', he wrote in late September 1815, 'there have been very violent rains, and I lay my account with hearing of some mischief they have done.'[1] The winter of 1818 brought further anxious days, for reports had reached him of a great flood in the Glenmoriston district, the same which brought John Mitchell hurrying north from Dunkeld to repair the damage at Torgoyle and Drumnadrochit. The bad weather that year lasted far into the spring, and in the last weeks of April Hope was writing, 'By all accounts the snow on the Black Mount has been beyond all experience.'[2] 'Our thaw', he wrote to Rickman in the early weeks of 1820, 'has been as rapid as in the South, but not attended with rain. We look with anxiety to the safety of the bridges.'[3] Sometimes the winter storms held up even the posts from the south. 'Our storm is extreme', Hope wrote on 7 February 1823, 'and the snow falls heavily at this moment. We had four mails from London due.' A few days later the mails had got through, but anxiety over the fate of the roads and bridges was not allayed. 'We had six London mails due at one time and our Country more shut up than it has been for twenty-five years. . . . Yesterday and today the thaw is complete and rapid—with wind—so that we may well dread casualties in the North. . . . I have got no newspapers. The whole were much hashed in the bag.'[4] The autumn of 1824 brought more anxieties to Hope. 'There is reason', he wrote to Rickman in October, 'to apprehend further casualties if the weather of the last 48 hours should have been general in the

[1] Hope, 27 September 1815
[2] Hope, 25 April 1818
[3] H. of L. Hope to Rickman, 25 January 1820
[4] H. of L. Hope to Rickman, 7 and 12 February 1823

North; but all this season rains and storms have gone in zones. This district has escaped the whole season, but we are now getting it in a concentrated state.'

If fate dealt hard blows to the roads and bridges, the eighteen years which saw the virtual completion of their construction brought relatively few changes among the men on whom had fallen the main burden of the work. Duncombe's place as Chief Inspector had been quickly and adequately filled by John Mitchell the Morayshire mason, while on the Canal, John Telford's work at the western end had for long been in the capable hands of Alexander Easton. Rickman, Telford and Hope still carried, with few visible symptoms of weariness, their multiple burdens, while even among the members of the two Commissions the passing years had left few gaps; but changes were soon to come. The transfer to the Commissioners of the responsibility for the upkeep of the military roads had meant added work for Telford and all his colleagues, but for none more than for John Mitchell. Mitchell's early years as a mason on the Canal, hard and toilsome as they were, had called for little but the rude health and physical strength of which he had plenty, and even the hardship of working throughout the winter months had not come his way. With his appointment to succeed Duncombe as Chief Inspector of Roads, constant travel took the place of the healthy toil of a working mason, with the added and unaccustomed burden of responsibility, of correspondence and of office work. Long tours of inspection in all weathers were now his lot, and on his return from each, he and Andrew May must spend many weary hours in the bleak and fireless office in Inverness completing reports for Telford, for Hope and for the Commissioners. Years later when John Mitchell's son looked back on his own forty years of work as Chief Inspector of the Highland Roads, his hard life in the service of the Commissioners seemed easy in comparison with that of his father. 'On top or inside of coaches,' he wrote 'in gigs, in carts, on horseback, on ponies, on foot, in boats or in ships and steamers, by night or by day, I had to make my way, and many a snow-storm and bitter blast and wet jacket I had to endure; still I had generally good roads and tolerable inns with the advantage of youth and health. How different was my poor father's life! Traversing the country where there were no roads of any kind, crossing dangerous rivers and streams, travelling in wet clothes and for

shelter living in small and wretched huts where oatcakes with whisky were the chief and only refreshments. His enthusiasm overcame every difficulty, but his iron frame fell a sacrifice at last at the age of forty-five to the privations and hardships he had to endure and the duties he had to perform.'[1] Though the signs were not yet apparent, the hard life was taking its toll and the time was fast approaching when Joseph the son was to be called to take his father's place.

Joseph Mitchell had been born at Forres when his father was still a humble mason spending the working season on the Canal and the winter months at home in Morayshire; but when John Mitchell was chosen by Telford to supervise a section of the new roads under construction in the Great Glen the family moved to Fort Augustus, and later, on John's appointment as Chief Inspector, to Inverness. The choice of road engineering as a career for the boy seems never to have been in doubt. Telford, realising the benefit which his own early training as a mason had been to him in his subsequent career, urged that every young engineer should acquire some knowledge of practical work either as a mason or as a mill-wright, and on his strong advice, Joseph at the age of seventeen was sent to work with the masons engaged on the locks of the Caledonian Canal, first at Fort Augustus and later at Kyllachy near Loch Oich. 'The works at this point', wrote Joseph many years later in his *Reminiscences*, 'extending from the west end of Loch Ness to Loch Oich, a distance of about eight miles, were in full progress. There were five locks at Fort Augustus, two others westward and a large number of men were employed. All the masons were from Nairn or Morayshire; all the labourers were Highlanders. As my father was known to all the foremen and principal people about the works I was kindly received and treated with consideration; but I felt the work oppressive and I don't think I should ever have been a good workman. I was placed under a steady man to learn the mysteries of the trade. The foreman of the masons was a John MacPherson. Mr Thomas Rhodes and his brother were ships carpenters from Hull and had come to erect the lock gates. Thomas Rhodes was the chief. He had educated himself, and under the Rector of Inverness Academy had acquired a good knowledge of mathematics and drawing. He took a paternal interest in me, and every evening after working

[1] Mitchell, p. 320

165

hours I used to change my mason's apron, dress and spend two hours with him in drawing and other instruction. We worked together, he at his problems and I drawing part of the works. About 9 o'clock his wife laid on the table a bottle of strong Edinburgh ale of which he gave his wife and me a champagne glass full and I then took my departure.'[1]

Joseph soon developed some skill in draughtsmanship, and in 1821 in the course of one of his Highland tours Telford, who had noticed the lad's promise, set him to construct a panoramic picture of the Canal. When the completed picture reached London, Telford was inspecting Canal work in Wales, and anxious weeks passed while Joseph awaited the verdict on his work. The day when Telford's reply at last reached Fort Augustus was a happy one, for not only was Joseph's work warmly approved, but he was invited to go to London to work for Telford himself. The offer was eagerly accepted, and before many weeks had passed Joseph reached London after a six days' voyage in one of the early steamers sailing from Aberdeen, a passage for which he paid the modest fare of twenty-one shillings.[2]

Shortly before Joseph's arrival in London, Telford had set up house in Westminster, moving from the rooms in the Salopian Coffee House at Charing Cross which he had occupied for so long and with such profit to the management that, on acquiring the premises shortly before, the present landlord had also acquired Telford as part of the goodwill. Joseph now found himself ensconced as a permanent part of Telford's bachelor establishment at 24 Abingdon Street, within a stone's throw of the scene of the labours of John Rickman at St Stephens. Here young Mitchell, with John Gibb the son of the Superintendent of the Harbour Works in Aberdeen, and later George May son of the hard-worked clerk at Inverness were soon deeply immersed in the huge volume of engineering work on which Telford was engaged, and helping as best they could in the entertainment of engineers and soldiers, poets and politicians and many another who came to the house in Abingdon Street. Among those who visited Telford's house at this time was Count von Platen, who had come over from Sweden to discuss with Telford certain technical problems in connection with the Gotha Canal. Telford was on one of his frequent visits to Wales when von Platen arrived, and Joseph

[1] Mitchell, pp. 68-69   [2] Mitchell, p. 86

Mitchell and young Gibb, who had been charged by Telford to treat the Count with all consideration, had to face the formidable task of acting as hosts while striving to assume the detailed knowledge of the technicalities of canal-building with which their distinguished guest credited them.[1]

The variety of Telford's work at this stage in his career was almost incredible. The Menai Bridge and Holyhead Harbour, with the new road from London to Holyhead, the Highland roads and the Glasgow to Carlisle road were all under construction. So too was the great drainage work of the Bedford Level, with the Gloucester and Berkeley Canal and the Caledonian Canal, besides harbours at Dundee and Lynn. A letter from Telford to John Mitchell written from London on 23 November 1823 gives some idea of his busy life. 'I have examined and settled the Glasgow and Carlisle and Lanarkshire roads,' he wrote, 'a road near Edinburgh and the Waterworks; examined the River Clyde at Glasgow and set Gibb (senior) on a survey of that river and country to Hamilton; perambulated and set agoing a survey of the present and new line of road between Glasgow and Portpatrick; travelled through the Galloways, met Pollock [his Lanarkshire Surveyor] at Lockerbie and am now here.' With all this, Telford's young assistants had their hands full indeed, and Joseph can have found little leisure to write the letters home which John Rickman franked for him, saving him the postage dues of 1s 1½d to Inverness. Among his many duties none gave him more interest and pleasure than his attendance with Telford at the meetings of the newly-formed Institution of Civil Engineers, of which Telford was the first President. At one of the early meetings, Joseph made, for his own interest, notes of the discussion which followed the reading of a technical paper. Telford chanced to see the notes, of which he highly approved, and at his suggestion

[1] More than fifty years later Joseph Mitchell wrote of Telford's establishment in London, 'His house was handsome, quite suited for his requirements, and in accordance with his professional position and he was very proud of it. After having lived in lodgings and hotels all his life, he appeared gratified and delighted at the additional comfort and conveniences of his new residence. When any friend called and complimented him on his new quarters he used to say "Oh you must see my house", taking them over the principal apartments pointing out the solid mahogany doors and marble chimney-pieces. "Below", he would say, "I have a perfect village", and opening the door of the apartment in which we worked he added, "and here are two raw Scotchmen." He usually finished by observing, "It is a singular coincidence that I, a bridge-builder, should occupy the house of the Engineer of Westminster Bridge, La Bayelle; and there in a panel above the chimney-piece in the dining-room is a picture of the Bridge by Canaletto."' Mitchell, p. 88

these were transcribed and adopted as what were probably the first formal Minutes of the Institution.

Joseph's time in London was as happy as it was busy, and it was a sad day for him when in July 1824 a letter reached him from Scotland with the news of the serious illness of his father. In this emergency Telford and Rickman took counsel as to what arrangements should be made, and Joseph Mitchell was sent north to carry on as best he might with the road maintenance work during his father's illness; but the change was no temporary one for on 20 September 1824 John Mitchell died. 'We never can expect', wrote Hope to Rickman on John's death, 'to see his place filled with the same nerve and capacity, but it is a comfort that Joseph Mitchell promises so well', and in that same month of September 1824 Hope was forwarding to Rickman a copy of a letter which Joseph had written to an angry Highland laird with the comment, 'It is so discreet and yet has so much of the nerve which poor [John] Mitchell had that I think you will have satisfaction in the perusal of it.'[1]

Before six months had passed Joseph, thanks to no small extent to the knowledge of mason-work which he had painfully acquired as a lad in the Great Glen, had shown to the satisfaction of Telford and the Commissioners that he was a fit permanent successor to his father, and so at the age of twenty-one he took up the burden which he was to bear until the close of the Commissioners' work nearly forty years later. On his appointment to succeed his father, Joseph Mitchell's salary was £300 per annum out of which fifty pounds was retained each year as a contribution to the Superannuation Fund which Rickman had lately set up for the benefit of the Road Inspection Staff. His salary, together with the interest on the £1,700 which his father had left, supplemented by a contribution of £300 from the Commissioners, had to suffice for the support of himself, his mother and her younger children; but the travelling expenses allowed him by the Commissioners and the modesty of the charges then made by Highland inns stood him in good stead, and from his annual salary he was able to save not far short of £100 a year.[2] Subsequently Mitchell's salary as Chief Inspector to the Commissioners was augmented by payments for work in connection with Highland

[1] H. of L. Hope to Rickman, 22 and 27 September 1824
[2] Mitchell, p. 144

harbours and the building of manses for ministers of Highland parishes, and he has left it on record that at its height his fees and salaries from all sources reached a total of £1,000 per annum.[1] Of this period in his life Mitchell subsequently wrote, 'James Watt, when inventing the steam-engine, contrived what he called a governor, the functions of which were to regulate the discharge of the steam and establish uniformity of action in the engine. I fortunately had two governors: first, the fear of being found unfit for or unworthy of the trust reposed in me at so early a period of life; secondly, the fact of my Mother and seven young children being mainly dependent upon my exertions for their support.'

But if finance presented few problems there was no lack of worries in Joseph Mitchell's early work. While the Government were contributing one half of the cost of construction of roads in the Highlands, local support and local enthusiasm were assured; but when after the passing of the Act of 1814 it became apparent that a large part of the cost of maintenance would fall on county funds, the Highland counties soon revised their views, while the depression which immediately followed the French Wars made the prospect doubly unwelcome. Rickman thought ill of the new trend of thought. 'I foresee', he wrote to Southey in April 1823 with his usual vigour of language and mixture of metaphor, 'I shall conquer the absurd reliance which the semi-barbarous have imbibed that they are not to pay for the maintenance of their roads. They have been indulged so much as to believe that they do me a favour in suffering me to repair their roads; but it has come to such a pass as this that I have turned upon them sharply enough to convince them of their error, and all will be well. They are spoilt children learning to kiss the rod. . . .'[2] Hitherto the local proprietors had readily acquiesced in the control of road work by the servants of the Commissioners, but now that these proprietors were to be liable for a large part of the cost of upkeep, they began to expect and demand an increasing voice in expendi-

---

[1] Shortly after Joseph Mitchell's appointment as Chief Inspector, the Government, at the urgent request of Dr Chalmers, agreed to build and endow forty churches and manses in the poorest Highland parishes. The erection of these churches was placed under the control of the Commissioners for Highland Roads and Bridges. In addition to these duties Mitchell became responsible for the erection of harbours to help the fishing industry, to the cost of which the Government contributed one half. Mitchell, p. 155

[2] Rickman to Southey, 4 April 1823

ture and management. To this Rickman was much opposed, but Joseph Mitchell showed himself diplomatic and tactful beyond his years, and by degrees a more democratic system of management was devised. From now on, plans for expenditure and road repair came for discussion before periodical meetings of the counties, while a system of tolls, and strict economy in repair work, helped to relieve the burden of assessments and so to silence local criticism. Even the conservative Rickman came at last to acknowledge the wisdom of the new plan.

There now started for Joseph Mitchell a long period of active, useful and happy life. His apprentice days with Telford in London short as they had been, had afforded him unusual opportunities for acquiring knowledge and experience in engineering matters of which he had taken full advantage, while the high reputation which John Mitchell had built up before him predisposed the Highland proprietors to respect the views and accept the advice of the son who had taken the father's place. So it came about that within a short space of time Joseph found himself firmly established, not only as the responsible agent of the Commissioners, but as a valued counsellor on road, bridge and allied problems throughout the Highland counties. His work inevitably brought him into close personal contact with very many Highland lairds, great and small, and soon he was accepted and welcomed far and wide on terms of confidence and friendship to a degree remarkable at a time when rank and social standing were still regarded as matters of some moment.

When in 1814 the Government decided to discontinue the whole upkeep at public expense of the military roads, Perthshire alone refused to undertake the share of the future maintenance cost which would thus fall on the local proprietors. The result of this refusal appears to have been that for some years after 1814 little attention was given to the military roads in the county, and since none of the roads built by the Commissioners were in Perthshire, this meant that the whole road system in that county rapidly fell into a state of complete disrepair. So bad did the Perthshire roads become that, as Southey records, the drivers of coaches bound for the north had to reassure their alarmed passengers that the sudden bumping signified not an accident to the vehicle, but its entry into that county.[1] The state of the

<hr>

[1] Southey, p. 26

Perthshire roads became so bad that shortly before John Mitchell's death the Duke of Atholl had asked the Commissioners to allow Mitchell to arrange for the repair of the roads, the expense to be met by tolls or by money advanced by certain of the local land-owners. On John's death, Joseph took up this work, and he has left on record that during the next few years a sum of about £180,000 was spent under his supervision on roads and bridges in Perthshire.[1]

Meantime the Highland road and bridge construction started in 1803 had almost reached an end, but two projects still remained unfinished, and to Joseph Mitchell fell the task of bringing them to completion. The serious floods which had occurred in the Glenmoriston district during the winter of 1818 had completely destroyed the bridge at Torgoyle over the River Moriston on the new road from Inverness to the west by Glenmoriston and Glen-shiel. As this was an essential link on the road to Skye, a tem-porary wooden bridge had been built, but a permanent stone one was essential, and its successful completion in 1828 was one of the earliest achievements of the young Chief Inspector. In Skye, a road from Sligachan to Dunvegan had been planned to complete the communications in the Island. The project which was long delayed was at length put in hand, the Commissioners by some special arrangement with MacLeod of MacLeod agreeing to pay half the cost, although the closing date for public contribution to new road construction had long since passed. MacLeod's road, as it was called, was not complete till 1826, and to Mitchell fell the task of making the final inspection in company with Mac-Kinnon of Corry near Broadford, grandson of that MacKinnon who had proved such an admirable host to James Boswell and Samuel Johnson at Corriechatachan more than fifty years earlier. MacKinnon occupied a position of great popularity and in-fluence in the island where, though no lawyer, he held the office of sheriff substitute. When Mitchell looked back on his many years of work with the Commissioners, he called again to mind the memory of that visit to Skye in the summer of 1826, when his companion, a shepherd's plaid thrown across his chest and a huge walking stick in his hand, would turn aside from his road inspec-tion to hold informal open-air courts, where his decisions, based on common-sense and natural justice rather than on knowledge

[1] Mitchell, p. 115

of the law, were accepted by the litigants as readily as any pronounced in the Courts of Edinburgh.[1]

From the start of the Commissioners' labours in 1803 Charles Abbot, now Lord Colchester, had as Chairman of the Commission for the first fourteen years, taken a close interest in the work. The Commissioners as a body seldom met except when Parliament was in Session. The presence of three Commissioners was necessary for the transaction of important business, and as the Chairman and Vansittart the Chancellor of the Exchequer were usually the only members on whom he could count, Rickman was often hard put to it to keep the wheels turning in London. William Smith, the Member of Parliament for Norfolk, who had been a Commissioner from the start, paid regular visits to Scotland, and in the summer of 1827 Lord Colchester himself came to Scotland accompanied by his son. Hope in Edinburgh received the news of the coming visit with mixed feelings. Telford had proposed that Hope should go with Lord Colchester on his tour, but Hope's plea that he was 'a deep-rooted plant . . . who thinks that nothing can go right in his absence from the office' seems to have been accepted, and it was left to young Joseph Mitchell, so early in his career as Chief Inspector, to act as courier to the party.[2] The tour took them from Inverness up the north-east coast to visit the new roads of Easter Ross-shire, and down the Canal to Fort William, south to Inveraray and the Argyllshire roads and out to Islay. From Mitchell's account the journey throughout was something of a triumphal progress for, despite the delicate question of future upkeep, the landowners of the Highlands were in their hearts not unmindful of all the Commissioners had done for them.[3] Lord Colchester was enthusiastic and full of plans for a further extension of road-making in Orkney, in Wester Ross-shire, in Mull and in Lewis, ambitious projects which were abandoned on his death two years later.

One of the Perthshire roads which soon called for attention was the old military road which General Wade had built leading from Dalnacardoch near Drumochter Pass to Crieff, by way of

[1] Mitchell, p. 128
[2] Hope, 4 July 1827
[3] Southey in the *Journal* of his tour in 1819 had quoted the postmaster at Dalmally as having reported that since the upkeep of the roads had been taken over by the Commissioners the normal load of a cart had more than doubled, while blacksmiths at Fort Augustus and Inveraray were complaining of the loss of profit from repairing coaches. pp. 237-8

Tummel Bridge and Aberfeldy. Though this road had long ceased to be of practical use as a military road, it happened to follow the most direct line for the droves of cattle and sheep which came through Drumochter Pass bound for the great trysts at Crieff and Falkirk. Throughout the greater part of the 18th century this droving traffic was largely a traffic in cattle for which open, roadless country was an advantage rather than an obstacle. With the turn of the century, however, sheep breeders from the Borders had come in increasing numbers to rent grazings in the Highlands, and soon sheep as well as cattle were taking the road south to the autumn markets. With the coming of sheep, roads on the routes of the drovers took on an added importance, easing the task of the drovers and providing, as parts of the King's Highway, established and recognised routes to take the place of the traditional drove roads many of which were falling out of use and recognition.[1] The reconstruction, mainly for the use of droving traffic, of Wade's old road by Tummel Bridge was a formidable task in which Mitchell was soon involved, while his burdens were further increased and his income augmented by his appointment to supervise the erection by the Government of churches and manses in remote Highland districts. So the days passed, filled with hard, varied and useful work. Year by year the reins which had fallen from the hands of John Mitchell came to be held ever more firmly by the hands of the son, whose growing knowledge and widening experience were soon to be tested by Fate's hardest blow.

The early summer months of 1829 were unusually warm in the north-east of Scotland. As July passed, wide variations in the barometer took place, with great displays of Northern Lights which were later to be recalled as having been portents of strange things to come, and Hope in his Queen Street office waited anxiously for the Lammas floods which so seldom failed. On 2 August Mitchell had left for Orkney and Shetland to arrange for the building of churches in the Islands, crossing from Thurso to Kirkwall over a Pentland Firth unusually calm and placid. Next day he set off on horseback to visit the site of one of the proposed churches at Tankerness some thirteen miles to the north. 'We had scarcely started', he wrote later, 'when it began to rain in torrents; then the wind got up and before we were able to return

[1] Haldane, *The Drove Roads of Scotland*, Chapter XI

to Kirkwall, two hours behind our time, it blew a perfect hurri-
cane. . . . In all my travels I never experienced such a deluge of
constant and persistent rain.' On the following day he started for
Shetland and it was not till the afternoon of 11 August that he
again reached Thurso. Here he found an Inverness paper and
read to his dismay of huge floods which had taken place in the
valleys of the Nairn, the Findhorn, the Spey, the Don and the
Dee. The extent of the disaster was clearly such that no time
could be lost in returning south, and within half an hour Mitchell
was in the mail coach bound for Speyside where he arrived after
many hours of continuous travelling.[1] Meantime, on 8 August
news of the floods had reached Edinburgh. 'Such disastrous news
never occurred from one night's rain in our days', wrote Hope,
and that same evening the London Mail carried Hope's letter to
the Commissioners with news of the disaster. 'We shall have
survived', he wrote, 'some of our most splendid works.'[2]

The full extent of the damage was even greater than Mitchell
had feared as he hurried south from Thurso. Torrential rain in
the Monadhliath Hills had raised the Spey to unprecedented
heights, while near Huntly on the upper Deveron the measured
rainfall in twelve hours was nearly four inches. The widespread
drainage of agricultural land which had been carried out in recent
years had led the water off with a speed which overtaxed the
capacity of streams and rivers, while in many places embankments
made by the Commissioners had dammed back the floods,
forcing through the bridges a mass of water far in excess of their
capacity.[3] On the Spey the magnificent bridge at Fochabers which
had been completed soon after the start of the Commissioners'
work had been destroyed, while the 150 feet of iron arch with
which Telford had spanned the river at Craigellachie now hung
almost by a thread. On the Dee, the new bridge at Ballater which
had twice escaped so narrowly from floating timber had been
swept away, in common with those over the Findhorn at Forres
and Corryburgh, while others on Donside and on the Upper Spey
were gone. The damage to private property, to trees, crops, stock
and buildings was very great. The loss of life was small, but to
many thousands the Moray Floods brought serious loss then and

[1] Mitchell, pp. 159-60
[2] Hope, 8 August 1829
[3] Dick Lauder, *The Moray Floods*, Prelimary Chapter

in the months to come, and even today the rains which fell during the night of 2-3 August 1829 are remembered as among the most grievous natural disasters suffered by the Highland counties. Only for a few did the floods bring fortune. It is recorded that while the salmon fishing on the Findhorn, perhaps owing to the muddy water brought down by the floods, was ruined for the remainder of that season, that on the nearby Nairn was correspondingly improved, while above Randolph's Leap on the Findhorn the under-gardener at Relugas with the aid of an umbrella caught a stranded salmon at a point fifty feet above the normal level of the river.[1]

The permanent repair of the damage was to occupy much of Mitchell's time for the next three years, but so hard did he and his staff work that by the end of the first week in October, and despite a second serious flood within three weeks of the first, temporary repairs had been made to keep the roads open, and Craigellachie Bridge had been saved. 'Up to that time', wrote Mitchell many years later, 'I was like a doctor during an epidemic not knowing where to turn, moving to and fro in excited anxiety.'[2] Yet, as so often, the public were impatient and hard to please. 'I must, however, say', wrote Hope in the last weeks of September to correspondents in the north-east, 'that the complaints of the public should be at the elements, and I must consider that as usual such complaints as have reached you as regards Craigellachie against all and sundry for supineness and neglect in not making a more speedy and efficient repair originate in thoughtlessness. To meet the wishes of all is impossible. . . . If the Commissioners cast bridges as fast as the Mint cast sovereigns there would have been a demand for them all in the expectations of your northern friends.'[3]

The full reckoning for the Lammas Floods of 1829 was a heavy one. By the autumn of 1831 the cost to the Commissioners had already reached over £5,000, and with new bridges over the Dee at Ballater and the upper Findhorn at Fairness the total was soon to rise to over £10,000, a large sum in those days. On Mitchell had fallen a great burden of added labour, and the sum of £20 which was paid to both him and May, his assistant, was little more than a token. Hope deprecated the idea of financial reward,

---

[1] Dick Lauder, op. cit., ch. VII   [2] Mitchell, p. 160
[3] Hope, 12 and 23 September 1829

knowing that as a loyal servant of the Commissioners Mitchell did not look for it. Yet, as Hope wrote to Samuel Smith, now secretary to the Commission, 'Between the Public and their servant there exists no reciprocity or feeling of individual gratitude and the Commissioners have therefore no other way of rendering effectual their sense of his exertions.'

If the Commissioners' servants expected little, others were less reticent. For several years past, the burden of the cost of road repairs falling on county funds had been lightened by tolls collected at toll-bars erected on the roads of the northern counties. To ease the problem of collection, many of these toll-bars were let by auction to tenants who paid rent to the Commissioners, making what profit they could on the tolls collected. Some tenants on the less-frequented roads, considered the collection scarcely worth their labour, finding their profit rather in the sale of home-made whisky or in road-contracting. Southey reported that on the new Lovat Bridge over the Beauly, though the Inverness-shire County Council had the right of levying tolls they did not think it worth their while to erect a toll-house, while at Helmsdale the tenant of the toll-bar paid his rent and made his living from sales of liquor alone; but for others the tolls represented a real source of income. In Morayshire and on the roads immediately around Inverness the interruption of traffic caused by the fall of so many bridges in the floods of 1829 meant real loss. Toll-bar tenants over a wide area were not slow in seeking a reduction of rents, and to Mitchell's burdens was added the problem of distinguishing the real sufferers from those who only sought to profit from the misfortunes of their neighbours.

Plate 12 Highland Drovers

Plate 13   Loch Leven from Ballachulish Ferry

11

LIFE ON THE ROADS

WHEN in the autumn of 1822 the efforts of Thomas Telford and his colleagues had brought almost to completion the work on roads and Canal, nearly fifty years had passed since that September day of 1773 when James Boswell and Samuel Johnson had crossed to Skye on the first stage of their journey to the Western Isles. These fifty years had witnessed in the Highlands changes far exceeding in speed and in magnitude any which had gone before, and now, while troubled times still lay ahead, life and movement had come to the glens to a degree undreamed of by the London travellers as they rested tired, ill humoured and ill fed in the inn of Glenelg. In the half century which had passed, increasing interest in and concern for the Scottish Highlands had brought north in ever-growing numbers travellers on many errands from the south. New methods of agriculture spreading from the Scottish Lowlands had brought farmers, some to study and some to exploit, the fertility of Highland glens and hills. Growing interest in coastal fishing had brought enthusiasts and advocates to urge its claims and its possibilities, while the poet, the journalist and the ordinary citizen had come to visit, to study and to admire an area hitherto virtually unknown.

The new age which was dawning for the Highlands was the golden age of the social economist and the statistician, and before the 18th century had ended, the printing presses of the south were already working overtime to remedy long neglect and profound ignorance of Scottish affairs. Sir John Sinclair, enlisting the aid of the parish clergy, had gathered from every quarter of Scotland and had made available in the Statistical Account, a wealth of detail and information hitherto unequalled for any part of Britain, while from nearly every Scottish county were coming surveys of contemporary agriculture and plans for its improvement. It was an age too of the letter-writer, the diarist and the journalist, and few who then came north to the Highlands on journeys of substantial extent or serious purpose failed to record for the benefit of their friends or for a wider public, their impressions, their opinions or the incidents of the road.

When Wade built the first Highland roads, little thought had been given to their use by civilian traffic, and the records of the military road-makers who succeeded him contain few references to provision for the ordinary traveller. As time passed and the needs of the army receded, a small number of inns were here and there established, but these were few in number and even the attraction of a Government subsidy was hardly sufficient to tempt men into the inn-keeper's trade on roads where few passed but drovers and their cattle. The cattle indeed seem to have had the best of it. For them, as the drovers well knew, nightly resting places, food and water at carefully spaced intervals must be provided on their southward journeys. Men and women on the roads, it seemed, must do without or at best must be content with wayside houses not worthy to be called inns, where the accommodation was of the roughest and the fare often little more than porridge, oatmeal bannocks and illicit whisky. Even here, it is pleasing to read that in the latter part of the 18th century and indeed for many years to come, accommodation for horses received at least as much attention as that provided for their riders. The primitive state of the contemporary Highland inn is hardly to be wondered at, when it is considered that even in Edinburgh almost the sole redeeming feature of the best inns was the cheapness of the food and drink.

The inn at Glenelg on that September evening of 1773 had little to offer, and from Boswell's account of the standard of food and accommodation it is small wonder that he thought wistfully of the rude comforts of the nearby barracks at Bernera. Twelve years later John Knox undertook a six months' tour through the northern and western Highlands in the course of which he travelled nearly three thousand miles. His time and trouble were well rewarded, for in the course of his journey he is reported to have collected contributions not far short of five thousand pounds for the newly planned British Fisheries Society, the successful launching of which was largely due to his efforts. The success of his tour did not blind him to the lack of amenities for the traveller in the shape of roads and inns, and almost the only inn for which he had a good word was that at Dalmally for which, he reports, the inn-keeper paid an annual rent of six pounds.[1] Close on his

[1] Knox, *A Tour through the Highlands of Scotland*, p. 15

footsteps came Thomas Newte who found only one public house, 'of the worst kind', in Oban, while Kingshouse on the Moor of Rannoch had 'not a bed in it for a decent person to sleep in, nor any provisions but what are absolutely necessary for the family'.[1]

With the opening of the 19th century came Dorothy and William Wordsworth and their friend Coleridge. Their journey up Loch Lomond, by Loch Fyne and Loch Awe, Appin and Glencoe and back over the Black Mount was no trip for a sick man, and Coleridge was ailing.[2] Yet Dorothy, to judge from her journal, enjoyed the tour even when, as at Luss, the ill-humoured wife of the inn-keeper grudged them a fire. The inn at Taynuilt welcomed them not only with a good fire, but with a breakfast of eggs, preserved gooseberries, cream, cheese and butter which made up for the hard oatcakes which Dorothy could not eat. Supper was even better, for they had fresh salmon from the Awe and a fowl and were charged only seven and sixpence a head for supper, two breakfasts, drinks, bed and stabling; but Kingshouse Inn still lay ahead, and Kingshouse ran true to form. It was, wrote Dorothy, 'as dirty as a house after a sale on a rainy day, and the rooms being large and the walls naked they looked as if more than half the goods had been sold out'. Eggs, milk, potatoes and bread were not to be had and only 'a shoulder of mutton so hard that it was impossible to chew the little flesh that might be scraped off the bones and some sorry soup made of barley and water (for it had no other taste)'. A fire of wet peats did little to remedy the state of the damp sheets, while out in the stables where there were no stalls or bedding, William had to keep guard over his horse as it ate its corn lest it should be robbed of its meal by others 'standing like wild beasts to devour each other's portion.' Kingshouse Inn indeed held few attractions in that autumn of 1803, but the servant girl who complained to Dorothy that her employers were always changing little knew how strangely inverted would sound her grievance to 20th century ears.[3]

As the Wordsworths struggled over the Black Mount and faced the rigours of Kingshouse and Inveroran, in London and in Edinburgh plans for the new roads were fast taking shape, and before many years had passed, a traveller through the Highlands

[1] Newte, *Prospects and Observations on a Tour in England and Scotland*, 1791, p. 120
[2] Coleridge left the party at Arrochar on 29 August. Wordsmith, *A Tour in Scotland*, 1803, p. 289
[3] Wordsworth, *A Tour in Scotland* 1803, vol. I, pp. 334, 336

had a very different tale to tell. In the autumn of 1818 when the construction of the new parliamentary roads was all but complete, William Larkin left Perth on a journey which took him by Blairgowrie up Glenshee to Kirkmichael. Then crossing into Strathtay he went by Aberfeldy and Loch Tay to Tyndrum and over the Black Mount to Ballachulish and Fort William. Here he took the new road by Loch Laggan over which Telford, Rickman and Hope had laboured so hard, and came by Dalwhinnie and Blair Atholl to Dunkeld. His Journal shows the great changes which had taken place in the previous fifteen years. Many of the poor whisky houses, which had alone served travellers on the old military roads, had now been turned into good inns even if still lacking in what one traveller described as 'Metropolitan elegance', while the smaller wayside houses at least offered food, and stabling for horses. Larkin found a good inn at Tyndrum, but of Kingshouse the best he could say was that 'after a long stage of 19 miles those who take this road can hardly dispense with stopping here'. The growing tourist traffic in that autumn of 1818 must have taxed to its limits the capacity of the inns, for Larkin summarises the accommodation available throughout as being 'comfortable enough to satisfy those who possess a power of reflection and a fund of good temper sufficient to enable them to bear without repining or murmuring the inconveniences of a journey which are sometimes unavoidable particularly on the most frequented Highland routes where the inns are liable to be often crowded at certain seasons of the year'. Good temper and power of reflection had, it seemed, been especially called for at Dalwhinnie where the grouse-shooting season coincided with the arrival of crowds of drovers with their cattle on their way to Falkirk Tryst.[1]

The early autumn was fast coming to be recognised as the fashionable season for Highland travel, and in September 1819 came Robert Southey. Southey came to Scotland as the friend of John Rickman, and with Rickman himself, Mrs Rickman and Telford in the party it may be that the way was to some extent smoothed by the importance and authority of the travellers; but for all that, Southey's account of the trip leaves small room for

[1] Larkin, *A Tour in the Highlands of Scotland*, 1818, p. 326. Larkin records that in the autumn of 1818 Captain Barclay shot forty brace of grouse in one day near Dalwhinnie

doubt that their entertainment throughout at the inns they visited was little different from that available for every traveller; and almost everywhere it was simple, unpretentious but good. The road by Achnasheen to Strome Ferry had not been long completed, but even here good mutton chops, excellent potatoes, herrings, barley cakes with soft curds, cream and butter were on the menu, with tea and good smuggled whisky for drink. The few weeks of Highland travel seems to have brought about a rapid education in Southey's taste for unaccustomed dishes, for in Strathcarron he found sheep's head surprisingly good because of the skin and the flavour of singeing. Even the inn at Kingshouse for once earned modified praise, with lamb, hen's and turkey's eggs on the table, and cream with the tea.[1]

If tea, brandy and claret were coming to be numbered among the list of drinks at Scottish inns, the composition of the bill of fare was still largely dictated by local resources, and in many Highland districts the limits of variation were narrow; but sea, loch or river were at the door. Plenty was no bad substitute for variety, and who today, blessed with good appetite and sound digestion, would grumble at the breakfast menu offered to Joseph Mitchell a few years later at Sconser on the road to Portree? 'The breakfast table of the inn', he wrote, 'groaned with viands— salmon, cod, mackerel, fowls, beef and potatoes etc. At respectful intervals sundry stoups of whisky bitters with half-filled glasses standing beside them.'[2]

Contemporary judgments of the quality of Highland inns in the first quarter of the 19th century varied like—and perhaps with—the weather. If the sun shone for Southey in that autumn of 1819 others were less fortunate. Between 1811 and 1821 Doctor John Macculloch made a series of long journeys through the Highlands and Islands, recording his impressions and experiences in four volumes of letters addressed to Sir Walter Scott. One of his journeys took him to Strontian on Loch Sunart where he was unfortunate enough to arrive on a wet day when the old inn was in course of reconstruction. 'It was much the same', he remarks, 'out or in, for it had only half a roof being in fact a barn ... open to the sky. As the rain and wind came with a slant the walls did some good.' The Doctor's damp bed induced a critical mood. As Burt observed a century ago, 'in these Highland inns, whether you sleep under the sky, or a black roof, or a dimity tester, whether you have anything to eat or nothing, attendance or none, you must pay as much for the want of everything as you do for the enjoyment of everything at Ferrybridge or Barnbymoor.' [1] If the weather explains much of his ill-humour at Strontian the same cannot be said of his visit to Taynuilt where the morning was fine and the Doctor was all impatience to climb Ben Cruachan, an expedition which was nearly spoilt by a long wait for a poor breakfast. So the inn at Taynuilt goes down in his Journal as 'a vile pot-house', a description in which it is hard to recognise the establishment where Coleridge and the Wordsworths had enjoyed such good entertainment a few years earlier. [2]

Though traffic on the Highland roads was steadily on the increase, it was still very far from the point where inn-keeping could be regarded as more than a part-time employment, and most inn-keepers had some subsidiary source of income. Some were farmers on at least a modest scale. 'No inn-keeper', wrote Hope to Rickman in the spring of 1814, 'can exist without some farm at least.' [3] Some, like the Irishman who kept the inn at Beauly at the time of Southey's tour, 'speculated in road-making', while many supplemented their income by some form of smuggling. One of the most profitable forms of smuggling was in salt. The duty on salt was high, but this was remitted if the salt were used for salting fish for export. Much of the salt imported under this concession not unnaturally got diverted from its rightful purpose, and so a busy and profitable trade sprang up. When Southey went downstairs to breakfast in the inn at Fort Augustus on a September morning of 1819, he found within the doors of the inn six sacks of contraband salt which had been seized during the night, and Garrow, the Road Inspector for Argyll, told him of a former road employee who had abandoned road work for dealing in salt where he could make over 200 per cent on one deal. Kingshouse appears to have been a centre of the salt smuggling traffic. The inn-keeper, who had taken over Kingshouse Inn in 1809 with a capital of only £70, had in the course of ten years made enough to take a large farm and lay out £1,500 in stocking it. [4] Of his constancy at least the servant girl of 1803 could

[1] Macculloch, *The Highlands and Western Isles of Scotland*, vol. 2, pp. 182-3
[2] ibid, vol. 1, p. 268   [3] Hope, 2 March 1814   [4] Southey, p. 234

have had no complaints—if she herself had stayed the course!

If salt was a lucrative side-line with some, others found it more profitable to deal in home-made whisky, the illicit distilling of which in the first quarter of last century, despite and perhaps partly by reason of the Government policy of encouraging small licensed distilleries, was described as almost universal throughout the Highlands and Islands. 'Whisky', wrote William Larkin in 1818, 'is to the full as much a staple commodity as black cattle, sheep and wool . . . and the smuggling of whisky is the only resource for the regular payment of their rents. The heavy duties on home-made spirits having debased the quality while it has raised the price, the superiority of the smuggled article is so palpable that the demand for it is universal. . . .' The demand for home-brewed whisky made the temptation to manufacture it in the Highland glens almost irresistible. 'Some', wrote Larkin, 'carry it on in the valley and when anyone of those engaged in it observes the approach of the Excise Officers a concerted signal is hoisted and every illicit article is immediately concealed. Others, for greater security, retire to the hills, remote woods and recesses of the mountains.'[1] In Highland inns home-brewed whisky was the universal drink, accepted and enjoyed by all. Joseph Mitchell reported that in his boyhood in Inverness some of the shops even went so far as to erect signs to show that they dealt in home-brewed whisky, and Southey found that the yeast regularly used for baking bread in the town came from smugglers' stills in the Black Isle.[2] In his *Reminiscences* Mitchell has described how in the course of one of his many road inspections he met, in Glenmoriston, a band of smugglers with a string of twenty-five horses each loaded with two kegs of whisky, a meeting which caused some mutual embarrassment until Mitchell's identity and purpose in the glen had been satisfactorily established.[3] So widespread and so profitable was the trade, that more than one contemporary writer considered that the making of the Parliamentary roads had checked emigration by the unintended method of facilitating the import of barley from the Lowlands and the subsequent disposal of the home-brewed spirit.

To the hazards of a Highland journey in the early years of the 19th century the state of the ferries made no small contribution.

[1] Larkin, *Tour in the Highlands*, p. 116
[2] Southey, p. 141   [3] Mitchell, II, pp. 61-2

Construction of piers had been no part of the original plan when the Commissioners started their work, but on many roads ferries were an essential link, and soon their improvement came to be accepted as a necessary item in the cost of road construction. New piers at the Corran Ferry across Loch Linnhe were early added to the troublesome contract for the road through Moidart, and Telford and his inspectors were soon involved in supervising similar work at Kyle-Rhea, at Strome and at Kyleakin; but even in this, beasts rather than humans were the chief consideration, and in nearly every case the new work was designed more for the shipping of cattle than for the transport of vehicles.

Until Telford built his bridge at Bonar, the Meikle Ferry of 1½ miles across the Dornoch Firth had been a very real hazard on the drove road from the north. Joseph Mitchell has left on record a vivid description of the perils of the Meikle Ferry as it existed in his father's days. For three generations the ferry had been worked by a family of the name of Patience, whose mode of operation seems to have been singularly at variance with their name. The equipment of the ferry boat, according to Mitchell's description, left much to be desired. Broken ropes, torn sails and defective rudders appear to have been common occurrences, misfortunes less easily surmounted on the occasions when the thole pins had been left behind. In John Mitchell's day there was no landing place on either side, while shallow water on the north side of the Firth meant that heavily-laden boats must lie offshore until the tide was well in. Sometimes in crossing to the north side Mitchell had known the boat to be driven three or four miles up the Firth waiting for the tide. One of the worst accidents in the history of the Meikle Ferry took place in 1809, and only by the narrowest of margins did John Mitchell escape from being among the victims. Delayed in his journey from the south he reached the Ferry to find to his annoyance that the boat had just left. The day was stormy, the boat heavily laden, and as he watched, it was caught by the wind and overturned with the loss of over 100 lives. Had anything been needed to impress on John Mitchell the necessity and the urgency of the work of the Commissioners this must surely have supplied it. Southey reported in 1819 that the Sutherland man who praised so highly Telford's bridge, and whose father had been one of the victims of the accident, had been so shaken by what then took place that for ten years he had preferred being cut off from the south side of the Firth to setting foot in a ferry boat.[1] Perhaps Southey had the Meikle Ferry and its perils in mind when later in his journey he wrote of the Kessock Ferry over the Cromarty Firth, which he had been assured was the best in Scotland, 'but the best ferry is a bad thing'.[2]

As the spreading roads brought new life to the glens so did variety of class, of substance, of interest and of occupation show itself among those who used them or who thronged the homely but laden tables of the inns. Work on the new roads brought to the Highlands engineers, inspectors and surveyors and all the miscellany of adventurers, earnest, optimistic or purely speculative tempted by Hope's advertisements. The seasonal movements of labour so trying to the tempers of road contractors and Canal-builders alike meant a constant traffic of men seeking work, or others returning to their crofts and their fishing. With the new roads, too, came dealers and commercial travellers from the south. As late as 1824, wrote Mitchell, though the roads were all but complete, commercial travellers still rode on horseback. 'Portly old gentlemen with rubicund faces who wore top hats, blue coats with brass buttons; rode good horses, did their business in no hurry, had saddlebags behind for their cloths and samples and carried large whips'; but soon after 1824 younger men took up the work and gigs replaced the horses of the older genera-tion.[3] At the other end of the commercial scale were 'a variety of vagrants such as gypsies, ragmen, vendors of crockery, tin-smiths, egg dealers and old clothes men'. Writing in 1842 the New Statistical Account for the Parish of Strath in Skye, the parish minister estimated that by then the annual sale of eggs in the parish realised about £100, which to his sorrow was spent on tea-drinking and on the purchase of tobacco for chewing and smoking. From 1817 onwards the growing wool market at Inver-ness brought buyers and sellers to trade in the clip of the increasing flocks of Cheviot sheep in north and west, while late summer and early autumn brought heavy traffic of men and beasts bound for local fairs like the horse fairs at Contin, where dealers from the south bought hardy ponies destined for the pits of Northumber-land and Durham.[4]

But if a few of the fairs in the northern Highlands and Islands

[1] Southey, p. 129   [2] Southey, p. 167
[3] Mitchell, II, p. 75   [4] Southey, p. 147

were horse fairs these were the exception rather than the rule. From very early times one of the main products of the Highlands had been cattle. While any close estimate of numbers is impossible, it is certain that the cattle population of the glens had for centuries past been very considerable, a combination of cultivated land in the glens and large areas of hill ground for summer grazing being not unfavourable to the maintenance of large herds. For long the unsettled state of the Highlands made the transport of these beasts outside the territory of their owners virtually impossible. As with the early nomadic peoples of Europe and Asia the chief wealth of the clan for long lay in the possession and home consumption of animals, the only marketable products of which were the hides which could more readily be exported from the Highlands. By the start of the 18th century, however, the gradual emergence of more peaceful conditions had made it possible for cattle to be taken for sale to the Lowlands by long and perilous droving operations, and with the settlement of the Highlands after the Rising of 1745 this droving trade rapidly expanded. Its growth and prosperity were at this time greatly stimulated by the growth of London and of the industrial towns in the Midlands and north of England and the increase of population in central Scotland, and soon the growing needs of the navy and army still further increased the demand for Highland beef. From now on till other forms of transport and other means of marketing cut into the trade, the early autumn months saw growing numbers of cattle passing in slow-moving droves from all parts of the Highlands to the chief markets at Crieff and Falkirk and on across the Border to England. This droving traffic was hard and rough for men and beasts alike. It was highly speculative too. Money was often quickly made and as quickly lost. A few of the large dealers made fortunes, but for one who prospered there were many who failed, bringing down in their fall others inextricably involved with them in the peculiar complexities of droving finance. It was to meet the needs of this droving traffic that Telford, mindful of the effect of hard roads on the hooves of far-driven cattle, insisted on the use of plentiful gravel as road surfacing in the north, while to cut the costs and increase the profits of breeder and dealer alike he had planned the drove road over Rannoch Moor which came to naught.

From June to October each year this droving trade brought

to the inns of the north and west bustle and noise if little profit. 'The prices', wrote Mitchell, 'fluctuated like the price of money on the Stock Exchange. If there was an ample harvest, a sudden rain and a plentiful crop of grass in England, or prosperous times, prices went up; in other circumstances they declined. As there were no telegraphs the quickest drover was the person who had the best chance of buying low in the local markets and selling high at Falkirk. Hence the drovers, very sharp at bargain-making, were a rough, excitable set of men, who during the season rode night and day from market to market and many a night I have been disturbed at the inns with their noisy and riotous wrangling. There were some very respectable men among them and good judges of cattle, but as a class they were a rough set.'[1] Big dealers from the south had no lack of money in their pockets, much of it borrowed, but the smaller dealers and the working drovers had little to spend, and many an inn-keeper must have viewed with mixed feelings the advent of impecunious guests whose wordy arguments and noisy wrangles continued far into the night. If their fellow guests were farmers—and most of them were—talk of stots and heifers, turnips and dung, came in no way amiss, but for those less versed in these mysteries the evenings must indeed have dragged. Long experience of Highland roads and Highland inns had made Joseph Mitchell only too familiar with evenings so spent; but others were less fortunate. 'I am a little accustomed to such talk,' wrote Mitchell of a typical evening at an inn on the road to Wick, 'but Donaldson (an Edinburgh advocate) whose business is talking was destined to be a silent listener the whole evening.' There were times when even Mitchell had his fill. For Dorothy Wordsworth, the drovers and their dogs crowding the small inn at Inveroran on the Black Mount, on an autumn evening of 1803, had at least the virtues of novelty and picturesqueness, but for John Macculloch in Skye at a later date there were no such compensations for a lost night's rest. 'The inn at Portree', he wrote, 'is a laudable enough inn, but of what use is an inn when you cannot get into it or if, when in, it is to be in at a meeting of drovers or of Commissioners of taxes, roads or Excise.'[2]

On the gravelly roads of north and west the main traffic was still supplied by south-bound drovers, by small farm carts and by pedestrians, but south and east of Inverness and up the coast to

[1] Mitchell, I, pp. 334-5   [2] Macculloch, op. cit., vol. 3, p. 367

Wick new and faster traffic was soon on the move. At the end of the 18th century mails from the south bound for Inverness came three times a week by way of Aberdeen, but by the spring of 1811 daily coaches were running along the Moray coast to Aberdeen.[1] Two years earlier a direct coach had started running the 117 miles from Inverness to Perth, three times a week in summer and twice a week in winter, leaving Inverness at 5 a.m. and reaching Perth at 3 p.m. Years later when, thanks to the work of the Commissioners, Perthshire roads were very different from what they had been in Southey's time, Joseph Mitchell recorded his impressions of a coach journey from Edinburgh to Inverness. Perth had been reached in four and a half hours, including over half an hour at the Ferry. 'There was no lack of driving through the Vale of Athol. Down we swept one hill and the impetus brought us half up another. The quick turns were taken, sometimes within six inches of the stones placed to define the edge of the road, or the corner of a bridge; still neither these nor the bolting or kicking of some of the horses nor the darkness of the night diminished our steady pace of ten or twelve miles an hour. It was very dark till about two in the morning [9 August] and being an old traveller I dozed, well protected by great-coats, between two less prudent passengers. I like to ride outside, if well protected, on a summer night, the pure morning air being so fresh and grateful.'[2]

The road up the north-east coast to Wick and by Lairg to Tongue had caused the Commissioners no little worry. The long distances involving big and costly contracts had called for extra care and vigilance on the part of Hope and Rickman in scrutinising the offers. Here on this north-most road the variations in the offers were even wider than on the west coast and in the Islands, and for the road from Bonar Bridge to Tongue the lowest offer was £6,492 while the highest was £21,865. The final cost of these forty-eight miles of road was a little over £16,500 and even the heritors of Sutherland may well have felt some measure of relief that James Hope's prudence had ensured that the contract did not fall to the lowest bidder.

These northern roads were among the last to be finished, but by 1819 the Commissioners could report with some pride that a mail coach could leave Inverness at 6 a.m., reaching Thurso at

[1] Barron, *The Northern Highlands in the 19th Century*, I, p. 41
[2] Mitchell, I, pp. 343-4

mid-day on the following day. If the Commissioners took some justifiable pride in this development they were fully conscious of the limitations. 'It is not to be understood', they wrote in their 9th Report, 'that this Northern Mail Coach (or Diligence as it is usually called) is exactly the same thing in form or speed as those of the Southern parts of the Kingdom, but it appears to be well calculated for its purpose. It carries three inside passengers (one of them looking backwards) three outside passengers, the driver, the guard, the Mail and other luggage. The Coach itself is lighter by two or three cwts than a Southern Mail Coach and the speed required is no more than six miles per hour; but it is drawn by two horses in place of four, the horses generally, their provender always, of an inferior kind. . . . It would be unreasonable to expect that occasional snow-storms and sudden thaws, added to the general influence of a humid climate, and (more than any of these causes) the inexperience and want of accurate habits in the persons engaged in such an undertaking, should not sometimes delay the arrival of the coach beyond its stated time; but probably tacit allowance is made for such accidents, as we do not find that the Mail Coach has ever returned to Inverness so late as to retard the conveyance of its Letter-bags Southward.'

When in the autumn of 1828 Telford reported to his Commissioners on the general state of the roads, he was able to look back on the great changes which twenty-five years of work and worry had brought to the north-east. 'Previous to the commencement of the Dunrobin Road, the Bonar and Helmsdale Bridges in 1808, when I travelled into that quarter', he wrote, 'in surveying for the future Roads, it was with difficulty and not without danger that I could scramble along a rugged, broken, sandy shore or by narrow tracks on the edge of precipices frequently interrupted by rude and inconvenient ferries; and having for lodgings only miserable huts, scarcely protected from the inclemency of the weather; while the adjacent country had scarcely the marks of cultivation. Now in the year 1828 a mail-coach passes daily from Tain by Bonar Bridge, the Fleet Mound, Dunrobin, Helmsdale and the Ord of Caithness, to the extremity of the Island at Wick and Thurso without being interrupted by a single ferry. Along the coast of Sutherland there are commodious inns; at Golspie, near Dunrobin Castle, there is one equal to any to be found in England. Helmsdale has become an important fishing station where are two very decent inns, and a number of herring houses. At Brora there is an extensive new village, and the same at Bonar Bridge. Along the whole of the Road, the lands are laid out in regular farms, with proper dwellings and offices, some of them very extensive, the whole presenting a picture which must afford pleasure to every one who feels gratified in observing the prosperity of his Country.'[1]

[1] H.R. & B. 15th Report (Repair), 1829, Appendix B, pp. 8-9

12

ACHIEVEMENT IN RETROSPECT

When the inaugural voyage between Inverness and Fort William marked the official opening of the Caledonian Canal in the autumn of 1822, little more than a year had passed since the Commissioners for Highland Roads and Bridges had put their names to the Ninth Report recording the virtual completion of their constructional work. The two great projects had thus to all appearances run a close finish. Yet in reality the road and bridge-builders had won an easy victory. On the roads the work of the Commissioners in the years to come was to be little more than up-keep. On the Canal many years of effort, of mishap and of frustration still lay ahead.

In the first years of the century when Telford's Reports on the two projects were under discussion, the protagonists of each had to a great extent taken their stand on common ground. Distress and unemployment in the Highlands and the growing threat of emigration in each case weighed heavily in the balance. In that field the planners of roads and Canal could in the event claim an equal measure of success, and even the most caustic critics of the Commissions could hardly deny the work and wages which, over nearly twenty years, they had brought to the Highlands. In the constructional period each project had been called on to face steeply rising costs, but while on the roads much of the growing burden was carried by contractors, by guarantors and by local contributors, on the Canal the rising cost fell almost wholly on the shoulders of the public. Moreover, while rising cost was a common enemy to the projects there were other potent factors the impact of which was felt only in the Great Glen. Long before the Canal was finished the shadow of France had receded, coastal lights had taken much of its terrors from the Northern Passage, while above all steam was fast replacing sail. To lay on the planners of the Canal blame or responsibility for failure to see more clearly what lay ahead would be hard indeed. The spiral of inflation was unknown alike to the speech or the thought of the early 19th century. The issue of the French War had hung long in the balance, and he would indeed have been far-sighted who could have foreseen in the first rudimentary trials of a steamship on the Forth and Clyde Canal in 1803 the approaching end of the sailing ship.

The public enthusiasm which greeted the official opening of the Canal had not deceived Telford as to the true position, and despite the optimistic reports of his loyal subordinates at Clachnaharry and Corpach, doubts and forebodings grew. The huge rise in costs and growing criticism in Parliament had forced the Commissioners into opening the Canal in 1822 with a depth insufficient to take the ships engaged in the Baltic and American trade on which Telford pinned his hopes. A year later he wrote to Rickman that an increase in depth to 15 feet at a cost of £25,000 would serve the needs of this trade and make the Canal economic,[1] though there is reason to think that the Commissioners viewed the future of the Canal with more realism and less optimism.

If hope died hard it had indeed, in the years which followed the opening, little enough to keep it alive. Dues from commercial vessels using the Canal lagged far behind the annual cost of maintenance, and Telford and his colleagues were thankful to welcome the increased tourist traffic, which, if it brought little revenue to the Canal, went at least some way towards justifying its existence. Annual deficits and payments for further constructional work meant continual votes for money by Parliament, and as the cost grew so did the strength and bitterness of the criticism. Even to the sanguine Telford his great engineering achievement brought in his later years little of the satisfaction of success. Yet, if the rapid development of the steamship had upset radically the calculations of the Canal planners, it had in fact saved the Canal from total failure. 'The work', said a witness before a Parliamentary Commission a few years later, 'was considerably advanced before it was admitted that the navigation of these lochs was so precarious as to defy the certainty of safe and easy transport, and if steam navigation had not come into use the Caledonian Canal must have been a failure.'[2] Though the careful record of winds which had been kept year by year during the work in the Great Glen had shown that they presented no insuperable obstacle

---

[1] H. of L. Telford to Rickman, 24 November 1823
[2] Select Committee on Conditions in the Highlands and Islands etc. Minutes of Evidence, 1841

Plate 14 Moray Place about 1830

Plate 15   Joseph Mitchell

for sailing ships, the winds were, none the less, a factor of some importance especially for ships beating westward up Loch Ness, and by 1834 traders seeking to use the Canal were clamouring for the provision of tugs to save delays. That same autumn, floods had raised Loch Ness and Loch Lochy to the highest levels in living memory, and though serious damage to the Canal was narrowly averted, Joseph Mitchell wrote to Samuel Smith, Secretary to the Canal Commission, in a letter of some candour, 'It must, however, reluctantly be inferred that the design and construction of the Canal works adjacent to the whole of the lakes has been founded upon too brief and limited an experience of the floods to which this district of country is occasionally liable, . . . I have yet scarcely recovered from the alarm which this tremendous flood occasioned.'[1]

The damage caused by the floods of 1834 had made it clear that the Commissioners were faced with heavy expenditure even to maintain the Canal in usable condition, while each successive year made it more evident that without radical improvement it would be useless for the size and type of ship which was soon to be in common use. Telford had just died and the Government consulted James Walker, an eminent civil engineer, as to the cost of making the Canal really serviceable or even of destroying it, and Walker reported that a further expenditure of £150,000 was required to give the undertaking a fair chance of accomplishing its purpose. At that time the total expenditure had already grown to over a million pounds, and in the face of the great and growing storm of protest the Treasury hesitated to cut their losses or to throw good money after bad. Efforts to lease the Canal for a long period, even rent free, proved unavailing and it was only the occurrence of further serious damage on the western section of the Canal that forced the Government into decisive action.

For three years the Canal remained closed while extensive repairs were carried out and the depth increased to 17 feet at a cost of £700,000. But even this did not bring an end to the misfortunes in the Great Glen. Great floods in the early spring of 1849 raised the Spey to a level 18 to 24 inches higher than it had been even during the Moray Floods twenty years earlier.[2] Widespread damage was done to roads and bridges throughout the

<hr>

[1] H. of L. Mitchell to Smith, 24 November 1834
[2] H. of L. Mitchell to Smith, 7 February 1849

Highlands. The bridge over the River Oich was completely swept away and the Road Inspector at Fort William reported that three breaches had been made in the Canal embankment and that the River Oich was running in the bed of the Canal. For many years the Canal remained a frequent subject for acrimonious debate in the House of Commons, where in 1860 the Member for Lambeth said of it that it had been the subject of no less than seventeen Acts of Parliament and that he regarded the whole proceedings connected with its construction and repair as the grossest job that had in his time been perpetrated. It is outside the scope of this book to trace the later history of the Caledonian Canal. If its failure as a commercial enterprise must in all fairness be acknowledged, so must the grandeur of its conception and the unique quality of its original construction, and it remains today a living monument to the genius of a great engineer.

With the completion of the road which leads from Sligachan by Loch Bracadale to Dunvegan in Skye and the rebuilding of the bridge over the River Moriston which had been destroyed in the winter floods of 1817, the constructional work of the Commissioners for Highland Roads and Bridges came to an end. Plans for further road building in the Islands and in the far north-west were abandoned after the death of Lord Colchester, and though the Commission was to remain in existence for nearly forty years more, its future work was to be solely on the upkeep of roads and bridges which had been built. So it was that when in the early weeks of 1821 John Rickman started on the all too familiar task of drafting the Report of the Commissioners, the Ninth Report to which he then set himself was the last chapter in the story of the making of what came to be known as the Parliamentary Roads in the Highlands.[1] The roads to Kinlochmoidart and Arisaig which had caused so much trouble in the early days and the fishermen's roads in Cowal had long been completed. In Glengarry where Readdie had failed, the road to Loch Hourn had been finished and had been linked by way of Loch Loyne with the Glenmoriston road which now led down Glenshiel and through Kintail to Kyle of Lochalsh with a branch over the Mam-Rattachan Hill to the Kyle-Rhea Ferry to Skye where over 100 miles of island roads had been built. The building of the Laggan Road from Spean Bridge

---

[1] Many further Reports were issued by the Commissioners, but these were almost entirely confined to road repair

to the Upper Spey had at last been brought to costly but successful completion, while with the building of the new road on the north side of Loch Ness the communication between Inverness and Fort William was complete. Up the River Beauly and through Strathglass stretched twenty-three miles of new road, while through the centre of Ross-shire Dingwall was now linked with Kyle of Lochalsh by way of Achnasheen and Strome Ferry, with a branch northward to Kishorn. A traveller from Dingwall could now travel to Thurso on a continuous stretch of nearly 120 miles of new road made by the Commissioners or, turning northward at Bonar Bridge, could reach Tongue on the north coast by way of Lairg and Altnaharra.

Even before the work on the roads had been completed, the work of the Commissioners had gone far to meet Telford's criticism in 1803 that one of the chief weaknesses of Highland communications lay in the absence of bridges over the large rivers. The great bridge over the Tay at Dunkeld had long been complete, while the middle reaches of the Spey were now spanned by Telford's iron bridge at Craigellachie. To the north of the Great Glen the Orrin remained unbridged, but Lovat Bridge over the Beauly,[1] and the bridge over the Conon had been completed with others at Helmsdale and Wick, while further south the Dee had been bridged at Ballater and Potarch, the Don at Alford and the Findhorn at Fairness.[2]

These were among the fruits of eighteen years of hard, perplexing and unremitting labour on which Rickman could look back as he wrote his Ninth Report. A total of 920 miles of road had been constructed at an average cost of between £400 and £450 per mile, while a total of 1,117 bridges great and small had been built. Over £500,000 had been spent, £267,000 being contributed by the Government and the balance by the Highland counties and individual contributors. While the work on roads and bridges was in progress much work had also been undertaken on the improvement of Highland harbours and ferry piers under the supervision of the Commissioners. The total sum spent on this work has been estimated at £110,000, nearly half being contributed by the Commissioners from funds arising from the handing back of certain of the estates forfeited after the Rising of 1745.

[1] Bonar Bridge over the Dornoch Firth
[2] Many of these bridges remain in use today

With the completion of the constructional work and the termination of the fifty per cent grants by the Government, the work of the Commissioners was concentrated on the maintenance of roads in the Highland counties, with such small improvements as were from time to time required to keep them in serviceable condition, the annual grant by the Treasury being restricted to £5,000. Much of this money was required to meet the cost of administration and inspection leaving a large part of the expense of repair work to be met by annual local assessments. Landowners in the Highlands who had shared willingly in the cost of making new roads so manifestly to their advantage, bore with less enthusiasm the burden imposed by the more prosaic task of annual upkeep. The fall in agricultural prices after the end of the French Wars did nothing to lighten the load, while from owners of land on the west coast and in the Islands was heard the complaint that their annual contributions were determined by assessments fixed when kelp prices were at their height. County contributions, particularly in the west, were constantly in arrear and Joseph Mitchell was hard put to it to keep income and expenditure in balance.

If those in the Highland counties were finding increasingly irksome their yearly assessment, Parliament too came as the years passed to look less kindly on the annual contribution. In 1833 the annual grant of £5,000 had been extended for thirty-one years as a charge on the Consolidated Fund, but in 1854 it was transferred to the annual estimates, and from then on it came each year to be viewed with increasing disfavour. Memories of the days when Highland distress and emigration were urgent problems had grown dim. The Highland counties now enjoyed a prosperity undreamed of in the first years of the century. If the days of the fabulous kelp sales had gone, Highland proprietors were now reaping rich harvests from sporting rents, and with the rapid development of railways after the middle of the century the roads of the Highlands were coming to appear to the eyes of the public a local rather than a national concern.

In 1862 the annual grant was terminated by an adverse vote in the House of Commons and with the subsequent transfer of the roads to the Commissioners of Supply in the Highland Counties[1] the Commission for Highland Roads and Bridges came to an end. 'In resigning the trust', wrote the Commissioners in their final

[1] 25 and 26 Victoria, c.105

Report, 'which the Commissioners have had the honour of executing for a period of sixty years, they cannot but look back with satisfaction upon the result of their labours. They have watched with the deepest interest the improvement of the Country which it was the beneficial design of Parliament to civilise and enrich. They found it barren and uncultivated, inhabited by heritors without capital or enterprise and by a poor and ill-employed peasantry and destitute of trade, shipping and manufactures. They leave it with wealthy proprietors, a profitable agriculture, a thriving population and active industry. The value of the land has been incalculably increased and the condition of every class of the people improved. Nor have the contributions of the State in aid of local expenditure been without ample return in other forms. The Highlands, whence a scanty revenue was formerly drawn, now furnish their fair proportion of taxes to the National Exchequer. At the same time the improved agriculture of the Highlands, maintained by a scanty population, has served to meet the ever-increasing wants of the populous South and has contribut d largely to the general prosperity of the Country. By such results as these has the wise foresight of the Legislature been confirmed and its liberality rendered fruitful.'[1]

In the two decades which had seen the virtual completion of the main constructional work on roads, bridges and Canal, Fate had dealt kindly with those who carried the main burden. Telford, Rickman and Hope had all lived to see their work—on the roads at least—brought to a conclusion. But long before the Commissioners finally laid down their trust all but one of the great figures had gone. Lord Colchester, Chairman for the first fourteen years and always a stout champion of Highland road development, had died in the same year which saw the great floods in the north-east, and the previous winter had seen the passing of that formidable opponent of the Commissioners whom Rickman described as 'our arch-enemy Glengarry'. Telford had lived to see his roads and bridges complete and his dream of bringing life and movement to the Highland Glens triumphantly realised. On this he could look back with unmixed satisfaction, and if his later years were saddened by growing doubts as to the future of the Caledonian Canal he did not live to see those doubts confirmed. With the completion of the work on the

---

[1] H.R. & B. Final Report, 26 March 1863

roads his visits to Scotland had become less frequent, but the affairs of the Canal, the Don Bridge at Aberdeen, the Broomielaw Bridge in Glasgow and the Dean Bridge in Edinburgh still brought him north till 1830 and possibly till 1831. His last years were spent in preparing a detailed description of the very many engineering works to which his life had been devoted. When in August 1834 his remains were laid beneath the nave of Westminster Abbey he took his place among those whose service to their country will long be remembered. 'His noblest monuments', as his statue near the north door of the Abbey records, 'are to be found amongst the great public works of this Country.'

On John Rickman the burden of work for the Commissioners had weighed sorely. The Secretary was not one of those who take their troubles lightly. Year by year his letters to Telford and to Hope bore witness to the growing strain of holding in his hands the threads of countless undertakings, of keeping constant watch on finance and finally of marshalling in orderly form the records of work accomplished for inclusion in the Reports to Parliament which were his special pride but his yearly care. His work as Secretary to the Commissions, heavy as it was, was only part of the burden he carried. As Second Clerk Assistant to the House of Commons his day was already full enough. From 1820 he carried the full reponsibility of First Clerk Assistant at the Table of the House besides the burden of Census Returns in 1821 and 1831. With the completion of the road and bridge-building his correspondence grew lighter, his reports on repair work less detailed, but there was still no lack of worries and problems though his salary as Secretary had by 1827 been progressively reduced from £700 at its peak to £400. Delays and disappointments in the Great Glen lay heavy on him as on Telford, and with the outcome of Glengarry's claim still uncertain the Canal had become for him almost a nightmare. He had long hoped for release from the burden of his work for the Commissioners but had struggled on from year to year. In 1828 he reached the end of his tether and in the summer of that year wrote to the Chairman, 'I have been too much pressed this Season with an unbecoming degree of hurry (amounting often indeed to confusion) to continue in their [the Commissioners'] service.'[1] Hope in Edinburgh received with consternation the news of the coming loss of his stoutest ally,

[1] H. of L. Rickman to The Speaker, 18 June 1828

a loss which he described in a private letter to Rickman as 'the Department losing the engine which keeps it in work'.[1]

If his retiral as Secretary to the Commissioners brought Rickman some relief, the burden of his Parliamentary work continued and grew, and on his shoulders as the years passed fell another wearisome load. With Telford's death in 1834 had fallen to Southey and Rickman, as executors of Telford's Will, the task of preparing for publication the Autobiography to which Telford had devoted much of his time since 1830. This work, which in the circumstances might have been expected to have been one of great interest, proved, so far as concerned Telford's work on roads and bridges in the Highlands, to be little more than a summary of the material contained in Rickman's Ninth Report, but added to it were many detailed plates of engineering works. These were costly and difficult to reproduce, a difficulty greatly increased by the death of the engraver in the year following the death of Telford himself. The work of editing was slow and laborious. In 1837 and 1838 Rickman and Southey were in constant communication and, as was his nature, the late Secretary to the Commissioners made no light work of the problems. After the death of the engraver of the plates the work had been entrusted to a journeyman in the craft who proved unreliable, and Rickman found little time for editorship save when Parliament was in vacation. Technical terms used by Telford presented a further difficulty and Rickman found proof-reading far from easy, 'Mr Telford not being good at that kind of engineering'.[2] It soon became apparent that the financial prospects for the book were far from bright. 'We legatees must consent to lose by the publication of every copy sold', wrote Rickman to Southey in the spring of 1838, 'but as Telford himself expected this result and I cared little about it his Executors and Legatees must not quite flout his liberal intention, and as the book will go off the better at moderate prices perhaps the loss may be imaginary.'[3] By the summer of that year the outlook had grown no better. 'We lose', wrote Rickman, 'about £1,200 expended by Telford before his death on the plates and more if the books do not sell.'[4] By now Rickman's eyesight was failing and a threatened operation for cataract had been postponed to allow him to finish work on the book.

[1] Hope, 19 July 1828   [2] Rickman to Southey, 19 February 1838
[3] Rickman to Southey, 19 March 1838   [4] Rickman to Southey, 26 July 1838

John Rickman lived to see the publication of the Autobiography. If it brought little profit to Telford's legatees and could claim small literary merit it was to be at least a detailed and factual record of the work of the great engineer. Its completion and publication in the face of so many difficulties was a labour of love and a tribute by the man who was so soon to lie in the Church of St Margaret Westminster, within a stone's throw of the monument to his more eminent friend within the Abbey. John Rickman died in August 1840. Until the day of his death he remained First Clerk Assistant to the House of Commons, and on 3 February 1841 the House resolved 'that this House entertains a just and high sense of the distinguished and exemplary manner in which John Rickman, Esquire, late Clerk Assistant to this House uniformly discharged the duties of his situation during his long attendance at the Table of this House'. Today in the room in St Stephen's occupied by the present holder of the office which Rickman once held, hangs an engraving of his portrait by Samuel Lane. Rickman's left arm rests on a sheaf of papers, perhaps a Report for the Commissioners; his right hand holds the pen with which he laboured so hard; the clock behind him measures out the many hours he spent in service to the House of Commons, to the public and to the Highlands of Scotland, and below the portrait is the simple epitaph which none can grudge him, 'An honest man'.

The passing years had brought great changes in the life of James Hope and in the city in which he lived. As the 18th century drew to a close Edinburgh was entering on that period of her history which during the next thirty years was to bring her name and her fame to its highest point. In medicine and surgery her professors and teachers had already acquired an international reputation and to her Medical School came students from far and wide. In the art of the painter she could look with equal pleasure and pride on the work of Allan Ramsay, David Wilkie, Colvin Smith and Andrew Geddes, while already Sir Henry Raeburn was depicting for the delight of future generations the features, rugged or fair, of the men and women among whom he moved. In architecture the two brothers Adam were at work introducing into the houses of the New Town and far beyond the limits of Edinburgh and of Scotland those details of design and decoration which still delight the eye. For the legal profession, too, the turn of the century was a notable time, and in the List of Bench and

Bar were to be found the names of men prominent both in law and letters. While chief among them all moved the yet unknown author of the Waverley Novels there were others whose names were to be remembered. Literature and litigation went almost hand in hand in an age when each was in its glory. To the Parliament House behind St Giles' Church came litigants and men of letters, and the Hall where less than a century earlier had assembled the last Parliament of Scotland was now the meeting place of men like Scott, Lockhart, Jeffrey, Cockburn and Brougham, men whose varied interests reflected many sides of the cultural life of Scotland.

The city itself was changing fast. When Hope had made in 1803 the arrangements with the Bank of Scotland which were to ease so greatly the path of the Commissioners, the Bank still occupied the premises in the Lawnmarket where it had been since 1700, but two years later it moved to its new building near the top of the Mound. From then on, Hope in the long coat and tall hat, white cravat and tight fitting trousers of the new fashion would be a familiar figure as he made his way up the Mound to confer with the staff of the Bank or with the advocates and court officials in the Parliament House beyond. Here great building changes had taken place. Gone were the narrow passage that led from the High Street to Parliament House, the goldsmiths' and jewellers' shops which clung like barnacles to the south side of St Giles' Church; but gone also was the pleasing façade of Parliament House with its Gothic windows, its turrets and battlements. In their place was a cold classical building with colonnades along the west and south sides. Already to the west of the Square the old houses in Forrester's and Liberton's Wynds were being demolished to make room for the buildings which were soon to house the Advocates' Library and the Library of the Writers to the Signet, to which, year by year, Hope added the latest record of the work to which he gave so much.

To the north of the Old Town and linked to it by the north Bridge and the Mound, well-built houses and broad streets were taking the place of the narrow wynds and crowded tenements of the High Street, the Canongate and the Grassmarket, and to them the more prosperous citizens were fast moving, attracted by the space and convenience of the new buildings, and not least by the boon of piped water within them. By 1814 the building of the

New Town had reached Queen Street, but the northward trend continued and already the builders were at work in Heriot Row and Abercromby Place. In 1803 when James Hope began his work for the Commissioners, his house and office had been in that section of Princes Street which lies between Hanover Street and South St David Street, and so within a stone's throw of the Turf Coffee House where Telford lodged on his way to the Highlands; but soon the growing stream of Hope's letters bore his new address at the west end of Queen Street. Here for over fourteen years he lived and worked during the period when the work of the Commissioners was at its height, but on 1 January 1825 came Hope's first letter to Rickman from his new address in Moray Place. 'I have changed my quarters,' he wrote, 'driven from my former by want of room, approach of buildings, shops etc. I am now 500 yards to the north-west of my former house; a new place formed in the fields to which we used to look with admiration, but now studded with houses. We are on the top of a bank above a ravine—which must exclude building for five or six hundred yards at least in rear.[1] I have got all my papers moved and most of my books. The old H.R. & B. which occupied a considerable portion of my space I intend to deposit in boxes with due package and labels—probably never to be again opened—but still accessible.'[2]

From his desk in the Moray Place house, Hope could look over the Dean Valley and up to the village of Dean watching the progress of work on the Dean Bridge which was to be almost the last of Telford's works in Scotland. By now the volume of Hope's correspondence over the making of Highland Roads and Bridges had dwindled, but maintenance and repairs still brought their problems, and the continuing succession of his letter-books bore witness to his industry and to the labours of his copy-clerks. Like Joseph Mitchell he was still a prey to the vagaries of Highland weather, and seldom a year passed without reports of floods and

[1] Lord Cockburn writing of this period so described the land which was to become Moray Place: 'It was then an open field of as green turf as Scotland could boast of, with a few respectable trees on the flat, and thickly wooded on the bank along the Water of Leith. . . . How glorious the prospect on a summer evening from Queen Street! . . . How can I forget the glory of that scene! on the still nights on which, with Rutherford and Richardson and Jeffrey, I have stood in Queen Street or the opening at the North-West corner of Charlotte Square, and listened to the ceaseless rural corn-craiks, nestling happily in the dewy grass.' Cockburn, *Memorials of His Time*

[2] H. of L. Hope to Rickman, 1 July 1825

damage to roads and bridges. 'The Spey appears to be determined not to let you rest', he wrote to the Chief Inspector only two years before the great disaster of 1829.[1]

With the passing of the years the hard conditions of their employment was taking its toll of the old inspectors. Some had died in harness, while failing health had forced others into retirement. Despite the Superannuation Fund which Rickman had started long ago, provision for them and their dependants was small enough, and the Commissioners with the Treasury at their back could do little to supplement it. Hope and Rickman did what they could, and Mitchell too lent a helping hand. Martin, the Lochaber inspector, had died at the end of 1824. In the following spring Hope wrote to Rickman that Mitchell had been helping with the education of the family,[2] and when several years later Garrow, the Argyllshire inspector whom Hope had once described as a peripatetic philosopher, at length retired after twenty-seven years of service, Hope and Rickman were at pains to advise the old man as to the best way of using the small gratuity which was with some trouble obtained for him.

If the volume and content of Hope's letter-books left small doubt of the burden he still carried, there was as yet little indication that the load was proving too heavy. Hope did not share with Rickman a yearning for release from work, and the only reference to personal well-being was in a letter written from the Moray Place office in the spring of 1832 when cholera was rampant in Scotland. 'We are still in this place', wrote Hope, 'free from the pestilence which surrounds us—a circumstance almost miraculous considering that it has raged for a fortnight within five miles of us.'[3] The first hint of failing strength came in the spring of 1837 when he wrote to Smith, Rickman's successor, that he was unwell and unable to sit at his desk. Five more years of work still lay ahead of him and it was not till the autumn of 1842 that the last of the great trio who had served the Commissioners so well passed from the scene. James Hope could at last lay down his burden in the assurance that he had played his full part in a

[1] Hope, 31 January 1827
[2] 'They are all prospering,' wrote Hope to Rickman, 'perhaps a little of the frenzy of the times of planning or aspiring beyond their reasonable situation . . . but they have escaped what I remember Dr Adam Smith called "the fate of the poor man's son whom Heaven in its wrath has visited with ambition",' Hope, 25 March 1825
[3] H. of L. Hope to Smith, 6 February 1832

great work for the Highlands, serving his country and maintaining the best traditions of the profession to which he belonged.

With the death of James Hope there remained only one of the men who had for long played a leading part in the work of the Commissioners for Highland Roads and Bridges. In the twenty years which had passed since the completion of Macleod's road in Skye, the work of Joseph Mitchell had been confined largely to the maintenance and repair of the new roads and bridges and the supervision of various harbour works for which the Commissioners had long been responsible. During these two decades there had, however, been one major project which, though never carried out, was to have an important influence on the future work of the Chief Inspector. Plans for shortening the road from Inverness to Perth by eliminating the lengthy detour through Drumochter Pass had long been in contemplation. As early as 1828 Telford and Mitchell had surveyed alternative routes through the hills further to the east, and nine years later Mitchell made for the Commissioners a more detailed report on the possibility of routes by Glenfeshie and over the watershed into Glentilt, or by Glentromie into Glenbruar. The high altitude of the watersheds in each case and the danger from snow led to the abandonment of these ambitious plans, but Mitchell's study of the problem had given him a detailed knowledge of the whole area, which was later to stand him in good stead.

As the second quarter of the 19th century drew to a close the frenzy of railway planning and railway speculation was approaching its peak. In the spring of 1838 Mitchell was employed by James Hope to survey an alternative route for part of the proposed railway line between Edinburgh and Glasgow which encroached on the property of his client the Earl of Hopetoun. Mitchell's survey came to nothing, but his thoughts now turned increasingly to railway construction and to the prospect of putting to a new use the wide knowledge of the Highland area possessed by the surveyors and engineers of the Commissioners. Soon Mitchell was at work surveying at his own cost a route in Perthshire for the Scottish Central Railway, but disagreement with the promoters of the Caledonian Railway led to the severance of his connection with this project. Mitchell took his disappointment philosophically. 'Perhaps as it happened', he wrote later, 'it was fortunate, for if I had continued Engineer to the Scottish Central

Railway, I should in all probability have been drawn into the vortex of railway speculation, which in that year (1845) was rife throughout the country, particularly in Perth and by which about half the well-to-do people in that City were damaged and many ruined.'[1] But few engineers of those days could for long resist the attraction of railway planning. His earlier survey for the Commissioners had convinced Mitchell that a railway line through Drumochter Pass reaching the Tay Valley by way of Glengarry and Pitlochry was practicable, and soon he was again involved, surveying this as an alternative route from Inverness to Perth in face of the determined opposition of the planners of a line by way of Aberdeen. After a long and costly hearing, the Parliamentary Committee before which the rival cases were argued preferred the Aberdeen route, and for a time Mitchell resumed his road work for the Commissioners, while engineers, contractors and speculators throughout the country, more deeply involved than he, suffered the crippling losses which followed the financial crash of 1847.

The crisis of that year had, however, done little more than check momentarily the flowing tide of railway promotion. Financial difficulties had prevented the construction of the line from Inverness to Aberdeen and seemed likely to delay indefinitely railway development of what was later to become the area of the Great North of Scotland Railway. In these circumstances Mitchell urged on his Inverness friends the advantages of a line from Inverness to Nairn. Little more than twelve months after the start of this work in September 1854 the Nairn line was opened, and four years later an extension to Keith was completed. Despite the earlier defeat before the Parliamentary Committee Mitchell had never abandoned his dream of a direct railway line southward to Perth. Delay in completing a through connection from Inverness to Aberdeen strengthened the pressure for the southward line and led in 1860 to a determined effort to revive the latter project. All opposition from the rival company was now at an end. The support of the Duke of Atholl, which was essential to the plans, was obtained. The Bill for the Highland Railway passed through Parliament in July 1861, and on 9 September 1863, less than two years after the start of the constructional

---

[1] Joseph Mitchell in his *Reminiscences* recorded that in 1845, when railway speculation was at its climax, no fewer than 620 companies were registered with a combined capital of £563,203,000. Mitchell, II, p. 158

work, the dream which Joseph Mitchell had dreamt more than twenty years earlier at last came true.

The excitement and anxiety of railway speculation, the rapid and violent alternations of elation and depression and the strain of working at high pressure took their toll of many caught in the toils of the railway mania, and Joseph Mitchell was among the victims. In the spring of 1862, while work on the Highland line was yet incomplete, he was seized with paralysis, and little more than a year later a second blow fell on him with the news of the ending of the Commission for Highland Roads and Bridges to which so much of his life had been given. 'I felt at the time', he wrote later, 'it was like a notice that the end was drawing near.' For a few more years Joseph Mitchell with the assistance of his partners continued work as a railway engineer, surveying and engineering the line from Dingwall to Strome Ferry and much of the line through Sutherland and Caithness to Wick and Thurso; but the end of his career as an engineer was fast approaching, and he has left on record that the year 1867 saw the close of his professional life.

As Telford had done before him, Mitchell devoted his last years to recalling and recording the achievements and incidents of his life in the Highlands. Few writers of Memoirs can have had richer material with which to work, and, unlike Telford, Mitchell possessed the power of instilling life and colour into the scenes of which he wrote. As he recalled the long years of an active life, the old inspector could look back on a period in which the life of the Highlands had changed almost beyond recognition. He had seen as a boy the first start of the Commissioners' work on Highland roads and the early days of the Caledonian Canal. As the son, and later as the successor, of John Mitchell the former Chief Inspector, he had himself shared the hopes, the disappointments and the ultimate triumphs of the planners. He had known Telford in his heyday, had shared with the great engineer his labours, his problems and his dreams, and had lived to see a large part of those dreams come true.

He could remember Inverness in the days when coaches were a rarity, a journey to Perth or Aberdeen an adventure. He had lived to see it the growing centre of coach and rail traffic to north, south, east and west. He had heard as a boy of the first experimental steam boat on Dalswinton Loch, and had seen for himself, on his first long journey from home, the power of steam, little dreaming of what it was to mean for his country, his profession and his own life. The lad who had sailed in Bell's *Comet* on her first voyage on the Caledonian Canal little guessed that he would live to see Oban, Fort William and the Outer Isles linked with Glasgow by *Cygnet*, *Lapwing* and *Plover* and other small stout ships of the growing fleets of Burns, Hutcheson and MacBrayne.

He had seen the spreading roads bringing new life and movement to the Glens, but with them new methods of farming, new ideas and new men to compete with and finally to oust the clansfolk clinging to the old ways of a life which was passing. He had seen the clearances from Sutherland and many another Highland district, the sad spectacle of emigrant ships sailing from the Hebrides, and the forced movement to the coast of many who stayed at home displaced and disillusioned.

He had seen the misery and hunger which came to north and west with the potato failures of the late 'forties. In his time, too, the high hopes of coastal fishing had proved all but illusory. As he gleaned the scattered memories of an octogenarian the day had long passed when the minister of an island parish could write of summer evenings when the Sound of Raasay was dotted with the sails of countless fishing boats from coastal villages of Invernessshire and Wester Ross. Even as he wrote, Lord Napier and his colleagues on the Crofters Commission were putting the finishing touches to the report which was at least to bring hope to the victims of a great social upheaval.

He had seen the cattle-droving industry rising to its peak in the days when Corriechoillie and the other great drovers of the time brought their beasts in hundreds and thousands to the markets at Falkirk, and had lived to see the drove roads almost deserted. He had known the Disruption of the Established Church, the selfless loyalty of displaced ministers and the devotion to principle of Dr Chalmers, and had himself taken a full part in the building of new manses throughout the Highlands. In Mitchell's time the rent roll of the Highlands had grown by leaps and bounds with the spread of sheep-farming, the short-lived boom in kelp and the growing cult of grouse, salmon and deer; but the rising rents had too often been ill-spent and wasted, and he has recorded that in his lifetime two out of every three Highland estates had seen new owners.

In the changes which had come in Mitchell's time his own work had played no small part, and if these changes had brought sorrow to some he must, on a wide view, have had few regrets. In a changing scene one thing at least had not changed, and on it he could look back with lasting pleasure. His wandering life throughout the Highlands had stored in his memory pictures of natural beauty to which he was far from insensible. As he wrote the last pages of his book, he recalled an early summer's day when the still waters of Loch Maree reflected the green of young birch on the southern shore. He remembered the stern and rugged magnificence of Glen Shiel as he had seen it on an autumn morning when all was silent but for the sound of the river and the call of sheep on the hill. He lived again that same September day when, having climbed the hill from the Ferry of Kyle-Rhea on the Skye side, he had seen in the evening light the blue outline of the Cuillins; below him the white cottages on the shores of Broadford Bay, and across the waters of the Bay the hills of Applecross and Torridon.

THE END

APPENDICES

APPENDIX I

Memorial respecting the Glendaruel Road

Unto the Honourable the Commissioners appointed by the Act of the 43° Geo.III. c.80, for making Roads and building Bridges in the Highlands of Scotland.

> The Memorial of William MacLeod Bannatyne, of Kaims, one of the Senators of the College of Justice, John Campbell, of Southall, Duncan Campbell, of Glendaruel, John Campbell, of Ormadale, Angus Fletcher, of Dunnans, Donald MacLachlan, of MacLachlan, Esquires, and others;

Humbly sheweth,

That the counties of Argyll, and of the Island of Bute, are much connected in the trade of fishing, and are still more connected in civil and military policy, the circuit courts for both being held twice in the year at Inverary, and the counties having only one regiment of militia between them.

That the making of a proper Road between Inverary and Island of Bute would therefore be highly beneficial to the Public, as well as accommodating to the Inhabitants of these parts, by shortening the communication of land not less than 97 miles out of 117, the present Post Road from Inverary to Rothsay in Bute, by Dumbarton, Glasgow, Greenock, and Largs, being 117 miles, whereas the Road proposed to be opened by the Memorialists will only be 20 miles; besides the Ferry from Bute to Largs, in Ayrshire, which is the line of the present Post Road, is five or six miles wide, and often not passable, whereas the Ferry from Bute to the proposed new Road is not a quarter of a mile wide, and is passable at all times.

In Loch-Fine not fewer than 500 large herring-boats are annually employed; and the Town of Rothsay annually sends out from eighty to ninety large vessels for the bounty-fishing; which sufficiently shews the importance of establishing an easy communication between these places, not only as enriching the country by the quantity of fish caught, but also as affording an extensive nursery for hardy seamen to the Royal Navy.

That in order to accomplish these very desirable national objects, the Memorialists propose that a Road shall be made from the Ferry of Cuilintrive, nearly opposite to the Town of Rothsay, along the

Keiles of Bute, and through the Valley of Glendaruel, to the line of Road on the East side of Loch Fine, which leads to Inverary, and communicates nearly in a straight line with the great line of Road leading to Fort William and the Caledonian Canal.

That by making this Road the Communication between the Continent of Argyllshire and the extensive Islands of Bute and Arran, as well as the Fishing Towns of Inverary and Rothsay, would be rendered much more certain, easy, and direct, to the great advantage of the numerous fishermen, as well as the other inhabitants of these places, who are often put to much inconvenience in attending Circuit Courts and other public Meetings at Inverary, owing to the want of Bridges, and the almost impassable state of the tract through which it is proposed to carry the intended Road.

That besides these great national and local advantages, this Road would open up an extensive district of country, well adapted to the purposes of Agriculture, and other Improvements.

That the extent of this proposed line of Road, as already said, is about twenty miles; and the expence of making it is computed at £2,500.

The Memorialists propose to raise one-half of the sum necessary; and they hope the Honourable the Commissioners will think the undertaking deserving the public Aid, and will contribute the other half; the Memorialists being bound to finish the Road and Bridges, and to keep them in repair.

May it therefore please you to order the foresaid proposed line of Road to be surveyed, and that the necessary steps be taken for compleating it.

(Signed) JOHN CAMPBELL , qrtus

Writer to the Signet
Agent for, and authorised by the Memorialists

December 1804

APPENDIX II

Memorial respecting the Leckan Road

Memorial of the Committee appointed in the District of Argyll for conducting the Leckan Road;

> To the Honourable the Commissioners for making Roads
> and building Bridges in the Highlands of Scotland;

Sheweth,

That there is a tract of moor in the centre of the county of Argyll, about thirty miles long, and extending from Cladich on Loch-Awe side, to near Loch-gilp-head, commonly called the Muir of Leckan.

That hitherto no Road fit for carts or carriages has been made across any part of this long tract of moor, which is attended with much inconvenience to the inhabitants, as they are obliged to cross it daily in various directions on foot, and over the whole of that tract there is only one path in which a person on horseback can travel with any safety, being that much-frequented path from Achindraine by Craig-nure to the Foord.

To remedy this inconvenience an application was made, signed by almost the whole land-owners in the district of Argyll, for having a line of Road through the moor of Leckan inserted in the new Road Act for the county, which was approved of, and the said line was inserted under the following description; viz. 'From Achindraine 'through the muir of Leckan till it intersects the Road from Kilmartin 'to the west end of Loch-Awe.'

This line, if accomplished, would open a short and easy access between the low country and the county town of Argyllshire (Inverary) on the one hand, and the fertile and populous district called the Strath of Argyll on the other, and would save persons, having carts and carriages, the trouble and delay of a long circuit by the Loch-gilp-head Road, which, besides the length, is in many places steep and ill executed.

Auchindraine, where the line in question commences, is about the middle of the long tract of moor before-mentioned; and the other termination of the line not only accommodates the inhabitants of the Strath of Argyll towards the Foord, and towards Kilmartin and Kilmichael, but it also connects very closely with two other great lines; viz. that from Kilmartin by Crinan to Knapdale, and to the ferries

213

which cross over to Jura, Islay, and Collonsay; and 2ndly, that towards Craignish, North Lorn, and the adjacent islands; the inhabitants of which districts and islands, with their cattle for the markets, are now in the habit of going to the Low Country by the path beforementioned, with hardly a single exception; and it is moreover proper to state, that several useful branches, towards Loch-Fyne and Kilmichael, may afterwards be easily ingrafted on this line.

These circumstances render the execution of this Road an object of particular importance to the inhabitants of these parts of Argyllshire, and accordingly the trustees of the district of Argyll have been very anxious for its completion; various surveys have been made by professional men, and committees of the trustees have been appointed to examine, and to report, with the assistance of these surveys, as to the most level, cheap and useful line, and to obtain estimates of the expense thereof, all which they have done. The description of the line contained in the Act of Parliament was suggested by the particular nature of the ground in that part of the moor of Leckan, which is much more low and level than any other part, while both terminations afforded the most general facility and accommodation to the inhabitants of the country.

But useful as the Road is, the execution of it has necessarily been for years delayed by want of money, as the small stent, or tax, exigible from the heritors of the district, is allocated or mortgaged for payment of prior advances, which will take some time to pay off.

The estimates obtained were made according to the specifications prescribed by the Government surveyors in some Roads now making in Argyllshire, and from these it appears that the sum of 2,341L will be necessary.

The length according to the survey approved by the trustees of the district, is twelve miles one furlong and some falls, and the Memorialists have reason to hope that one-half of this sum can be raised by subscriptions of heritors and public-spirited individuals in the country, on the prospect of future indemnification from the county funds, if the Commissioners will have the goodness of aiding them with the other half: and from the circumstances stated, they have no doubt the Honourable Commissioners will consider this line very deserving of their attention in the distribution of the Government aid.

(Signed)   NEIL MACGIBBON
JOHN CAMPBELL
DUN. CAMPBELL

May 1806

APPENDIX III

Memorial of His Grace the Duke of Argyll and others

Unto the Honourable the Commissioners appointed for the purposes of an Act of the Forty-third of His present Majesty, intituled, 'An 'Act for granting to His Majesty the sum of Twenty thousand Pounds, 'to be issued and applied towards making Roads and building Bridges 'in the Highlands of Scotland; and for enabling the Proprietors of 'Land in Scotland to charge their Estates with a Proportion of the 'Expense of making and keeping in repair Roads and Bridges in the 'Highlands of Scotland.'

> The Memorial of His Grace the Duke of Argyll; the Trustees of Sir James Riddell, Baronet; the Guardians of Ronald George MacDonald, of Clanranald, Esquire; Alexander MacLean, Esquire, of Ardgour; Lieutenant-Colonel Donald MacDonald, of Kinlochmoidart; James Forbes, Esquire, of Kingairloch; Alexander MacDonald, of Glenalladale, Esquire, and others:

Humbly states,

That a large district of country in the counties of Argyll and Inverness, comprehending His Grace the Duke of Argyll's property in Morven, the estates of Ardnamurchan and Sunart, Clanranald's estate of Moidart, the barony of Ardgour, Kinlochmoidart, Kingairloch, and others, the property of the Memorialists, labours under very great disadvantages from the want of a Road to the Low Country, in consequence of which, these districts are, in a manner, entirely shut up from all communication with the south.

The proprietors of these districts are therefore most desirous to open up the communication with that part of the country, by a line of Road from Lochmoidart (a large and spacious harbour in the county of Inverness) to the Corran of Ardgour, from whence there is a commodious and safe ferry to the Military Road from Fort William to the Low Country; and it is proposed, that the said line of Road should be from Lochmoidart to the Bay of Saline upon Loch Sunart, to the village of Strontian, and from thence to the Corran of Ardgour. The extent of this line of Road (it is supposed) may be from thirty to thirty-five miles, and the expense of making it, and of building the necessary Bridges over the rivers, it is believed, would not exceed 3,500L.

The Memorialists are humbly of opinion that this proposed line of Road would be of very great benefit and utility to the Highlands in general, and particularly so to the Western Islands, as it would render the communication with them to the Low Country much more safe; Lochmoidart being one of the best harbours upon the western coast of Scotland, from whence the communication to the Low Country, were this Road made, would be much nearer and more convenient than any other; and besides, there is every reason to believe that a very valuable fishery may be established in Lochmoidart, which would be greatly forwarded by means of good Roads.

His Grace the Duke of Argyll, and other heritors in the island of Mull, further beg leave to state to the honourable commissioners, that very great advantages would result to that part of the country, if a Road was opened up from Bunessan Loch, upon the west coast of Mull, to Auchnacraig, which is the great ferry from that island to the main land of Argyllshire, and which would open up a rich tract of country capable of very great improvement, but which at present is almost inaccessible for want of Roads.

The Memorialists, sensible of the great advantages which would result to the Highlands from the above proposed line of Roads, are induced to request the aid of the honourable commissioners for assistance under the authority of the aforesaid act of parliament; and they are most willing to comply with the regulations therein prescribed, if the honourable commissioners shall be pleased to approve of the proposed Roads, which they hope they may be induced to do from the public utility which the Memorialists are confident will result from opening up a communication to the Low Country with extensive districts, at present, from want of Roads, almost inaccessible.

(Signed)   HENRY JARDINE
Writer to the Signet

APPENDIX IV

Memorial respecting Loch-Laggan Road

Unto the Honourable the Commissioners appointed for the purposes
of an Act of the 43° Geo.III. c.80. (the Highland Road and Bridge
Act.)

> The Memorial of his Grace the Duke of Gordon, Aeneas
> MacIntosh, of MacIntosh, and Colonel Duncan Mac-
> Pherson, of Cluny.

Humbly states,

That a large district of Country, in the shire of Inverness, comprehending the whole of the higher and more remote parts of Badenoch
and Lochabar, the property of the Memorialists, labours under very
great disadvantages by the want of proper Roads and Bridges.

The Memorialists are therefore most desirous to open up the communication of that part of the country by a line of Road from the
Inn at Pitmain in Badenoch (where the present Military Road passes
from Stirling, Perth and Edinburgh to Fort George) by the North side
of Loch-Laggan to Fort William on the West Coast.

The Memorialists are of opinion that this line of Road would be of
infinite service to the inhabitants of Badenoch and Lochabar, and all
the neighbouring districts of the county of Inverness, and for the purposes of commercial intercourse among themselves; and they beg leave
to state, that when it is opened, and Bridges thrown across the Rivers,
it will make the best and safest, as well as the shortest and most ex-
peditious communication yet proposed, between the South of Scotland
and Fort William and the West end of the Caledonian Canal, being
nearly on the level through its whole course, and from its low direction
along the margin of Loch-Laggan (which seldom freezes) it may be
travelled in perfect safety at all times and seasons of the year, and even
in the deepest falls of snow that have happened in the memory of man.

From these considerations Lord Adam Gordon, when Commander
in Chief in Scotland, ordered a Survey to be made by George Brown,
in the view of a Military Road being made in that direction from
Stirling to Fort Augustus and Fort William, instead of the present one
by Garvamore over Corry-Arrick which from its height is at all times
dangerous, and generally impassable for four months in the year, to
the prejudice of his Majesty's service, and the loss of the lives of many

of his soldiers and subjects. And Mr Brown accordingly, in the year 1792, made a very minute and accurate Survey; and a Plan and Estimate of the Expence of making the said Road, and building the necessary Bridges thereon, were lodged with the Lords of the Treasury, by which it appears that the sum of £4,700.19s.9d. would then have been necessary for that purpose; but by the increased expence of labour, and the rise of the prices of all materials for building, since that period, a considerable sum more will now be requisite to execute the work in the same manner.

The Memorialists, sensible of the great advantages which would result from the line of Road now proposed, are induced to request the aid of the Honourable Commissioners in making the same, under the authority of the aforesaid Act of Parliament, and they are confident that the County of Inverness will approve thereof, and most readily contribute the one half of the expence of opening a communication of so much private utility and public advantage.

(Signed)   GORDON

Gordon Castle, August 9th, 1804

APPENDIX V

Memorial respecting the Isle of Skye Roads

Unto the Honourable the Commissioners appointed for the Purposes of an Act 43° Geo.III. c.80. (the Highland Road and Bridge Act.)

The Memorial of the Right Honourable Alexander Wentworth Lord MacDonald, for himself and other Proprietors of Land in the County of Inverness;

Humbly states,

That the Inhabitants of the very large and populous parts of the County of Inverness, comprehending the whole of the Isle of Skye and the Isles of Uist and Harris,* and the extensive grazing Estates of Glenelg and Lochalsh, have been always in the practice of sending their Cattle (the principal source of the Revenue of that Country) by the Ferry of Kyle-Rhea, Bernera, and along the Military Road leading by Fort Augustus to the markets in the low Country; indeed from the situation of the country, this has hitherto been the only practicable line for driving Cattle to market; and for want of Roads through Skye, and from the Military Road having gone into decay, the loss of Cattle has been very great.

That your Memorialist perceives from the Report made by the Honourable Commissioners to Parliament, that a line of Road has been adopted by them, and he understands now contracted for, leading from the Military Road at Loch-Oich near Fort Augustus, through Glengarry to the end of Loch-Hourn; and that Mr Telford in his Report of this Road, dated on the 21st December 1803, states, that 'this line of Road may be connected with Bernera, either through Glenelg or through Glensheal, and past the Sheal-House, or by both of these lines of Road. In this point of view it is of the utmost importance as a Drove Road from a very extensive tract of country.'

From this statement of Mr Telford, the Honourable Commissioners will perceive that the great advantage of this junction of the Road with Bernera by Sheal-house, and of course by Kyle-Rhea, did not escape the notice of that discerning Engineer, though his attention was not directed to it by any application from your Memorialist or the other Proprietors interested in that Line.

The Memorialist is humbly of opinion that this connextion of the

* Population of Skye 15,800; of N. and S. Uist 7,600; of Harris 3,000

Road, already begun through Glengarry, with Bernera and Kyle-Rhea by one or more Branches, as suggested by Mr Telford, would be of very great benefit and utility to that part of the Highlands, and in particular to the Districts above mentioned, and indeed to the whole Kingdom, by giving access to the Isle of Skye, and enabling persons to send for the breed of cattle of that island, now admitted to be the best in Scotland.

Sensible of the advantages which must result from opening as speedily as possible, and in the manner proposed by Mr Telford, a safe communication with the Isle of Skye by a Branch from the Glen-garry Road by Sheal-house, Bernera, and Kyle-Rhea; and being of opinion that without such Branch the Road from Loch-Oich to the head of Loch-Hourn would be of very little public benefit; The Memorialist is induced to request the aid of the Honourable Com-missioners under the authority of the aforesaid Act of Parliament, and he is ready to comply with the Regulations of the said Act for making the said Branch of Road.

The Memorialist begs to suggest the propriety of surveying the line of Road through the Isle of Skye (1) From the Ferry of Kyle-Rhea, by Broadford and Sconser, to Dunvegan and Stein; (2) a Branch from Sconser, northward by Portree to Aird of Trotternish; and (3) from Broadford, southward to Armadale and Ardavaser Bay in the district of Sleat, and the necessary breast-works at the Ferry, &c. on which Road and Ferry your Memorialist has already laid out a large sum of money; and if the Honourable Commissioners shall adopt this Line and the Branches therefrom above humbly recommended, the Memor-ialist is willing to make further efforts towards the completion of so great and essential an improvement.

Which is humbly submitted.

(Signed)   MACDONALD

July 1804

APPENDIX VI

Prospectus of a Canal from Fort William to Inverness

Gigha, 21st December, 1792

Sir,

In the Statistical Account of this parish, I hinted at the advantages of a canal across the isthmus of Crianan in Argyleshire, and of another between Fort William and Inverness. With regard to the former, it must afford pleasure to every lover of national improvements to understand, that the subscription for that important work is now completed, and consequently that there is a prospect of its being soon carried into execution. Besides the advantages resulting from it to the public, it will be attended with the happiest effects to the poor mariner, at this season of the year, when navigation round the Maoil of Ceanntire is so difficult and dangerous.

If it be not reckoned too great presumption, I would beg leave to mention some things which occur to me, respecting the inland navigation between Inverness and Fortwilliam. This tract I have had occasion to travel often; and, though neither my studies nor views were directed to such subjects, I could not resist a certain impulse which led me, repeatedly, to examine the ground, and still makes me ardently wish, that, some time or other, a national spirit of improvement would be excited to open this communication, which nature seems to have intended, as the most important object for commercial enterprise, that ever was undertaken in Great Britain.

There is no person of common observation that travels from Fort William, through Strath Lochy, to Inverness, but must be struck with the astonishing contrast, between a level, upwards of 60 miles long, extending across the island from sea to sea, and ranges of the highest hills in Scotland on both sides. This level, which is nearly in a straight line from N.E. to S.W. consists of land and water: so that nature not only favours such an undertaking (by the flatness of the ground), but has in fact completely finished more than one half of it already. Lochness is reckoned 20 miles in length, Loch Lochy 16, and Loch Oich 5; in all, upwards of 40 miles.

To enumerate all the advantages of this navigation, is a task I am not qualified to undertake; but to those who are conversant in the seafaring and commercial lines, and who have enlarged views of the present state of the country, they must be obvious and striking, even upon a bare inspection of the map. As they occur to me, the advantages of this canal may be considered in three points of view: First, As it respects the adjacent countries; Secondly, The commercial interest of England and Ireland; and Lastly, The improvement of the fisheries, and the introduction of trade and manufactures into the Western Isles and Highlands of Scotland.

I. On the north side of this level or valley, are the countries of Urquhart, Glenmorison, part of Abertarf, Glengary, and that part of Lochaber which surrounds Locharcaig and thence extends to the head of Lochial. On the south side lies Strathharrie, part of Abertarf, Letterfinlay, Keppoch and Glen-navas. All these extensive countries, abound with excellent woods (consisting chiefly of oak, ash, elm, birch and fir;) which at present, however, are of no great value to the proprietors, nor of any real advantage to the public, for want of water carriage to bring them to market. In all parts of these countries, bordering on the sides of the supposed canal, there are rivers, and copious streams of water, for working all kinds of machinery: and, notwithstanding the emigrations that have taken place from some of the districts, there are still many inhabitants, who, by habits of industry, might become a valuable acquisition to the manufacturing and seafaring part of society. The lakes and rivers are well stored with salmon and trout; the low grounds, for the most part, capable of being rendered very fertile; and the hills not surpassed by any in Scotland for sheep ranges. In short, this valley between Inverness and Fortwilliam, were the canal opened, and manufactures established on both sides of it, would soon become the centre of trade in the Highlands; where the mechanic, the merchant, and the manufacturer, would find sufficient employment, and the industrious labourer meet with due encouragement.

II. With regard to the commercial interest of England and Ireland, a canal here, on such a scale as to admit vessels drawing about 16 feet water, would be attended with most solid and permanent advantages. All ships from Ireland and the west coast of Britain, bound for the east coast, for Holland, or the Baltic, could perform their voyage in, at least, a third less time than now, and with greater safety. In like manner all the West India and American traders, from the east of Scotland and north-east coast of England, could avoid the circuitous and dangerous navigation of the Pentland Firth; and in time of war, could rendezvous at Inverness or Fortwilliam, protected by strong forts, and in harbours that may justly be reckoned among the safest and most capacious in the kingdom. Besides, a frigate or two, stationed in the Moray Firth between Peterhead and Fort George, together with as many on the west coast, between the sound of Mull and the north of Ireland, could afford greater protection to our trade in those quarters, than many times the number at present, when the navigation round the north of Scotland is so scattered.

III. As to the Western Isles, and the opposite coast of the Highlands, where every thing but proper encouragement from the government, contributes to raise them to the highest eminence, in a commercial and maritime view, the benefits of this canal would be immense. Thousands, who are lost to themselves and to the world, might be usefully employed. Many families, who pine in want, might live in affluence; and several, who, contrary to their inclination, are obliged to leave their native soil, and remove to other states, might contribute to the strength and wealth of their own country. Large tracts of land, now in a barren state, might be improved; and those parts, which at present afford but a scanty subsistence to a small number of inhabitants, might be so far meliorated, as, with the help of commerce, to support a numerous population.

That the above assertions may not appear too bold or exaggerated, let it be observed, that the herring fishing, which at present is entirely confined to one side of the kingdom, would, by means of this canal, become open to both; so that twice the number of hands might be employed in that branch: and the cod and ling fishing, which is yet but in its infancy, might be carried on as extensively as the herring fishing. In all the attempts hitherto made in the white fishing, people have been employed at great expense from the east country. These people, having no permanent place of residence on the west coast, are in general exposed to so much fatigue and danger on their journey over land, or in their passage round, through the Pentland Firth, and are liable to so many inconveniences, on their arrival, for want of proper lodgings, and other accommodations, that their exertions must be languid, and of course their success precarious. This being the case, it is no wonder, that adventurers in the white fishing, after being at considerable expence and trouble, should drop the plan as totally impracticable. Now, were the canal opened, all these obstacles might be removed. Large vessels, with every conveniency along with them, might be fitted out from Cromarty, Inverness, and other towns in the Moray Firth, which, in the course of a few days, might sail to the fishing grounds, where they could choose safe harbours in the neighbourhood of the best banks. Besides the advantage of having all their necessaries on board, the prospect of returning soon to their families and friends would double their industry and exertions. In this way, the white fishing would soon become successful: and the natives of the Western Isles, by their intercourse with the east country people, would acquire the knowledge of it in a short time, and be able to co-operate with their instructors in bringing it to such perfection, and carrying it on to such an extent, as to become a considerable object in the commerce of the kingdom.

By means of this canal, the salmon fishings on the west coast could also be improved, and have ready access to the London market. Thus they would become very valuable to the proprietors; though hitherto they have almost all been little attended to, except that of Lochy, near Fortwilliam, where it is principally carried on by men hired from Nairn, Findhorn, or Speymouth.

Thus it seems evident, that opening the Strathlochy Canal, would be productive of very great advantages to the Highlands, in respect of the fisheries alone. Besides these, however, there are many other articles of commerce, which would occupy the sailor, the handycraftman, and the labourer. Men of all these denominations would find constant employment, about the slate works of Eisdale and Balachaolais, the lead mines of Suanard, the copper mines of Kishorn (near Applecross), and the marble quarries of Tiree and Icolumcill: to which may be added, the limestone, shell sand, and kelp of the Western Islands, and all the oak woods of the west coast, especially those of Lorn, Appin, Morven and Ardnamurchan.[1] But, without dwelling any longer on particulars, it may be safely affirmed, that, by fishing and an interchange of commodities between the east and west coasts of Scotland, through this canal, exclusive of the advantages in trade and the number of people occupied in different works, fifty seamen for one now, at a moderate calculation, might be employed in those parts. Connected with the other two canals, this one would occasion a circulation in trade; which is as necessary to the existence of the commercial system, as the circulation of fluids is to that of the animal body. And, lastly, all the improvements in fishing, farming, mechanics, and manufactures, of the east country, might easily be communicated to the inhabitants of the west.

As some people, from confined ideas, may think, that the interest of those, concerned in the Clyde and Crianan inland navigation, would suffer, were this canal carried on; it will not be improper to observe, that the advantages to be derived from the former, can never be fully experienced, till the latter be opened. The three, taken together, as hinted at above, will form a chain, in the system of internal commerce which will be productive of advantages never to be derived from them singly, or from any two of them, without the third.

Let us now suppose, that, in any part of England, the communication from the east to the west coast were, for 200 or 300 miles, interrupted by high mountains, except in one place, where there was an opening or flat across the country; nay, let it be supposed, that, in such a situation, there were only two vallies penetrating from each coast into the country, and approaching in a straight line within a short distance

[1] Several of the articles are manufactured already, but not near so extensively as they might be, were the communication with the east coast, through this canal, opened. The proprietors of those places are deeply interested in promoting this plan.

of each other, where their junction was interrupted by a cross ridge of hills: In this case, where nature had done so much, though she did not complete the whole level, the enterprising spirit, for which our southern neighbours are so justly famed, would, long since, have been exerted to surmount every difficulty, in order to open such a communication; not only by cutting a canal in the level part of the ground, but also, by piercing through the hill or mountain which occasioned the interruption. What shall we say, then, of ourselves, for our want of attention to this great object of national improvement; where nature has, not only given us a continued level from sea to sea, but has likewise performed more than one half of the work to our hand, by a chain of lakes, where ships of the line could sail with safety?

Besides the above advantages, for facilitating this great undertaking, nature has been favourable in other respects. There is hardly any continuance of frost in this valley to interrupt the navigation in the winter season. Lochness never freezes, and Loch Lochy seldom. Now, if the canal were made on a large scale (from 16 to 18 feet deep), there would be almost a certainty of its continuing always open; especially when we take into the account, the number of springs which abound at the bottom of such high mountains, many of which must be opened in the tract of the canal.

Another thing worthy of notice is, that the summit (or highest ground at Lagan-achandrom', between Loch Lochy and Loch Oich, which is a flat, about two miles long, and half a mile broad), could be constantly supplied with water from both sides by two burns; one shelving down the hill on the south side, about the middle of the ground, and another larger one on the north side, which runs into Loch Lochy at the west end of the summit, but which could easily be brought into the canal, if found necessary.

Upon the whole, the facility of accomplishing a work of such magnitude and importance, highly deserves the attention of every one who has the interest of his country at heart. May I, therefore, be permitted to indulge the pleasing hope, that one, who has so eminently distinguished himself, in promoting national improvements, as Sir John Sinclair, will, at some seasonable time, use his influence to direct the attention of government and of the public to this great object? The happiness of thousands of virtuous and loyal subjects, as well as the internal wealth and strength of the British Empire, might be promoted by it. This, at least, is the persuasion of one, who, though little acquainted with the world, and confined to a retired corner, rejoices in the prosperity of his country, and, if in his power, would cheerfully promote it. This being his firm persuasion, he humbly hopes, it will be deemed a sufficient apology for the liberty he has taken in this address, and in attempting to write on a subject which, he doubts not, may have been communicated to Sir John Sinclair by persons much better qualified to do it justice, than the writer of this letter can pretend to be.

With the greatest respect,
I have the honour to be, Sir,
Your most obedient,
and most humble servant,
WILLIAM FRASER

APPENDIX VII

Memorial respecting the Loch-Tay Road

To the Commissioners for Roads and Bridges in the Highlands of Scotland.

The Memorial of sundry Proprietors of Lands in the County of Perth;

Sheweth,

That much inconvenience is experienced by the Inhabitants of the Country which is situated along the sides of Loch-Tay, from the want of a more direct communication with the Lowlands, than is afforded by the Roads which proceed from the extremities of that District, at Kenmore and Killin. These places are 16 miles (the length of Loch-Tay) distant from each other; and although they are connected by good Roads on each side of the Loch, yet the Inhabitants of the inter-mediate District in using these Roads as a communication with Comrie, Crieff or Stirling, make a very circuitous journey, compared with that which they would have to perform were a good Road made from about the Middle of the District, on the South side of the Loch through Glenlednaig to Comrie. The Distance from Stirling to Kenmore, by Crieff and Tay bridge, is 46 Miles, to which if 8 Miles be added as a medium Distance from Kenmore to the Country situated between Kenmore and Killin, the Total Distance from Stirling to that District will be 54 Miles; in like manner the distance from Stirling by Callender and Loch Earnhead to Killin, being 38 Miles, and 8 Miles more being added as the distance from Killin to the District opposite the Centre of Loch-Tay, the Total Distance of that District from Stirling by Killin will be 46 Miles. The Distance from Perth to Kenmore is 37 Miles, and 8 Miles more being added as above, the Total Distance from Perth to the District above mentioned is 45 Miles.

Stirling and Perth are the nearest, and the only Sea Ports with which Breadalbane is connected; and it is from these places that all the Coal used in that District is brought.

There is another District of Country, to the Southward of that which has been described, which sustains at present the similar inconveniences of a very circuitous communication with the Ports of the Forth and Coal Country situated along that River, while a much more direct communication might be made, viz. the Village of Comrie and that part of Strathearn, which is situated in its neighbourhood. The Distance from Stirling to Comrie by Crieff is 28 Miles.

To remove the inconvenience thus experienced by the Country situated along Loch-Tay, and by that around Comrie, it has been long and frequently proposed to open a Road from the South side of Loch-Tay near the Village of Ardeonich through Glenlednaig to Comrie, and to continue this Line of Road from Comrie through Glenlichorn by Ardock and Kinbuck towards Dunblane and Stirling. The effects of this Line of Road being carried through, would be, to reduce the Distance from Stirling to Comrie from 28 to 20 Miles, and to reduce the Distance from Stirling to the Centre of Loch-Tay, from 54 Miles by Kenmore or 46 Miles by Killin to 34 Miles, being a reduction of Total Distance of 20 Miles in the former and of 12 Miles in the latter case.

There exists at present, in the Course above described, unformed Tracks, and accessible only to Horses or the lightest Country Carts with very small loads.

The Expence of making these Roads, if wholly defrayed by the voluntary Contributions of the Landholders through whose Estates they pass, would very greatly exceed the benefit and advantage which would result to them individually from the execution of such a Work. At the same time the Memorialists are willing, to a certain extent, to devote to the Improvement of that part of the Country in which their Estates are situated, a very considerable portion of their private Fortunes, for the attainment of that object; and they are willing to subject themselves to the Condition of advancing One-half of the Expence, in Terms of the Act of the 43d of His present Majesty, provided the Commissioners appointed by that Act shall be of opinion, that the Circumstances of the Case which they have stated, fall under the intendment of that liberal and most beneficial Enactment.

The Districts above described would derive from these Roads their whole supply of Coal, which is of very great consequence to obtain at such a rate as to enable the Inhabitants along the sides of Loch-Tay to avail themselves of it for burning the Limestone with which the Country abounds. These Roads would form the great Lines of Communication with the Lowlands and with the Sea Port of Alloa, and they would facilitate to a great degree the intercourse of Districts of Country between which a very considerable Traffic would exist, arising from the exportation of Timber, Oak, Bark, Slates, Limestone, Wool, &c. and the importation of all sorts of manufactured Goods and Merchandize.

The Memorialists therefore pray that the Commissioners aforesaid will take the subject of this Memorial into consideration, and if they shall approve thereof, that they will authorize or direct the necessary

Surveys, Estimate and Reports to be made in order to their afterwards advancing in the manner and under the Conditions prescribed by the said Act of the 43d of His present Majesty, the One-half of the estimated Expence of making the said Road.

(Signed)   BREADALBANE
C. S. DRUMMOND
ROBT. DUNDAS
PATR. MURRAY

14th July 1807

APPENDIX VIII

Memorial respecting Ballater Bridge

Memorial of the Right honourable the Earl of Aboyne; Captain James Farquharson, of Invercauld, R.N.; Peter Gordon, Esquire, of Abergeldie, and William Farquharson, Esquire, of Monaltrie;

To the Honourable the Commissioners for Roads and Bridges in the Highlands of Scotland;

Sheweth

That the river Dee is well known to be the third in Scotland, and equal in rapidity to the Spey, though not so large. It runs from the high mountains which divide the counties of Aberdeen and Inverness, to Aberdeen, a distance of about seventy miles, nearly in a straight line; passing through the Grampians for the first thirty miles, and thereafter along the north side of these mountains. From the Bridge built by Government in Braemar, to Aberdeen (a distance of fifty-six miles) there are only two Bridges, the nearest of which, to Braemar, is thirty-seven miles; and the other within two miles of Aberdeen, on the great post-road from Edinburgh to that place. It is obvious, therefore, that the intercourse between the south and north of Scotland is very much obstructed by the want of Bridges across this large and rapid river; and so much was this felt so far back as the year 1726, that the Memorialist's predecessors did everything in their power to procure money enough to build a Bridge over the Dee, near to Ballater, where it passes through the united parishes of Tullich, Glengarden, and Glenmuick, but without success.

In the year 1776 another attempt was made; and by private subscription, (chiefly within the county) with the aid only of 300L. from the Board of Forfeited and Annexed Estates, a handsome Bridge was begun and completed (after occasioning much trouble and expense) in 1783, where it had been originally intended, and cost 1,700L. But, unfortunately for the country, to a great extent, both south and north of it, and particularly so to a great part of the counties of Aberdeen, Angus and Kincardine, this beautiful and useful Bridge was carried away by an uncommon flood, on the 30th August 1799, and now lies in ruins.

Repeated attempts have been made by the Memorialists to raise as much money as would rebuild a work, the loss of which is most severely felt; but, as it would now cost a much larger sum (as will be seen by the plan, specification, and estimate herewith presented for the inspection of the Honourable Commissioners) from the difference in the expense of labour and materials since the former Bridge was built, and the manner in which the foundation of a new Bridge must be executed to prevent a similar disaster; and notwithstanding that all ranks of people in the neighbourhood are willing to contribute to the utmost of their abilities, and several noblemen and gentlemen who live at a distance have contributed very handsomely, the Memorialists are afraid it will not be possible to rebuild this Bridge without public aid.

The Memorialists therefore beg leave to submit the whole circumstances of the case to the Honourable the Commissioners for Roads and Bridges in the Highlands of Scotland; and request that they will have the goodness to take the same into their consideration together with the plan and specification of the intended Bridge, and thereafter be pleased to order an engineer to examine the matter herein represented, and to report thereupon.

(Signed)   ABOYNE
WILLIAM FARQUHARSON
PETER GORDON
JAS. FARQUHARSON

May 1806

APPENDIX IX

Memorial respecting Potarch Bridge

Memorial of Alexander Brebner of Lairnie, John Gordon of Craigmile, Lewis Innes of Balnacraig, John Douglass of Tillywhilly, for themselves and in name of many other Proprietors of Land in the County of Aberdeen.

To the Honourable the Commissioners for Roads and Bridges in the Highlands of Scotland.

The great Military Road leading from Brichen by Fettercairn, Kincardine O'Neil, and Boat of Forbes, to Huntly, and which is commonly called Cairn O'Mount Road, from its being carried through a very difficult pass of the Grampians, has been long very much frequented by Travellers, and by the Military in their passage to and from Fort George, and in general is of the greatest consequence to the Commercial Interests of a large district of Country to the Northward, in so much as the distance from Brichen to Huntly is thereby shortened at least twenty miles. This Road is intersected by the river Dee near Kincardine O'Niel, and by the River Don at the Boat of Forbes, as will be seen delineated in the large Map of Scotland published last year by authority of the Right Honourable the Commissioners for Roads and Bridges.

Both these Rivers are large and rapid, particularly the Dee, generally reckoned the third River in Scotland. This River descends from a mountainous and highly elevated District, and either when in Floods in the Summer and Autumn months from heavy falls of rain, or in Spring from melting of the snow in the upper District, or in Winter when gorged with ice, the passage of Kincardine O'Niel is rendered extremely precarious, and often impracticable altogether for days. The interruption occasioned to, and the danger incurred by, Travellers on this Road, from the want of Bridges on these Rivers, has been long severely felt, and for more than a century past it has been in contemplation to build a Bridge over the Dee, at a place called Potarch, a little below Kincardine O'Neil, and in the Line of this Road. This place possesses superior advantages for the site of a Bridge to any other situation on the river Dee, and perhaps almost any other River whatever. Here a ridge of solid rock extends completely across the River through a fissure or opening, in which the River in its ordinary state flows.

This description sufficiently evinces the natural facilities this situation presents, and accordingly, whenever a Bridge in this part of the Road was in contemplation, this site naturally offered itself.

The Memorialists and their Predecessors, fully sensible of the necessity for such a Bridge, have made frequent attempts to raise Money by Subscription for that purpose, but unfortunately these attempts have always hitherto proved abortive, and the accomplishment of this desirable object, from such repeated failures, was almost despaired of. The Memorialists however, encouraged by the aid promised by Government to such necessary undertakings in similar situations, have again set on foot a Subscription, which they have no doubt will soon be filled up; but that no time may be lost, they have obtained a Plan, Section, Specification and Estimate of a Bridge, including the necessary Embankments, proposed to be built over the river Dee at Potarch, which are herewith forwarded and humbly submitted to the consideration of the Commissioners; and the Memorialists hereby pledge themselves immediately to contract with the Commissioners for building the said Bridge, upon their receiving one-half of the estimated Expense out of the Funds appropriated by Government for such purposes.

The Memorialists therefore humbly hope, that the Honourable the Commissioners will be pleased to extend their patriotic views to the improvement of this part of the Highlands, and that upon receiving the Report of their Engineer, approving of the site proposed for the Bridge, and Plan, Section and Specification herewith transmitted, with such alterations as he may see proper, they will accede to this proposal.

The Memorialists understand that a similar application has been made by the Proprietors on the river Don for building a Bridge over that River at Boat of Forbes, which is said to have met with a favourable reception from the Honourable the Commissioners. Should these two useful Bridges be obtained by these means, the communication by this Road would be uninterrupted, and the importance of so substantial an improvement to this Northern District, will be universally felt and gratefully acknowledged.

(Signed)   LEWIS INNES
              JOHN DOUGLASS
              A. BREBNER
              JOHN GORDON

Aberdeen
20 June 1810

BIBLIOGRAPHY

MANUSCRIPT SOURCES

Public Record Office. Papers, Ref.T.86.I
House of Lords Record Office. Papers in connection with making of Highland Roads and Bridges, Caledonian Canal etc. 1803-51
Letters from John Rickman to Robert Southey (Copies in possession of Sir A. Gibb's Executors)
Letters from Thomas Telford to John Rickman, 1803-11. (In possession of Ministry of Transport)
Account Book of Lord Macdonald, 1813-1818 (In possession of Edinburgh Public Libraries)
Letters of Thomas Telford to Andrew and William Little (In possession of Mr W. J. C. Little, Craig, Langholm)
Letter Book of John Telford, Engineer in Charge at West End of Caledonian Canal (In possession of Mr Frank Whyte, The Blue House, Ditchling, Sussex)
Letter Books of Joseph Mitchell, 15th March 1830 to November 1834, 3 vols (In possession of Institution of Civil Engineers)
Letter Books of James Hope, W.S., 14 vols, 1803-38 (In possession of Hope Trustees, Edinburgh)
Papers in connection with Highland Roads and Bridges (H.M. Register House, Edinburgh)
Bank of Scotland. Private Minute Books vols 1-4
Dempster, George, of Skibo. Heads of a Plan for improving the waste lands in the Highlands of Scotland (Among letters of Sir John Sinclair, Bt, Thurso Castle)
Dunlop, Jean. The British Fisheries Society 1786-1893 (Unpublished Thesis, 1952, Edinburgh University Library)

OFFICIAL PUBLICATIONS

Reports of Commissioners for Highland Roads and Bridges 1803-1863
Statement respecting Origin and Future Repair of Highland Roads, 1814
General Report of the Agricultural State etc. of Scotland 1814
Reports of Commissioners for Caledonian Canal, 1803-1920
New Statistical Account of Scotland, 15 vols, 1845
Papers concerning Bridges, Canals, Roads etc. in Scotland 1782-1841 (In British Library of Political and Economic Science)
New Annual Register for 1803
Arrowsmith, A. Memoir of a Map of Scotland. Jan. 1809 (Printed with 3rd Report of Commissioners for Highland Roads and Bridges)
2nd Report of Select Committee on Conditions in the Highlands and Islands and practicability of Relief by Emigration, May 1841
2nd Report (Roads and Bridges) and 3rd Report (Canal) of Committee appointed to consider Telford's Survey and Report, 1803

BIBLIOGRAPHY

Hansard's Parliamentary Debates, vols XXXIX, XLIX and LVI
Crofters Commission Report 1884

BOOKS

Alexander, Wm. *Notes and Sketches of Northern Rural Life in the 18th Century* (1877)
Anderson, George and Peter. *Guide to the Highlands and Islands of Scotland* (1834)
Barron, James. *The Northern Highlands in the 19th Century*, 3 vols (1903-1913)
Day, J. P. *Public Administration in the Highlands and Islands of Scotland* (1918)
Gibb, Sir Alexander, *The Story of Telford* (1935)
Graham, Henry G. *Social Life in Scotland in the 18th Century* (1901)
Grant, Mrs Anne of Laggan. *Letters from the Mountains 1807-1845*
Grant, Mrs Elizabeth of Rothiemurchus. *Memoirs of a Highland Lady 1807-1898*
Haldane, A. R. B. *The Drove Roads of Scotland* (1952)
Knox, John. *A Tour through the Highlands of Scotland and the Hebrides Isles in 1786*
Lamb, Charles and Mary. *Letters* ed. Lucas (1935)
Larkin, William. *Sketch of a Tour in the Highlands of Scotland in 1818*
Lauder, Sir Thomas Dick. *An Account of the Great Floods of August 1829 in the Province of Moray and Adjoining Districts 1830*
Macculloch, John. *The Highlands and Western Isles of Scotland*, 4 vols (1824)
Mitchell, Joseph. *Reminiscences of My Life in the Highlands*, 2 vols (1883)
Newte, Thomas. *Prospects and Observations on a Tour in England and Scotland in 1785*
Salmond, J. B. *Wade in Scotland* (1938)
Smiles, Samuel. *Life of Telford*, 2 vols (1867)
Society of Writers to H.M. Signet. History (1890)
Southey, Robert. *Journal of a Tour in Scotland in 1819* (1929)
Telford, Thomas. *Life of Thomas Telford, Civil Engineer, written by himself*, 2 vols, ed. John Rickman (1838)
Webb, Sidney and Beatrice. *The Story of the King's Highway* (1913)
Williams, Orlo. *The Life and Letters of John Rickman* (1912)
Wordsworth, Dorothy. *Journals, 1798-1828*, ed. Wm. Knight (1924)

ARTICLES, PAMPHLETS, ETC.

Adam, M. I. 'The Causes of the Highland Emigrations of 1783-1803'. *Scottish Historical Review* vol. XVII (1920)
'The Highland Emigration of 1770'. *Scottish Historical Review* vol. XVI (1919)
(Anon.) 'Caledonian Canal'. *Blackwood's Magazine* vol. VII (1820)
Brewster, Sir D. Review of *Life and Works of Thomas Telford, Edinburgh Review* vol. LXX (1839)
Brydges, Sir S. E. 'Observations on the 3rd Report of the Commissioners for making New Roads in Scotland', *Censura Literaria* vol. IX (1815)
Dempster, George. *A Discourse containing a Summary of the Proceedings of the Directors of the Society for extending the Fisheries . . . since 25th March 1788*
Fraser, C. I. 'A "New Deal" of the 18th Century', *Scots Magazine* vol. XXV (1936)
Highland Society of Scotland *Transactions* vol. I (1799)

Irvine, Alex. *An Inquiry into the Causes and Effects of Emigration from the Highlands etc.* (1802)

Mackenzie, Sir Kenneth. 'General Wade and his Roads', and 'Military Roads in the Highlands', *Inverness Scientific and Field Club Transactions* vol. v (1902)

Rickman, John. 'Obituary' *Gentleman's Magazine* n.s. vol. xv (1841)

'Scottish Forfeited Estates Papers, 1715, 1745', *Scottish History Society* vol. LVII (1909)

Selkirk, Earl of. *Observations on the Present State of the Highlands etc.* (1805)

Thomas, John. 'The Remarkable Valley', *Blackwood's Magazine* vol. CCLXIX (1951)

LEGAL PAPERS ETC

Macdonell v. Caledonian Canal Commissioners. 1825-30. Session Papers. Signet Library Collection Vol. 205 No. 418

Papers in connection with Abolition of Heritable Jurisdictions (Signet Library, Edinburgh)

INDEX

Abbot, Charles 35, 38, 95, 172, (Lord Colchester) 197
Aberdeen 118, 128, 138, 188, 198, 205
Aberdeenshire, contracts placed in 88; labour from 82; proprietors agree to repair highways 3
Aberfeldy, Wade's bridge over river Tay 5, 6, 118, 173, 180
Abernethy, valuable timber at 126
Achanalt, Loch 10, 98
Achnasheen, new road by 98, 99, 104, 107, 111, 112, 124, 140, 158
Advocates' Library 201
Agriculture 30, 94, 197; changes in 19–22, 23, 29, 33, 126, 138-9, 177; diverts labour from Canal and Roads 16, 19–22, 82, 83, 185; sheep-farming 22, 29, 33, 94
Ainslie, John 62
Alford, bridge over Don at 195
Altnaharra 195
Amulree 10
Anderson, James 25
Aonach 10
Appin 82, 88, 179
Ardavasar Bay 68
Ardelve 70
Ardentinny 67, 106
Ardeonaig 94
Ardgour 67
Ardnamurchan 67, 97
Argyll, Duke of 18, 68
Argyll and Inverness-shire, Memorial regarding roads in. *See* Appendix III
Argyllshire, Assessment Bill 134; roads in 66, 141; sub-inspector's area 75, 161; woods cut for charcoal 126
Arisaig, road to 55, 57, 64; contractors' difficulties 65, 66, 71, 95, 96, 120, 194; damaged by drovers 157; labour for Canal from 82; Telford's estimate inadequate 136
Arkaig river 87, 124, 127
Arnisdale 26, 72
Arnisort 68
Arran 25, 94, 102
Arrochar 10
Arrowsmith, Aaron makes map of Scotland 62, 135, 141
Assessments, local, for road construction 51
Assynt 25
Atholl, Duke of 18, 119, 120, 171, 205
Aviemore 10

Ayrshire, tenders for new roads from 54

Badenoch, district a sub-inspector's area 75
Baillie, Evan, of Dochfour 153, 155
Ballachulish 13, 81, 87, 141, 180
Ballater, bridge over Dee at 127, 128, 130, 174, 175, 195
Ballater Bridge, Memorial respecting. *See* Appendix VIII
Balmacara 99
Banff harbour 116
Bank of Scotland, Commissioners' account with 45, 47, 72, 83, 89, 113, 115; Commissioners acknowledge help 73-4; gains and losses on exchange 45; issue of notes by 49, 73; offers advances to local landowners 50–1, 106, 121, 201; system of cash credits 49
Barilla, imports of 27
Barnbymoor 182
Bayne, John 110
Beauly, bridge over 104, 118, 129, 134, 176; Firth 87, 142; valley of 131, 195
Bernera, road to 10
Berwickshire, tenders for new roads from 54
Bills, Bank accepts them as security 50, 51; increasing use in commerce of 48–50
Black Isle, smugglers' stills in 183
Black Mount 10, 13, 163, 179, 180, 187
Black Watch, The 23
Blair Atholl 10, 180
Blairgowrie 8, 10, 180
Boat of Bridge ferry 132
Bona Ferry 143
Bonar Bridge, road from 188, 189, 190, 195; Telford's iron bridge at 104, 131–3, 184, 189
Boswell, James, journey to Skye with Samuel Johnson 10, 11, 171, 177, 178
Boulton and Watt 88
Boyle, Lord Justice Clerk 155
Braemar 8, 10
Brahan Castle 121, 140
Bran, River 119
Brander, Pass of 13
Breadalbane, Earl of 18, 94
Bridges
— Aberfeldy 5, 6, 118, 173, 180
— Alford 195

239

NOTE ON THE MAP

This map is based on Arrowsmith's Map which was published by the Commissioners for Highland Roads and Bridges in 1828 after the completion of the constructional work.

In addition to the roads constructed by the Commissioners, there are shown on the map as published those stretches of old military road for which the Commissioners became responsible in 1814. As explained in the text, the 308 miles of military road then transferred to their care comprised only part of the old military road system, the remainder being left to the care—and in certain cases to the neglect—of the counties through which they ran. For the sake of clarity those stretches of military road existing in 1814 but not transferred to the Commissioners have been added by the Author and are shown by broken lines.

The road from Glasgow to Carlisle, with a branch to Cumbernauld was engineered by Thomas Telford but is outside the scope of the book.

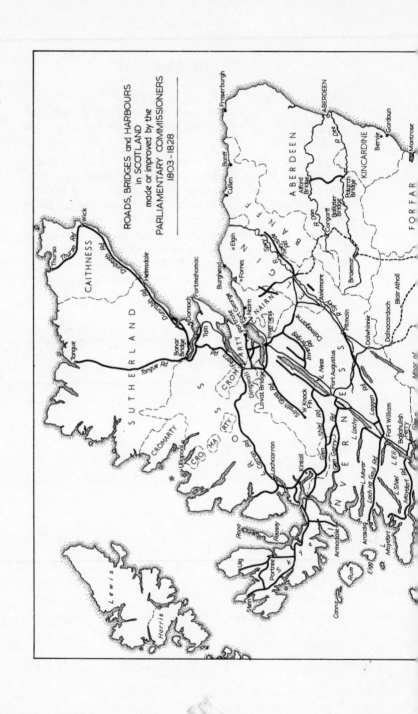

ROADS, BRIDGES and HARBOURS
in SCOTLAND
made or improved by the
PARLIAMENTARY COMMISSIONERS
1803-1828

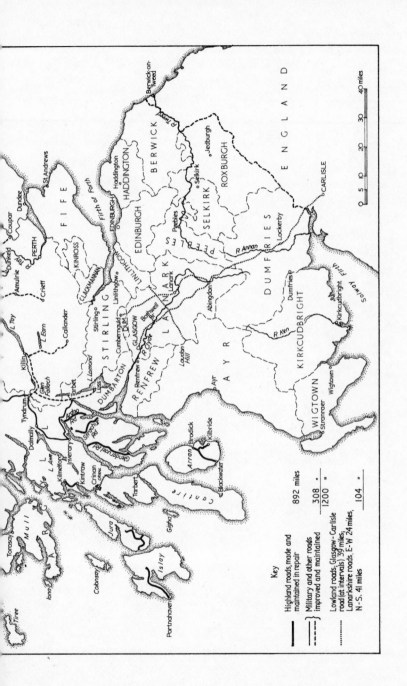